George Sand's
Theatre Career

Theater and Dramatic Studies, No. 28

Oscar G. Brockett, Series Editor

Leslie Waggener Professor of Fine Arts
and Professor of Drama
The University of Texas at Austin

Bernard Beckerman, Series Editor, 1980-1983

Brander Matthews Professor of Dramatic Literature
Columbia University in the City of New York

Other Titles in This Series

George Sand's Theatre Career

by
Gay Manifold

Associate Professor and Chairman
Theatre Department
University of LaVerne
LaVerne, California

U·M·I Research Press

Ann Arbor, Michigan

Produced and distributed by
UMI Research Press
an imprint of
University Microfilms International
A Xerox Information Resources Company
Ann Arbor, Michigan 48106

Library of Congress Cataloging in Publication Data

Manifold, Gay, 1943-
  George Sand's theatre career.

   (Theater and dramatic studies ; no. 28)
   Bibliography: p.
   Includes index.
   1. Sand, George, 1804-1876—Dramatic works. 2. Sand,
George, 1804-1876—Knowledge—Performing arts.
3. Theater—France—History—19th century. 4. Dramatists,
French—19th century—Biography. 5. Little theater
movement—France. I. Title. II. Series.

PQ2419.M3 1985   842'.7   84-28098
ISBN 0-8357-1653-8 (alk. paper)

For James

Il n'est pas bien honnête, et pour beaucoup de causes,
Qu'une femme étudie et sache tant de choses.

. . . régler la dépense avec économie,
Doit être son étude et sa philosophie.

Les femmes d'à présent sont bien loin de ces moeurs:
Elles veulent écrire, et devenir auteurs.

Molière, *Les Femmes Savantes*

George Sand Performing Role of Claudie at Theatre of Nohant,
8 August 1850.
Illustration by Maurice Sand in *Recueil de principaux types crées
avec leurs costumes sur le Théâtre de Nohant*, 2 vols., Bibliothèque
Nationale, Département des Estampes, Réserves, Tb471; 1:161;
hereafter referred to as *Recueil*.
Phot. Bibliothèque Nationale, Paris.

Contents

Illustrations

Foreword

I suppose that all specialists in a particular author are exposed to the same temptations. Their main project is well on its way, but the list of additional studies seems never ending: they always see new ones that ought to be done, ones that they want to do, that they sketch out, that they baby along over the years. They have gotten ahold of unpublished documents, which change the picture, and render null and void certain past efforts. In particular, rediscovered correspondence modifies some of their perspectives, for it bears precise details on the evolution of their author, elucidations on her thought, on the reception of her work by contemporaries. What a temptation to use all these materials, to incorporate them in future planning, in addition to the volumes already awaited by the public* (by virtue of a tacit agreement, to respect above all else), to write other works, torchbearers of definitive statements. "Am I not in the best position," one says to oneself, "to treat this subject? There is no one else who could do it better than I. Allocate the time so as not to be behind." But art is long, and time is short. Years pass, and there comes a day when, in a bookstore or a scholarly journal, the book or article jealously brooded over appears, but... under the name of a colleague.

Here two cases present themselves to our imagination. In the one we see the birth of an implacable and overdone spite, secreted by the ravenous specialist, the abusive monopolizer, with regard to his upstart rival. Or else, in the other case, the one who has no pretensions to a monopoly, who welcomes the work of his colleague, closes up the dossier which has become useless, and every now and then breathes a sigh of relief in making another check mark on the excessively long list of work to be done.

Being in this latter category, how can I not say "Bravo!" to the book by Madame Gay Manifold? Like others, I have planned long-term projects, for projects prolongate life in stretching it towards the future: counted among those intentions, those prospects, a study on the connections of

---

*[Note that Georges Lubin has published eighteen volumes of George Sand's correspondence to date and has another thirteen years of her life to go. G.M.]

George Sand and the theatre. *Et voilà*—done! These connections, which had their ups and downs, have been the subject of several uneven works and a number of articles. Certain ones treated the subject with condescension. There has been talk of an unfortunate obstinacy, an insinuation that the novelist had a great love for the theatre that was not reciprocated. That is far from being just, and fails to take into account the large number of her plays produced on Parisian stages; while they received mixed reviews, certain among them achieved genuine success and profit. Granted, George Sand's theatre does not offer a guarantee for eternity, but it has in that respect the same sort of posterity as the output of many other dramatists of the nineteenth century. To get an idea of the numbers lost, it suffices to glance over the invaluable inventories of Charles Beaumont Wicks. Which ones survive, of the two or three hundred plays by one or another celebrated playwright, ruler of the stage which enriched him?

Just as there is beauty for each epoch (the phrase is Baudelaire's), there is also theatre for each epoch. What amused the parents hardly makes the children smile. What made the tears flow yesterday, appears laughable today. Mentalities, ideologies are at opposite extremes from each other. The kind of situation that once was a matter of conflict in mores, and thus in drama's domain, has long since found a solution to dispel it. The unwed mother is no longer banned by public opinion as was Claudie in the play of that name. There are no more country folk comparable to the ones George Sand put on the stage: the agricultural worker reduced to extreme poverty, the handyman who made his living doing pickup work who no longer exists, but has gone off to increase the population of the cities, to join the ranks of the unemployed. The theatre audience of 1864 could be moved by the plight of a young woman of good family reduced by poverty to an almost servile position *(Le Marquis de Villemer);* that type of woman companion has completely disappeared. She is a model or cover girl.

Another thing: the theatre of George Sand sought to provoke emotion. People cried while listening to *François le Champi* or *Le Mariage de Victorine*, so the chroniclers inform us, and so do the letters of the author herself. "All her dramas are sincere moral dilemmas; the dialectic of the heart has not a more sagacious interpreter." (H. Taine) How could our century, which shuns emotion and rejects moral lessons, how could it welcome those plays which had their day at the Odéon and the Gymnase?

But one must not stop at this partial understanding of George Sand's connections with dramatic art. Few writers have practiced that art as directly, have reflected on it as much, written as much, tried out ideas on the problems of staging and interpreting as much—to the point of consecrating an entire novel *(Le Château des Désertes,* dedicated to the

English actor William Charles Macready) to a lively meditation on that art. The "pocket theatre" that she created in her Nohant mansion, which first served as her laboratory, became an end in itself, to borrow the expression of Madame Gay Manifold, who analyzes perfectly the role it played, its effects, and the prophetic inspirations of an author very much ahead of her time, specifically with reference to her evocations of Copeau, Antoine, Ibsen, Strindberg, Stanislavski, Artaud, and Bertolt Brecht.

Here is something to make us open our eyes wide at those who judged their contemporary George Sand as inept at the craft of dramatic author, something to restore interest in her by our own contemporaries, whether they be actors, directors, or simply lovers of the theatre.

GEORGES LUBIN

Preface

George Sand (1804–76) wrote not only plays, but also essays and novels on acting theory and theatre practice; and she produced and directed plays, constructed costumes, and even acted. At least twenty-five of her plays premiered in the big professional theatres of Paris (1840–72), and she staged dozens more of her scenarios and plays on the little stage of her private theatre at Nohant (1846–63). This study provides a history of that astonishing output, a comprehensive overview of a theatre career virtually unknown to theatre historians, language and literature scholars, and students of women's studies.

One of the most prominent writers of nineteenth-century France, George Sand, pseudonym for Aurore Dupin Dudevant, was known to her contemporaries primarily as a novelist. The twentieth century has largely ignored if not altogether forgotten Sand as an artist. Today a large part of her fame rests on her life, her love affairs with Chopin, Musset, and Marie Dorval, her wearing of men's clothing, and her cigar smoking. Only in the last decade have her novels begun to receive much attention. And interest in her theatre work has just begun.

This study attempts to provide the first full account of Sand's theatre career and achievements. It pulls together information previously available only in French in scattered published and unpublished sources. On-site research at Gargilesse and at Nohant, where Sand's private theatre remains intact, and examination of unpublished documents in several collections in France have provided much of the material. Only two books exist which focus on Sand's dramas, both in French: Fahmy's abundant but chaotic literary and biographical approach to many of Sand's plays and some of her other writings on the theatre,[1] and Wentz's well-organized discussion of five of Sand's Nohant plays analyzed from a literary point of view.[2] Rather than taking a literary or biographical approach, this history draws heavily on contemporary accounts and especially Sand's correspondence in order to place her full range of plays and scenarios, her other writings on the theatre, and her actual theatre experience in both a historical and a performance context. To appreciate Sand's contributions in drama and theatre fully we need to view them in relation to nineteenth-century stage practice.

Sand worked in the vanguard of three major movements: romanticism, realism, and the experimental little theatre movement. This history surveys the romantic dramas Sand wrote in the 1830s. Her first play, *Une Conspiration en 1537,* Sand gave to her lover Musset, who used it to create *Lorenzaccio.* In *Gabriel* and *Cosima* Sand raises the issues of women's inferior education and restrictive marital status, thirty years before Ibsen's *A Doll's House.* In the 1840s Sand's admiration for the isolated romantic hero waned; her disgust with contemporary theatre practice grew; and she turned her attention to socialism and her novels. The study chronicles how Sand's participation in the 1848 Revolution spurred her efforts to create a people's theatre. This aim culminated in her innovative realistic folk plays *François le Champi* and *Claudie,* in which Sand makes use of Berrichon folk songs, customs and dialect rhythms, fifty years before Synge's similar treatment of the Irish peasantry. Sand encountered frustrations common to professional playwrights: fickle audiences, substandard drama critics, difficult theatre managers. She had the added problem of being a woman working in an exclusively male arena. Then the Second Empire (1852–70) forced Sand to suppress her socialism and make her plays conform more to bourgeois taste, which she did, and achieved some notable commercial successes. Finally, with a theatre of her own in the Nohant country manor house, Sand could experiment more freely. Her work in commedia dell'arte and the uses of improvisation, in psychological realism and the one-act play form, in ensemble acting and modern directorial techniques prefigures the little theatre movement of the 1890s.

I would like to express here my profound gratitude to Georges Lubin, not only for his extraordinarily scholarly and sage contributions, graceful writing and good humor, in the editing of Sand's complete correspondence (now in eighteen volumes), but for his generosity in writing a foreword to this study, and taking the time to give my manuscript a careful reading.

Special thanks too, to Oscar Brockett of the University of Texas, Austin, and to Professors Carl Mueller, Eric Gans, and Michael McLain of UCLA for their assistance.

Library staffs have been most kind in assisting me to find materials for this study, especially Marie Odèle Gigou at the Bibliothèque Historique de la Ville de Paris, Monsieur Suffel with the Lovenjoul collection in Chantilly, and others at the municipal libraries of La Châtre and Châteauroux, and the Bibliothèque Nationale.

To my husband James, for his unflagging support and kindness, thank you.

1. Two Pictures of George Sand.
    Top: George Sand in 1837.
    Lithograph by Julien Boilly.
    From postcard, Phot. Bibliothèque Nationale, Paris.
    Bottom: George Sand as Molière, c. 1865.
    Photograph by Nadar.

1

From Romantic Youth to Proletarian Pierrot

George Sand once remarked with satisfaction, "There is none of the bourgeois in my blood. I am the daughter of a patrician and a bohemian."[1] Sand's father, the patrician Maurice Dupin, had on his side of the family tree a king of Poland, the Maréchal de Saxe, and the owners of the Chenonceaux château. Sand's mother, Sophie Delaborde, could be called a bohemian as she came from the lowest ranks of society and her father made his living selling birds along the quais of the Seine. Sand's parents met while her father was serving in Napoleon's army and her mother was mistress to Maurice's commanding officer. They married a month before their daughter, George Sand, or rather, Aurore Dupin, was born in July 1804. Maurice Dupin's fatal fall from his horse in 1808 left little Aurore's fate up to two women who were extremely hostile to one another: her mother, Sophie, and her paternal grandmother, Sand's namesake, Aurore Dupin. When the recently widowed Sophie left the Dupin country mansion in Nohant to return to her own relatives in Paris, little Aurore wanted desperately to go with her. But the grandmother insisted she stay with her at Nohant where she would have the benefits of a better education and milieu. Grandmother and daughter-in-law concluded their argument by fiscal means: in exchange for a generous monthly allowance Sophie relinquished her daughter to the grandmother.

Sand's love of the lower classes, embodied in the figure of her absent mother, developed alongside her aristocratic upbringing. Then, too, Sand's childhood in the Berrichon countryside included peasant playmates such as hog tenders, sheepherders and farmers' children. Sand's older bastard half brother, born of a peasant woman, taught her to ride horseback the way boys do. Sand's grandmother, a kind, liberal-minded, well-read, refined, and responsible eighteenth-century patrician, gave Sand a private tutor, music lessons, and free access to a fine library. At twelve Sand read Homer and Tasso. At sixteen and seventeen she discovered Rousseau,

Byron and Shakespeare. She felt a particular kinship to Hamlet and Jacques, and to Molière's *Misanthrope,* which she says became "her code" for that period of her youth when she relished the melancholy and "romanesque."

From the age of fourteen to sixteen Sand attended a convent school in Paris where she learned English and fell in love with the Italian language. In her autobiography she tells how she organized amateur theatrics at the school. The only one in the convent to have read Molière, a familiar pastime with her grandmother, Sand composed Molieresque scenarios from memory, then cast and directed her classmates in the stage business; dialogue was improvised. The performances proved highly entertaining. Since Molière was forbidden in the convent, Sand let the nuns believe that the scenarios were her own work, though not without a twinge of guilt. Sand remembers specifically playing the role of Monsieur Purgon in her version of *Le Malade imaginaire.*[2]

Out of school, back at Nohant, Sand continued her amateur theatrics and enjoyed attending the theatre whenever possible. She and a few friends staged a Carmontel *proverbe,* the kind of short play that had been popular in Sand's grandmother's youth, for her grandmother's birthday celebration. Sand played the role of the young male lover. She says she performed it as well as possible and very seriously so as not to offend her grandmother, who disapproved of her dressing in a man's attire. Sand and her friends went to the local town of La Châtre whenever a theatrical troupe came through on tour. That way she learned all the songs from the popular comic operas. From her grandmother she learned to appreciate Mozart.

But these golden days of melancholy literature, amateur theatrics, and carefree theatre excursions were cut short by the death of Sand's grandmother at the end of 1821. Sand was seventeen. The grandmother's will gave the Nohant estate to her granddaughter, and stipulated that Sand's guardian would be her cousin Villeneuve, owner and resident of the Chenonceaux château. But Sand's mother had other ideas; she rushed from Paris to Nohant and, exercising her legal rights as the mother, took Sand back with her to live in Paris. The experience was disenchanting, and in less than a year Sand was married to Baron Casimir Dudevant, and another year later she had a son, Maurice.

At nineteen, mother of an infant, Aurore played a comic old woman in a sixteenth-century vaudeville. Joining her on the makeshift stage at a friend's house was the actor from the Comédie Française, Michot-Antoine, aging, but "very known and esteemed" (*Corr.* 1:114). A few years later, as an increasingly bored young housewife in her early twenties, Sand received encouragement from a childhood friend who referred her to the dramatic proverbs of Leclercq, and advised Sand to convert the

Nohant château salon into a theatre space (*Corr.* 1:381). After twenty more eventful years Sand did just that in 1846.

George and her husband spent much of their early married life at Nohant. After the marriage fell apart Sand had to fight for Nohant in the courts. Wise to the ways of the world, Sophie had insisted that Sand retain title to the estate in the marriage contract. So eventually the courts ruled in Sand's favor, though not without her paying a high sum of money as penalty to her husband. Nohant remained the one constant in Sand's adventurous life.

Sand's change from provincial housewife and mother of two small children to struggling professional writer living in a small Parisian apartment paralleled the political revolution of 1830. Her disillusionment with marriage was compounded by her dashed hopes for the revolution and a republic. Having been excessively enthusiastic about the revolution's chances, Sand was left feeling foolish when political change failed to materialize:

> In our time enthusiasm is the virtue of dupes. . . . I laugh at myself because I was duped by my own desire to believe in goodness. I see now that hardly anything has changed . . . the absurdity of fooling myself regarding possible results of a three-day revolution (*Corr.* 1:721, 724).

Retreating to private life and personal affections somewhat comforted the would-be revolutionary: "I concentrate my life on the objects of my affection. I surround myself with them like a sacred battalion, which makes my black thoughts afraid to show themselves" (*Corr.* 1:721–22). But that solace was short-lived. In December of 1830 Aurore came upon a testament written by her husband and addressed to her to read after his death; she of course read it forthwith, and discovered to her chagrin a diatribe of maledictions and recriminations. Compatibility with the unfaithful, hard-drinking, obsessive game hunter Dudevant had long ceased to be a possibility. But the sudden shock of seeing how intensely bitter was his animosity toward her stirred a profound change in Sand. Jolted into a new sense of self, the twenty-seven-year-old woman recognized that her life had changed "irrevocably" (*Corr.* 1:724). In spite of Dudevant's recantings and promises of docility, Sand made plans to live in Paris for half of every year, three months at a time, in order to become a professional writer. To begin with, she insisted upon an allowance of 3000 francs from her dowry of 300,000. Her eight-year marriage to Dudevant henceforth continued to exist in name only. Divorce was out of the question because France did not make it legal until 1884, eight years after Madame Dudevant's death.

In January 1831, when Sand installed herself in Paris, her career was launched: "I am finally free" (*Corr.* 1:776). Work would be her salvation: "A passion is necessary in life. . . . I have a goal, a task, let's say the word, a passion" (*Corr.* 1:814, 817). In February she wrote of her plans to make a living at writing, nothing more, absolutely no fame: "Since I have no ambition of being well known, I won't be" (*Corr.* 1:801). Yet hardly more than a year later, in May of 1832, with the publication of Sand's first novel, *Indiana,* George Sand became instantly famous.

Sand's output and experimentation during that short year of literary apprenticeship, 1831, pertained mostly to the theatre. Even before she set out to write for and about the theatre, Sand had strong opinions about theatrical productions in Paris; in general, she did not like what she saw: "The bad, the false, the stilted have, in my opinion, invaded the stage and literature." The plays "are detestable and the theatre is in decadence." She especially objected to the violence and exaggeration. After seeing one particularly bloody assassination on the Odéon stage, she wrote,

> It's the latest genre. . . . I'm beginning to accustom myself to it. Every evening I see an execution, a hanging, a suicide, or at least a poisoning with accompanying cries and convulsions of agony. It's charming. I'm getting a little blasé and my sensitivities are so blunted that I laughed like a fool . . . at the red currant jam smeared on Monaldeschi's chest to simulate blood (*Corr.* 1:639–40).

But an opera performance featuring the famous soprano Malibran gave Sand what she was looking for: "That woman is the leading genius in Europe, beautiful as a Raphael virgin, simple, energetic, naïve, she's the leading soprano and the leading tragedian." Malibran's performance in *Otello* at the Théâtre des Italiens made Sand "cry, tremble, suffer just as if I were witnessing a scene from real life" (*Corr.* 1:789).

Throughout her long career as both playgoer and playwright, Sand measured the worth of an actor's performance by the degree of its simplicity, energy, and truthfulness to real life. She wanted actors with a wide range of expression who could elicit a strong emotional response from the audience.

George Sand recalls the experience at the opera in her first published work. The short story "La Prima Donna" (*Revue de Paris,* April 1831) tells of a soprano, Gina, who abandons her stage career for a man. Regretting the sacrifice, she longs to perform again. Given the opportunity, Gina's bursting joy proves too great for her fragile frame and she dies after the performance. Sand describes Gina's effect on the audience as refreshing and yet torturing.[3]

Readers and editors of Sand's first literary efforts judged them as "too moral and virtuous to be found probable by the public" (*Corr.* 1:818), so she decided to write what the public wanted: "It will be bad, and I'll wash my hands of it." "If monsters are à la mode, we'll make monsters" (*Corr.* 1:826). In this spirit Sand began her first play in June 1831: "I'm working on a sort of literary and dramatic trifle, black as fifty devils, with conspiracy, executioner, assassin, dagger blows, agony, death rattle, blood, swearing and curses" (*Corr.* 1:893). As the work progressed Sand warmed up to the play: "this good and beautiful drama . . . will make all the pregnant women in the boulevard theatres abort from fear" (*Corr.* 1:901), a reference to the story of an Aeschylus play that so frightened a woman in the audience that she aborted.

This first play by Sand, *Une Conspiration en 1537,* never appeared on the stage in spite of her intention to make it a sensation on the "boulevard du crime." The play was finally published in 1921.[4] But even though it did nothing to advance Sand's ambitions for a theatrical career, the play gave genesis to one of the greatest of nineteenth-century French dramas, Musset's *Lorenzaccio.* When Sand gave the manuscript of her *Conspiracy* to Musset during their tempestuous love affair (1833–34), he transformed and transcended the original, turning it into a modern masterpiece. Sand's text provided Musset with most of his principal characters and events, the historical setting in Renaissance Florence, and the sensational assassination scene on stage, Lorenzaccio's murder of Duke Alexander de Medici. Because of Sand's burgeoning concept of a revolutionary, Lorenzaccio became one of dramatic literature's first antiheroes, contemporary with Büchner's Danton and Woyczek.[5]

Sand's characterization of Lorenzaccio reflects her own political fervor and disenchantment with the 1830 Revolution in France. Angry with the royalists and their crowning of Louis Philippe, a bumbling, bourgeois king, Sand fears she could have been a political assassin herself had she been born a man: "Thank God I'm not a man, because I would have said or done something stupid" (*Corr.* 1:724). Sand believed that political assassination could be justified if it rid society of a tyrant, or even just a bumbler like Louis Philippe.[6] Her frustration with being a would-be anarchist and her despair with the failure of the 1830 Revolution left Sand feeling that all political causes are desperate and futile:

> Me, I hate all of them, kings and republicans, absolutists, moderate pretenders, I mix them all up in my mistrust and aversion. There are moments when it would make me happy to hurt them all. My only tranquility is when I can forget them (July 1831; *Corr.* 1:917).

Sand's character Lorenzo experiences the same despair:

> Do what you want with the people, I will do nothing. I hate them. . . . I have no interest in flattering them because I don't want anything from them. . . . To make a conspiracy you need just two things, a man and a dagger.

Once Lorenzo has assassinated the Duke of Florence in Sand's *Conspiration,* he gives a long litany of justifications, but his ultimate reason is actually a passion, not a reason: "The dream caressed me all my nights, the need devoured my soul, the goal of my destiny . . . to quench my thirst." Once the deed is done, the dream fulfilled, the thirst quenched, he wants nothing. Wouldn't he like to be duke now? "I would do good without any pleasure and maybe evil without any remorse."[7] To paraphrase an observation by Eric Bentley on the fate of political revolutionaries, Lorenzo's joy of rebellion has turned into the gall of disenchantment.

After her first play, Sand collaborated with her young lover Jules Sandeau on a novel, entitled *Rose et Blanche,* in December 1831.[8] They placed their joint authorship under the name "J. Sand." So when Sand published *Indiana* in May 1832, she kept the "Sand" and chose "George(s)" for her new first name in the nom de plume. Sand proceeded to make of her new persona a kind of theatre piece, wearing top hat, tails, trousers and boots, all specially made to fit her petite form. Reflecting on this masculine attire some twenty years later, Sand emphasized how much more comfortable and practical men's clothes were; she could walk from one end of Paris to the other without getting her feet wet or her neck cold, and she often made such walks going to the theatre. Disguised as a boy, she could take a place in the stalls with the young dandies and men of letters, and become "one of the boys," just another struggling young writer in Paris. George was one of France's first female professional writers; given the choice to dress and behave like another writer or like another woman, Sand chose the former at this stage of her career.

A young woman disguised as a boy, who haunts the theatre, plays the prominent part in Sand's novella "La Marquise" (December 1832). The nineteenth-century Danish critic Georg Brandes considered "La Marquise" Sand's masterpiece: "An absolutely charming fusion of the spirit and mores of the eighteenth century with the timid and exalted passion of the nineteenth." Brandes not only admired Sand's synthesis of eighteenth- and nineteenth-century sensibilities, but also her economy of expression: "George Sand never wrote anything more graceful . . . the artistic form has the concision of immortal works. 'La Marquise' merits a place in the masterpieces of French literature."[9]

The story, written as a dialogue between a young man and the old marquise, reads more like the eighty-year-old woman's monologue. This brittle and proper marquise recounts her story of the one and only great passion she ever felt, which occurred sixty years before (1770) the time she is narrating (1830). When she was a twenty-year-old, tall, svelte, proud, unsmiling, a huntress-nymph type of beauty, she experienced passionate, albeit platonic, love for an actor named Lelio. During the first two years of this five-year-long passion the marquise would disguise herself as a boy so that she could go as often as possible to the theatre to see Lelio perform without anyone recognizing her (she could not shame her noble rank and class).

Lelio, in his thirties at the time, an Italian actor who spoke excellent French, excelled in playing Corneille's twenty-year-old heroes. But, explains the marquise, Lelio never received the acclaim due him because the eighteenth-century public considered his acting in bad taste:

> In that time, one played tragedy decently; it was necessary to have *bon ton*, even with a slap in the face. Dramatic art was fashioned to conform to the manners of high society; the actor's speech and gesture kept rapport with the panniers and the powder which dressed up Phèdre and Clytemnestra. . . . Tragedy bored me to death. . . . I listened to those pompous tirades with coldness and restraint.[10]

Lelio neither sounded nor looked like the eighteenth-century ideal. His voice was "penetrating, nervous, accentuated, rather than sonorous." His physique was small and thin. He did not have beautiful facial features, but he had a proud and melancholy expression. There was beauty "in the irresistible grace of his attitudes, in the abandon of his approach. . . . It was for him the word charm was invented. . . . He cast a charm on me." There was nothing contrived, artificial or egotistical in his performance: "He moved, spoke and acted without method and without pretension, he would cry with the heart as much as the voice, he would forget himself in order to identify himself with passion" ("La Marquise," p. 16). Lelio exercised an electrifying power over the marquise, which she likened to ensnarement; she, the huntress-nymph, was hunted down and seduced by his acting:

> Like a vulture taking a partridge in his magnetic flight, just as he leads her breathless and immobile into the magic circle that he traces around her, the soul of Lelio . . . enveloped all my faculties and plunged me into a torpor of admiration ("La Marquise," p. 22).

Lelio's power could affect other actors performing with him on the stage, such as Mlle Clairon, not a favorite of the marquise's, but who would become inspired and impassioned under the influence of Lelio's genius.

On one occasion the marquise, still disguised as a boy, followed Lelio after his performance from the theatre to a café. What disenchantment; her illusions were shattered. Lelio had just finished playing Corneille's hero Rodrigue in *Le Cid,* so "frank, loyal and tender"; but now as himself in the café he appeared tired, older than his years, ignoble in bearing and coarse in speech. The marquise rushed out of the café, and upon her return home fell deathly ill. Several weeks later, and under duress from her doctors and well-wishers, the marquise returned to the theatre. Surprisingly, she again fell under the spell of Lelio's magic charm. That night she finally understood her love for Lelio; it was an intellectual passion, "romanesque":

> It was not him I loved, but heroes of ancient times which he knew how to represent . . . through him I was transported to an epoch of virtue since forgotten. . . . Lelio was no more to me than the shadow of the Cid. . . . He had to be in costume on the stage in order to be that which I loved. Stripped of all that, he returned for me into nothingness. . . . Off the stage he held not the slightest attraction for me. It was like contemplating a great man reduced to ashes in a silver urn ("La Marquise," pp. 27–28).

So for the next three years the marquise went to the theatre in her own person with her aristocratic equipage, and from a box hanging over the side of the stage gave to Lelio's performances her passionate attention. From such close proximity the actor and the marquise communicated by looks and emotions their passionate admiration for one another, for by now Lelio had fallen in love with the marquise. He performed for her as if no one else existed in the theatre.

At the end of five years the marquise received a love letter from Lelio. The actor dared defy social convention and express his love for the noble woman because he was about to emigrate from France and would never see her again. She consented to meet him in secret to bid farewell. At their appointed time and place they met. Lelio arrived in haste from the theatre, still in his costume and makeup for Molière's part of Don Juan. He looked extraordinarily handsome: "Velazquez would have thrown himself prostrate before such a model." After tearful adieux, the marquise compelled herself to depart. She looked back one last time; he had become old again, decomposed, "no more than the shadow of a lover and a prince" ("La Marquise," pp. 43–44). A delicate touch of humor between the old marquise and her young listener in the concluding dialogue is reminiscent of Marivaux, whom Sand admired and emulated.

"La Marquise" gives a clear picture of Sand's early views on the theatrical experience. First, Sand appreciated the visual aspects of the theatrical experience, as seen in her detailed descriptions of Lelio's costumes and the gowns worn by the marquise, which could form the basis of a costume manual for the eighteenth century. Second, Sand describes her ideal actor in the person of Lelio, who does not play himself, but loses himself in character roles which are larger and more idealized than he is himself. He rebels against the eighteenth-century taste for measured movement and "pompous tirades," and instead harkens back to Corneille's epoch, the seventeenth century, when, Sand imagines, men were more frank, passionate and tender. A third area of the theatrical experience that Sand explores in "La Marquise" is the relationship of spectator to actor, the magnetic effect a compelling performer can have on a receptive audience. The emotion and passion Lelio arouses in the marquise are intensified by her own discriminating taste and vivid imagination. She discovers that real life cannot equal the theatrically intensified life of the imagination. She willingly submits to the actor as hunter, seducer, and magician. She is his victim, concubine, and enchanted by his magic spell, as long as he remains at a distance. Lelio uses only two of his senses, sight and sound, to lure his victim into the magic circle, to magnetize, electrify, and make love to her; the rest is imagination and thought. Theatrical art mirrors life at the highest intellectual and imaginative levels; it must not step off the stage onto the physical plane and reproduce life with all the senses, or do so at the expense of the illusion of the ideal. Thus "La Marquise" provides us with the groundwork of Sand's objectives for actor and audience.

The marquise's theatrical experience parallels Sand's own response to the leading romantic actors of the early 1830s, principally two. Of the four most famous French actors of the romantic period (1827–44), Marie Dorval, Pierre Bocage, Jean-Gaspard Debureau, and Frédérick Lemaître, Sand became intimate friends with the first two (and had more than a passing acquaintance with the latter two). Dorval and Bocage were already famous when the unknown Aurore Dupin Dudevant arrived in Paris to begin her writing career. Before she met them personally, Aurore stood in the audience and cheered the two actors' triumphs, particularly the 1831 productions of Dumas' *Antony* and Hugo's *Marion de Lorme,* in which Bocage and Dorval together played lovers. In January 1833, a month after the publication of "Marquise," Sand met Dorval and they were instantly friends.[11] A month later, in February 1833 Sand met Bocage in the audience of a performance of *Lucrèce Borgia* starring Dorval. Sitting next to one another, the thirty-year-old writer and thirty-three-year-old actor responded to the performance as a single entity, their passion and sympathies in unison.[12] Clasping hands at that first meeting they began a thirty-year partnership in theatrical art.

Because Sand admired Marie Dorval contemporary to her writing "La Marquise," and because Sand and Dorval are said to have had a love affair (which would have been after the writing of "La Marquise," however), some biographers find it irresistible to identify the marquise with Sand, and Lelio with Dorval.[13] Certainly Marie Dorval had in common with Lelio a husky voice, a frank and energetic acting style full of emotion and passion, and a light and supple body, which Sand compares to the "wing of a voyaging fairy."[14] Another interesting parallel between the real actor Dorval and the fictional one Lelio: the marquise says Lelio played for her as if no one else existed in the auditorium; the same has been said of Dorval. Before Dorval would make her entrance onto the stage, she would peer through a hole in the curtain and choose one individual in the audience and then direct all of her persuasion and passion of the performance to that one person rather than to an anonymous crowd.[15]

But the similarities which exist between Lelio and the actor Pierre Bocage are more striking than between Lelio and Dorval, particularly in the details of their acting careers. Bocage was more controversial. Critics complained that Bocage lacked all the primary qualities one looked for in a leading actor: "manner, tone, diction and taste."[16] Only after his great successes of 1830–31 did the Comédie Française finally admit him into their ranks, where he remained only one year (1831–32), because of his difficulties and differences with that bastion of tradition. Sand's story of the fictional actor Lelio could well be a defense of Bocage against his detractors. Bocage spoke with a raspy, nasal voice; he moved with too much energy and gesticulation for the general taste; he was not conventionally handsome, but his eyes were fiery, and the overall impression Byronic. Some years later (1850), George Sand observes that Bocage

> didn't always have a beautiful voice, but it was profound and sympathetic. He spoke with an intelligence that neither Frédérick Lemaître nor Bouffée had, the greatest actors of their time along with Bocage. . . . He had true beauty, of the eyes and the face (*Corr.* 9:677).

And five years after Bocage's death Sand recalls the actor's outstanding features in a published play review she wrote in 1867:

> Bocage was the representative in flesh and bones of the exuberant literature of our times. His person and his form had the beauty and strangeness of that school. He had an aspect of suffering, gauche or excessive; but his face had the intellectual beauty of a strong inspiration, and his gaze burned with the sacred fire.[17]

Thirty-five years could not erase the powerful effect Bocage's acting performances had on the impressionable spectator. And Sand's memory, coming from the aging writer in her sixties, echoes the marquise as she remembers Lelio.[18]

Bocage reappears rather often in this account of Sand's theatre career, because of their lifelong association in the theatre, he as director and actor, she as playwright and muse. But they were also personal friends, and very briefly, in 1837, lovers.

Just as "La Marquise" explores by means of fiction a contrast in acting styles between the more contrived and self-conscious eighteenth-century heritage and the newer, freer and more natural style of the romantic actors, Sand's next piece on theatre, a critical review of an actual performance, applies the same contrast to living actors. The article, "Mars et Dorval," was first published in *L'Artiste* (17 February 1833), a month after Sand's friendship with Dorval had begun. Sand wrote about the event of two famous actresses performing together on the Comédie Française stage in one act from Beaumarchais' full-length play *The Marriage of Figaro*. Mars (stage name of Anne-Françoise Hippolyte Boutet, 1779–1847) played the witty and intelligent serving woman Suzanne, and Marie Dorval (1798–1849) the melancholy Countess Almaviva.[19] For Sand, Mars represents the more studied manner of eighteenth-century acting, and Dorval the more inspired nineteenth-century approach. Mars' "charming mincings of her fan" are contrasted to Dorval's "inflammable sensibility." Mars' type of passion is systematic. Dorval, the more supple of the two, has greater confidence in inspiration than in theory. "As to the intelligence of Madame Dorval, study and rules are too short a leash. Inspiration reveals all to her that instruction gives to the other."[20]

In developing and identifying with her character of the countess, Dorval not only deals with her present problem but remembers her past and dreams of her future. At present the countess is melancholy because the count is unfaithful. But she remembers when she was a simple young girl whom the Count Almaviva wooed so tenaciously and won in *Barber of Seville*. And she becomes animated by the lively imaginings of a future love in the affections of young Cherubin. Sand applauds Dorval's clear understanding of her character, based on close textual analysis and perception of Beaumarchais' intentions. Dorval's countess is an

> uncertain, frightened, impulsive woman whose past battles with her future, struggles against her reason and against her heart. One understands all of that in very little time because in reading Beaumarchais, Madame Dorval all of a sudden seized the intimate thought.

This "intimate thought," the character's inner life, distinguishes Dorval from Mars as the more modern actor. Sand's description of Dorval's character, "nonchalant on the outside and passionate on the inside," who connects the simplicity of her girlhood with the complexity of experienced disillusionment, anticipates the concept of "subtext" developed later by Stanislavski. Dorval's outer behavior communicates her rank, pride, nonchalance; her subtext or inner life communicates to the audience thwarted passion, restlessness and confused passion for a young boy who worships her.[21]

Mars' characterization of Suzanne, on the other hand, lacks Dorval's honesty and truthfulness, says Sand. Miss Mars, with her correct and studied grace, works too hard to please the audience; she has difficulty ridding herself of that urbanity. So in the role of Suzanne, Mars becomes almost equal in social rank to the countess. Sand points out that the Suzanne created by Beaumarchais is a saucy soubrette who provokes strong desires in men. But with Mars' interpretation, Sand thinks that the Count Almaviva must be very fatuous and stupid to think he can seduce a Suzanne who is so elegant in manner, chaste and modest. Thus Sand finds Mars too willing to sacrifice truthfulness to her role in order to keep her *bon ton,* which pleases a certain elitist class of spectators. But this falseness to her character "diminishes the power of her effects on the masses." In contrast to Mars' playing to please a certain segment of the audience, the audience forgets about Dorval per se, and becomes more absorbed in her interpretation of the role. The artist Dorval penetrates so deeply into the dramatic situation that she forgets herself entirely; she abandons herself to the task of being an artist.

Sand prefers Dorval's natural and fresh acting, her sense of immediacy, to Mars' studied and calculated manner. With Dorval's unexpected "always searing burst of impressions," one never anticipates her next word or gesture. There is nothing in the action of her muscles, in the rising of her breathing, in the contraction of her features, no preparatory effort which reveals to the spectator the next peripety of her internal drama, because she composes that drama herself, obeying the prompting of her own genius.

Sand concludes that the two actresses reign by different means: one by exquisite qualities and attractive graces and a prodigious beauty given her by nature; the other by a more vast apportionment of dramatic instinct and expansive sensibility, by a more thrilling vigor and a more commanding revelation of her specialty.[22] Thus we see how Sand sets up the same opposition in this review as she did in "La Marquise": the older, classical manner of acting characterized by control and good taste, opposed to the newer, more romantic, conscious abandonment of the actor's own persona in order to create a more natural and truthful character. However, Sand has provided a deeper analysis of the actor's craft in her critical review in discussing subtext.

Within a few months of "Mars et Dorval" George Sand began her second play; *Aldo le rimeur* was published in the *Revue des Deux Mondes* on 1 September 1833. Aldo, a Thomas Chatterton figure, fails in his search for self-expression and for love. In a structure which strictly alternates between monologue and dialogue, between Aldo's interior poetic life and its irreconciliation with the external, more vulgar world, Sand's unhappy artist contemplates suicide as the only solution to his misery. The first of two acts takes place in Aldo's poor Parisian garret, where he is visited first by the queen's fool, a dwarf who tries to corrupt the artist by hiring him to write a play that the fool will then claim as his own and have produced at court. But the poet refuses to become a hack rhymer. Alone, late that night, Aldo sleeps fitfully on his workbench, trusting that his sick mother sleeps upstairs in the loft. But his sleep-talking syncopates his mother's stumbling down the stairs. He awakes to find her dead. Aldo hopes that Jane, his young girlfriend, will comfort and console him, but instead she makes demands; she wants him to marry her. Disillusioned by Jane's self-interest, Aldo abandons all hope for love and life and leaves the garret to drown himself in the river. Act I ends when the queen and the fool float by in a little boat and pull Aldo from the river. In Act II Aldo fails to keep the queen happy; she finds him too moody and idealistic and returns to her more cheerful coterie of lovers. Again Aldo contemplates suicide, this time interrupted by the court astrologer who persuades him to wait until he has seen the full eclipse of the moon that evening, a sight worth living a little longer in order to behold. In the final scene we see Aldo and the astrologer climbing a mountain to their point of observation, all the time in fervent discussion about the merits of science and poetry. They discover that science and poetry are the same thing—truth.

Aldo le rimeur is Sand's first *drame fantastique,* a genre she also calls *drame du monde intérieur* and *drame métaphysique,* and later defines fully in her essay entitled "Le Drame fantastique," published in *Revue des Deux Mondes* (1 December 1839). Discussing that essay now, out of chronological sequence, will be useful in order to illustrate how *Aldo* fits her definition of a dream play. Sand's essay compares Goethe's *Faust,* Byron's *Manfred* and Mickiewicz's *Konrad.* What Sand says about these predecessors applies with equal force to her own *Aldo.*

The main character represents the "moi," or the subject, the self. All of the other human characters represent the "non-moi," or the object, the other than self. Any fantastic, supernatural beings constitute the self's efforts to relate to the non-self; they are allegorical manifestations of such self-expression as passion or despair. In other words, the drama's fantastic beings reveal the combat of the self's conscience; they are its struggles dramatized in visible forms. The ideal for the poet and the self is to arrive at an equilibrium of artistic (sensual) and philosophic (intellectual) faculties.[23]

For Aldo, his mother and Jane constitute his "non-moi," while the more mythical and allegorical figures of the dwarf-fool, the queen, and the astrologer are manifestations of struggles and temptations in his own conscience. In spite of Sand's claim that she had not finished the play,[24] the resolution of Aldo's internal struggle satisfies Sand's goal for a fantastic drama. Aldo reaches an equilibrium between artist and philosopher when he finds his scientific alter ego in the court astrologer.

Classified as an armchair drama, *Aldo le rimeur* was never staged during Sand's lifetime, and apparently has not been fully produced since that time.[25] Nevertheless, not only are there no inherent difficulties in staging *Aldo* (such as length, complicated set changes, or too great a number of characters), but the play lends itself to a highly visual interpretation of vivid images and, for the time, an innovative use of stage space. Just as Sand said of Goethe's *Faust,* that it could be staged by simply cutting some of the monologues and choreographing the black sabbath as a ballet,[26] so, too, could *Aldo.*

Sand's use of the staircase in Act I of *Aldo* was staged, even if the play was not. Going back to look at the scene in more detail, we see that late at night while the discouraged Aldo sleeps fitfully stretched out on his wooden bench placed downstage, his mother Meg, herself cold and starving, emerges from her loft at the top of the stairs and proceeds to grope and stumble down the old staircase. She can no longer see or hear very well, and while trying to find a place to sit down in the dark shadows she falls to the floor in a heap. George Sand may have shared this scene with her close companion, Marie Dorval, between the time *Aldo* was published in September of 1833, and the premiere of Alfred de Vigny's *Chatterton* in 1835. Dorval, who was Vigny's mistress during this epoch, played the role of Kitty Bell in *Chatterton*'s first production. The designer of that historic production, Charles Sechan, remembers Dorval's creation of Kitty Bell on the staircase. Having just discovered the dying Chatterton, a suicide by poisoning, in the upstairs room, Dorval's Kitty stumbles towards the stairs:

> She turns her face filled with terror and despair toward the audience. She recoils, her back to the bannister. That obstacle stops her and seems to communicate a shock which folds her in two; her head and chest fall forward into empty space, her lower back is propped against the railing, her legs droop over the edge of the stairs. No muscle contraction holds up this poor inert being, it slides rapidly and coming to the bottom of the stairs, falls like a wounded bird.[27]

The parallel with Sand's stage directions for Meg in *Aldo* is striking. Kitty Bell's famous staircase scene, attributed to Marie Dorval's invention, exercised a strong influence on nineteenth-century theatre history. When Emile Zola saw a revival of *Chatterton* at the Comédie Française in 1880, he observed that the staircase was the most important character in the play:

> My preoccupation, my only big preoccupation, during the evening, was the famous staircase. And I left with the conviction that that staircase is an important character

of the drama. . . . If the staircase didn't exist and everything was played on the same flat level . . . the effect would be diminished by half. . . . One recalls that it is an invention, a happy idea of Marie Dorval. That great artist, who certainly had a highly developed dramatic sense, must have sensed only too well the scenic poverty of *Chatterton* . . . that monotonous elegy. . . . She had an inspiration, she imagined the staircase which plays the most real and most lively role in the drama.[28]

Recognition is due to George Sand for having made this imaginative use of a staircase in her play *Aldo le rimeur* a couple of years before her friend Marie Dorval used the same idea in *Chatterton*.

From late 1834 through 1836 there is no sign of Sand writing for or about the theatre. Other preoccupations filled her life. Contemporary with the publication of *Aldo le rimeur* in 1833 George Sand and Alfred de Musset fell in love. Following a sojourn in Fontainebleau together they ran off to Italy for the winter months of 1833–34, when Sand gave her play *Conspiration* to Musset. Their first rupture, caused first by his unfaithfulness and then by hers, led to Musset's return to Paris while Sand remained in Venice with her Venetian doctor. When Sand returned to France, Musset and Sand resumed their famous love affair, but it came to an end in March of 1835. In the meantime Sand wrote more novels and began her *Lettres d'un voyageur.*

Sand's contacts with important musicians inspired her to take her two young children to Switzerland in the fall of 1836. She joined her friend Franz Liszt and Liszt's mistress, Marie d'Agoult, for a donkey ride through the French-speaking corner of the Swiss Alps. Back in Paris in November of 1836, Liszt introduced Sand to Chopin. But two more years would pass before Sand and Chopin became close companions.

The publication in January 1837 of her article "De Madame Dorval" marks the resumption of Sand's professional interest in the theatre. This article, or rather reverie, resembles both "La Marquise" and "Mars et Dorval," with the addition of some new thoughts on acting and the actor/audience relationship. Of critical importance to Sand's development of an improvisational theatre ten years later, is the fact that she is already talking about improvisation in 1837. She observes that a good actor, such as Dorval, can compose phrases suited to her character better than playwrights can:

It's not the words she pronounces. All those poets who dictate to her passion are beneath her. If they left her free to improvise her role she would speak better than they what should be said. But no matter! Happily she has a voice more powerful than their genius.[29]

In her autobiography Sand recalls how often playwrights' artificial lines bothered Marie Dorval. Faced with long tirades, and such lines as "What do I see?!" at moments of surprise, Dorval said she would have preferred to improvise "from one end to the other, if they'd let me do it" (*Histoire de ma vie* 9:129).

Mario, the narrator of Sand's reverie "De Madame Dorval," is a struggling young writer who worships Dorval from a distance, sitting on his bench in the theatre. Dorval is his muse, his energy, his soul:

> That pale and sad and beautiful form is my soul. . . . Her passion and suffering are not pale reflections like the words I use. . . . Inspiration, the flaming breath of God, passes through that soul in order to cool down.

The nature of Mario-the-spectator's communion with Dorval-the-actress has reached more mystical proportions than the marquise's communion with Lelio. Whereas the marquise sublimates her amorous and erotic attraction to Lelio in aesthetic imagination, Mario, the would-be artist, an empty vessel longing for completion, is filled with Dorval's light and energy, completing a mystical union:

> It's me you see there; it's my soul in that woman. . . . the god which possesses her is in me too; it's the same god; but she is a pythoness and I'm not. . . . I exist in all my pores . . . I communicate, I escape my prison, I break the sepulchre of ice where the divine flame has slept for such a long time. Give me my pen . . . I am the first of poets.

But when the curtain goes down and the candles are extinguished, the poet's genius goes down and is extinguished too. This provokes Evan, Mario's companion sitting next to him on the theatre bench, to burst out laughing. The consternated Mario slips back into the inert being of his ordinary life. Dorval, the powerful artist who just dispensed so much energy to Mario's profit, has taken it all with her in departing.

In this work Mario, as perhaps George Sand's spokesman, makes it clear that theatrical art is superior to written literature:

> To write, my friend, is life's torment. . . . it's a struggle without repose between desire and impotence, it's always rolling a stone that never gets to build the palace in one's imagination. O, Sisyphus! poor poet![30]

The writer, working alone forever and hopelessly, yearns for completion, a unity, a consummation with higher powers, an experience that is possible in the theatre, even if only for an instant.

Sand's concept of the theatre as temple, actress as priestess, and audience as devotee participating in a mystical experience, a kind of

Eleusinian mystery, gave impetus to her next play, *Les Sept Cordes de la lyre,* and her next essay, "Le Drame fantastique." The essay, conceived as early as September 1837 (*Corr.* 4:180–81), but not published until December 1839, has been briefly outlined above.

Sand began writing *Les Sept Cordes* in August 1838, and sent the completed manuscript to her editor at the *Revue des Deux Mondes* the following October. Editor Buloz didn't like it and held off publishing the drama until April 1839. Like *Aldo le rimeur, Les Sept Cordes de la lyre* is a *drame du monde intérieur,* a fantastic fable. But whereas *Aldo* relies primarily on visual effects to dramatize the conflicts in the main character's internal conscience, in *Sept Cordes* Sand utilizes strong aural effects as well as visual ones. Harp music and choral singing, attached to the muse-priestess character Helene, alternate with dry and skeptical discourse attached to the philosopher-teacher Albert. Lacking a score, this libretto can only suggest the strong musical possibilities in a stage performance; the work has never been produced. Sand's liaison with Chopin had commenced in June 1838, and one would do well to imagine his music while reading the play.

Albertus the philosopher has denied himself everything but philosophy, a search for truth. Before the action of the play Albertus has been instructing three male students in his philosophy, and trying to teach a fourth, female student, Helene. But she, the daughter of a musician, responds intuitively to art, not reasonably to science and logic. In order to cure Helene of this "madness" Albertus deprives her of the lyre left to her by her father.

The first of five acts, the longest (over a third of the entire play), entitled "The Lyre," takes place in Albertus' chambers. In the course of several scenes Mephistopheles emerges from an extinguished lamp and debates with infernal and celestial spirits while Albertus sleeps nearby. Later in Act I when Helene is alone, Mephistopheles enters disguised as a rich Jewish merchant, and attempts to buy the lyre from her. He then brings on a comic assemblage of poet, painter, composer, and critic, hoping they will be able to play the lyre and take it away. Because of the lyre's magic, the devil cannot touch it himself. But none of the false artists is able to make music on the lyre or to carry it away. But when Helene simply holds the harp it plays beautifully and mysteriously without her touching the strings.

The aural progression from everyday reality to fantasy moves from dry discussion and reflective monologues to the first sounds of the lyre, first just isolated pings to Albertus, then cacaphonous disharmony in the hands of false artists, and finally celestial harmonies in the arms of Helene. Each of the succeeding acts is progressively shorter, reflecting structurally the process of elimination taking place as Albertus breaks the strings of the lyre two at a time (two per act), thus destroying their symbolic function and deconstructing the lyre's musical harmonies. When Helene breaks the last string in the last moment of the play and releases the spirit of the lyre from its prison, she frees her soul from her body so that it can fly off to join the lyre's spirit.

The philosopher Albertus breaks the strings in an effort to understand rationally the musical dialogue that takes place between Helene and the spirit in the lyre. A musical dialogue forms the central focus in each of acts two through four. The fullest and most beautiful musical exchange occurs in Act II because the lyre still has all seven strings; it takes place on a garden terrace, Helene languishing upon cushions. This zenith of harmony and understanding disappears when Albertus breaks the strings of gold which represent faith and contemplation of the infinite. In Act III Helene and the lyre spirit play a song called "Resigned Hearts" in the evening on a river bank; it is destroyed when Albertus breaks the strings of silver which symbolize hope and nature's beauties. The visual setting of the fourth act foreshadows Ibsen's *Master Builder*: Helene climbs with her lyre to the top of a church spire where she sits on a pedestal of the archangel's statue and plays on the three remaining strings. The dialogue that Helene and the lyre's spirit play this time can be understood by the common man because it sings of man's work. The lyre's spirit optimistically sings of man's inventions, his monuments, ships and trains, his industry. But Helene answers in mournful tones that man's presence on earth is destructive; she paints a dischordant picture of wars, violence, injustice and cruelty, and throws the lyre from the top of the tower. Albertus recovers the harp and breaks the two strings of steel. In Act V, "The Bronze String," Helene stares vacantly, silently out the window of her chambers. The desperate Albertus recognizes his love for Helene when she breaks the last string, the string of love, and dies. He acknowledges that "love is the only thing which can be infinite in the heart of man," and thus is liberated from his false philosophy and dreams. The play ends with Albertus returning to his classroom and students, saying, "The lyre is broken, but its harmony has passed into my soul. Let's get to work!"

Sand's poetic morality play looks forward to Strindberg and Maeterlinck, relying on an interchange of symbols and senses that Baudelaire later called "correspondances." As Sand says in her mystical play:

> Everything is harmony, the sound and the color. Seven tones and seven colors interlace and move around you in a celestial marriage. Absolutely no color is mute. The universe is a lyre. Absolutely no sound is invisible. The universe is a prism.[31]

The socialist-evangelist critic Pierre Leroux, who formed a close professional association with Sand during this epoch, first defined poetry as a language of symbols, a system of correspondences, a network of vibrations.[32] Sand's drama of *Sept Cordes,* an enactment of Leroux's theory, fell on deaf ears; for, like *Aldo le rimeur,* it received little or no public notice following its publication, and fell into obscurity.[33]

Sand intended that her next drama please her editor and others of "common sense" who did not like her metaphysical reveries. *Gabriel,* written in the spring and published in the summer of 1839, received high praise from Balzac, who found *Gabriel* ravishing, "a piece of Shakespeare; and I don't understand why you haven't put it on the stage."[34] *Gabriel,* too, has yet to be performed.

Sand promised that *Gabriel* would not be philosophical, fantastic or metaphysical, but rather "romanesque" (*Corr.* 4:642). To her friend Charlotte Marliani, she confided that the drama's philosophy and metaphysics were disguised enough not to scare anyone away; and that the moral of the play would please Charlotte, "because the woman plays the biggest role, however, I'm not as ambitious as you, I only profess to equality" between the sexes (*Corr.* 4:634). To illustrate her theme of woman's equality, Sand gives her main character, Gabriel/Gabrielle, a man's education and male identity. We find out in the Prologue that Gabriel's grandfather, Prince of Bramante, some vaguely Renaissance Italian principality, has ordered Gabriel's tutors and guardians to raise the child as a boy. Her/his education has included hunting and athletic training, along with a classical education in languages, philosophy and science.[35]

In the play's Prologue, on Gabriel's seventeenth birthday, her grandfather visits. He has returned to this secluded castle after several years absence in order to tell the half-suspecting youth about her true gender and his reasons for keeping it a secret—he does not want the other side of the family, which has the legal male heir, to inherit his principality. Outraged with her grandfather's dishonorable deception, Gabriel sets out to find her cousin Astolphe, the legitimate male heir. In Act I Gabriel and Astolphe meet in a tavern where the dissipated cousin spends much of his time. A drunken brawl breaks out and Gabriel, still clothed as a boy, saves Astolphe's life by killing a man. The two cousins are taken to prison, where, in the next scene, they watch over one another, sleeping in turns; a tender affection arises between them and they become close companions. Act II divides the action between Astolphe's chambers and another grand house where a party takes place. The cousins get ready for a ball. First Astolphe preens before his mirror arranging an elaborate costume, teased by his mistress, Faustina, who is impatient to depart. Then Gabriel looks at herself in front of the mirror, putting the final touches on her "disguise" as a female. Astolphe's confusion at seeing how beautiful his friend looks in a woman's costume is further compounded at the party when he sees how the other men are attracted to Gabriel. She, too, feels a disconcerting attraction to Astolphe. When they return to their chambers at the end of the evening, Astolphe happens upon Gabriel as she undresses and discovers the truth. Act III takes place in Astolphe's rather delapidated country seat, where the now married lovers Astolphe and Gabriel have secreted themselves. While Astolphe hunts outside in the nearby forest, Gabrielle embroiders in the somber and gloomy sitting room, forced to listen to the bickerings of her mother-in-law and a priest. Gabrielle's true identity is kept from Astolphe's mother, who nevertheless treats her daughter-in-law with jealous hostility. Act IV finds Gabrielle even further isolated, in a country cabin at the foot of the mountains, sketching the scene out her window. When it comes time for her to return to Florence and resume her princely duties, Astolphe, out of jealousy, asks her to stay. Because of his own roving nature, Astolphe suspects Gabrielle of like infidelities. In Act V, set in Rome at carnival time, Astolphe and his old mistress Faustina sit together in a cabaret while the carnival revelers pass by. Gabriel sees them and retreats. Her mission to the Vatican has succeeded; she has secured the relinquishment of her title and estates in favor of her cousin. At four in the morning, leaving her stuffy room to walk her dog, crossing a bridge over the Tiber, Gabriel is stabbed to death by her grandfather's hired assassin.

Posing the problem of the equality of the sexes in both education and love places *Gabriel* (1839) well ahead of its time. While Sand's Shakespearean drama of a female prince does demonstrate that a boy's education can produce equal effects in a girl, for Gabriel proves that she can think and fight with the best of men, the play raises questions but gives no answers on how to maintain equality between the sexes in a romantic love relationship. Astolphe, the man, cannot help being overly possessive and suspicious of women; and though love ennobles him for a while, he nevertheless sinks back into his wastrel ways. Gabriel, the woman, cannot reconcile her profession as prince with being a devoted wife; she must alternate between the two roles, and being almost superhumanly generous and noble, she is too idealistic and too demanding of others. Sand's play has the advantage of giving a clear and colorful presentation of these conflicts without pretending to clear them up other than to resolve them in the almost gratuitous death of the principal character.

Sand's next play, *Cosima,* written in the summer months of 1839, followed hard upon *Gabriel,* and continues to explore the same problem posed in

Gabriel. Although this play is set in the Italian Renaissance as well, Cosima has not had an education equal to a man's. She has been raised to be a good mother and wife for her husband, a wealthy Florentine bourgeois businessman who, unlike Astolphe, is consistently kind, forgiving, noble and virtuous, completely unobjectionable. Cosima fully expresses what both she and Gabriel feel, confined in small, stuffy chambers, stifled and overprotected. In Act I the bored and unhappy housewife sits in front of her upstairs window staring out, her distaff idle on her lap. The young domestic, Neri, who secretly loves Cosima but is more faithful to his master than to his passion, complains to the brooding Cosima: "You used to love me like a brother, and now you mistake me for a guardian, a jailer." She answers, "It's boredom which devours me. . . . I don't live here, I suffocate."[36] Neri does not understand boredom; he never has enough time to do his work, a complaint to which Cosima responds:

> That's because you work. You don't know the anguish of leisure, you men! You have ambitions, you have duties! But for us, with what can we fill the emptiness of our days? Managing the house, you say? But that's a very little thing. Do you know that without leaving out a single task, each day I have three or four hours left and I don't know what to do. Do you know that the work is insipid (*she shows him her spinning wheel*) and that at each minute I'm seized with the desire to break this wheel? . . . Each of these skeins represents a week of my agony (*Cosima*, p. 34).

In conflict with Cosima's boredom is her husband's honor. The word "honor" functions as a leitmotif throughout the drama, a bitter refrain in Cosima's discourse:

> Always a propos of me, the honor of my husband. In truth, I admire the care taken here by everyone on behalf of that treasure, apparently so fragile. But I fear it's like every other precious thing, an indiscreet or clumsy hand will tarnish it (*Cosima*, p. 36).

And later, even more bitterly, she cries out, "Conjugal honor, fierce prejudice! you engender ferocity in the husband, shame in the wife and the ruin of the family" (*Cosima*, p. 46).

Threatening the husband's honor is Ordonio, a rich Venetian nobleman who has designs of seducing Cosima. Fascinated by Ordonio's attentions, Cosima fears she might be falling in love with him. In time we discover that Ordonio does not truly love Cosima, but, challenged by her virtue and pride, wants to bring her down: "Virtue has effrontery just like vice." When Cosima tells Ordonio that her place is near her husband, he is outraged that "at this instant" with victory in sight she has "the audacity to resume her role." "You play too big a role, madame, and you'll lose your part. . . . You have put me in defiance . . . and you will succumb thanks to your pride and mine" (*Cosima*, p. 58).

The most critical scene of conflict between Ordonio and Cosima takes place in Act IV in Ordonio's palace, in a dark, windowless boudoir; one small door upstage is barred and bolted shut. The room, elegantly furnished, but "mysterious," evokes Cosima's stifled eroticism. Cosima has come to this chamber out of jealousy, because she fears she has a rival; but once in that strange room with no exit, she must confront not only Ordonio's falseness but her own misguided sensuality. First Ordonio tries to seduce her. When that fails he threatens her with violence. Cosima is ashamed that she could have believed she ever loved such a man, and once dreamed of leaving her good and decent husband in favor of such a one. With the baldness of her suppressed lust having reared its ugly head in the dark and plush boudoir, Cosima's romantic dream turns into a violent nightmare. She attempts to run away, but is prevented by a real jailer this time, whose self-interest is his only motivation. By means of a "romanesque" secret passageway, engineered by a deus ex machina (the duke), Cosima returns home. In Act V Cosima commits suicide to prevent a duel between Ordonio and her husband.

George Sand wrote *Cosima* expressly for the stage, rather than to be read as a novel in dialogue form. She wanted to have it produced and acted by her friend Pierre Bocage, but he could not oblige her. His theatre was too small, and he was otherwise engaged (*Corr.* 4:627, 751). Buloz, Sand's irascible editor at the *Revue des Deux Mondes* and recently appointed royal commissioner of the Comédie Française, begged her for a play he could produce at the national theatre. So Sand gave him what she called her "légume," *Cosima,* in August 1839. While she could not get Bocage for Ordonio, she insisted on Marie Dorval for Cosima even though Dorval was neither a member of the Comédie Française nor one of Buloz's favorites. The project, Sand's first stage production, started off with doubts and dissent which got worse as the months passed. Sand grew to detest the arrogance and lack of cooperation among the Comédie actors, and mistrusted Buloz's directorial judgment entirely. She tried to withdraw her piece, but without success. So, in spite of her wishes and better judgment, *Cosima* opened at the Comédie Française on 29 April 1840.

What happened at that first performance had a devastating effect on Sand's hopes for a professional playwriting career. The idealistic and perhaps too naïve Sand refused to follow customary procedures and have a "claque" of audience members organized and paid to applaud and cheer on opening night. Heine said she was too proud (*Corr.* 5:36n), but Sand disapproved of the practice. Though she saw in advance that her enemies (whom Heine identified as elements of the bourgeoisie and aristocracy who considered Sand and her works immoral) were organizing their own claque, she was helpless to prevent them. On opening night this claque of enemies interrupted and at times overwhelmed the performance of *Co-sima,* whistling, laughing, booing and hissing (*Corr.* 5:44n). The actors, shaken by this reception, performed poorly. Sand responded calmly, if a little sadly, the day after:

> I was there, tranquil and even a little gay. . . . the incident seemed burlesque to me. If there is a sad side, it's to see the grossness and corruption of taste. I never thought my play was beautiful; but I will always believe it is honest and the sentiment pure and delicate (*Corr.* 5:47).

Cosima closed on May 17, after only seven performances.

Sand had wanted *Cosima* to introduce onto the public stage a free discussion of the internal life of a household. She hoped that this production would habituate the public taste to witnessing a "change of emotions and an interest in little family events," and to following the "development of a passion without strange incidents, surprise or terror." The temptation of Cosima shows not only how weak and impressionable the woman can be, but how the man who poses as her protector, "the friend and doctor of her soul," is no less culpable. Sand thought *Cosima* would establish a new genre of theatre, psychological drama "analytic of intimate thought."[37]

Those critics who complained of *Cosima*'s immorality appear to have based their objections on Cosima's ingratitude towards her husband. Why, they ask, would any woman married to such a fine man want to dally with a dandy like Ordonio. Heine objects to Sand's tendency to rehabilitate women who fall into temptation.[38] Hippolyte Lucas' review in *L'Artiste* (3 May 1840) calls Sand's defense of such a woman as Cosima a "perfidy":

> What! a woman has for a husband a gallant man . . . full of zealous attentions for her . . . whose full-time occupation is to procure for her well-being and wealth, who is esteemed, respected and held dear by all around him, and that woman, one fine morning, gives in to a thoughtless caprice . . . to the first man who will . . . pass some hours under her window sighing with his hand on his heart! She will leave her sewing, renounce the cares of her domestics . . . in hopes of meeting this mysterious person who troubles her existence. Isn't that the limit of ingratitude? and virtue which is as fragile as glass! Resist more valiantly, Cosima . . . or else it's better you poison yourself (p. 332).

Cosima's defenders, two leading critics of their day, Sainte-Beuve and Théophile Gautier, found Cosima's predicament more sympathetic. Sainte-Beuve thinks that any young woman would be tempted to fall in love with a romantic young stranger, no matter how decent and good the husband; and Cosima's boredom, exacerbated by her feeling of being overprotected, makes the temptation all the more understandable. Sainte-Beuve compliments Sand on her sensitive character analyses in the characterization. He attributes the unsuccessful first night performance of *Cosima* to insensitive and mediocre male actors who lack *ensemble*; and to the public, or that faction of the public which looked for faults and double meanings at which to hiss and whistle. Sainte-Beuve's advice to the playwright: pay more attention to development, clarification, and symmetry in the construction (*Revue des Deux Mondes,* 1 May 1840, pp. 563–68).

Gautier's criticism of the *Cosima* premiere performance penetrates even further beneath its surface failure:

> *Cosima* is a study of woman that is perfectly true, and one that only Sand could do. That passion which ends in hatred is admirably observed and with a profound philosophical sense. But that finesse of nuance harms success. The public, wrong in this case as in others, can put up only with demons and angels in the theatre. An abandoned and impetuous lover who gives herself entirely would seem to the public more natural than the prudent and timorous Cosima; and yet every day you encounter Cosimas on their way to church in lace mantillas and satin hats.[39]

Because Cosima seems so true to nineteenth-century type, Gautier regrets Sand's setting her in Renaissance Italy, even though he sympathizes with the desire to have beautiful costumes and a picturesque stage setting. A modern setting would have had more "vraisemblance," and the audience would have "better understood Ordonio in patent leather boots and yellow gloves."

Another distinguished critic of the day, Jules Janin, after a lengthy summary of the play's plot (typical of nineteenth-century criticism), advises his reader to forget about Sand as a dramatist and go read her brilliant novels instead. She is too "ill at ease in the milieu of the theatre," where "her soul is compromised in that insipid atmosphere . . . without air, without space, without liberty."[40] Janin thinks that Sand's expansive soul cannot be contained in a dramatic structure. Sainte-Beuve thought Sand had not paid enough attention to dramatic structure; Gautier stated that she was too occupied with the play's carpentry and the story's complication, and complained that she was too afraid of being her lyrical, turbulent self. Now Janin dismisses the value of Sand's trying to do anything in the theatre.

At the time, Sand might have agreed with Janin; for as far as she was concerned *Cosima* marked the beginning and the end of her professional theatre career. Her hopes had been high: during one year, 1838–39, Sand had written four dramas: *Les Sept Cordes de la lyre, Gabriel, Cosima* and *Les Mississipiens.*[41] She had begun the last one immediately after writing *Cosima,* in the fall of 1839, and intended to have it produced with Bocage playing the lead. But some time during those nettlesome months of *Cosima*'s rehearsal at the Comédie Française, Sand changed her plans for *Les Mississipiens,* and simply had it published in March and April 1840. She waited almost a decade before writing another full-length drama.

Les Mississipiens departs from the other three plays written that year as radically as the first three differ from one another, attesting to how extraordinarily experimental Sand's turbulent imagination could be. With its more realistic focus on concrete problems of money and the materialistic conflicts between socioeconomic classes, *Les Mississipiens* points toward Sand's plays of the 1850s, rather than back to her dream plays of the 1830s. The play's characters subject women, love, and marriage to monetary interests. Their dialogue crackles with a bitter blend of Marivaudage and Robert Macaire. Greed makes love just another commodity to put on the auction block; exploitation rules human relationships.

The play's Prologue, set in the year 1702 at the end of Louis XIV's reign, shows a young man coming to the home of the woman he loves so that he can see her one last time; she is being married off to a rich old man. The young man, Leonce, has lost both his fortune and the woman he loves; so he plans to emigrate to America. A blasé duke, friend of the girl's mother, remarks to himself that there once was a time when women could love men for themselves alone, at least some women did; but now, thanks to the likes of Madame Maintenon, and her kind of devotion, women do not even give men a look without payment in solid gold.[42]

When, in Act I, Leonce returns years later, in 1720, during the corrupt times of the Regency, he is not the stereotypical poor emigrant boy who returns from America rich and famous; but instead he has become George Freeman, famous for writing books against slavery. He appears on the stage dressed in simple, scholarly attire:

> Costume of a philosopher, black hair parted in the front and combed naturally, brown suit without any trim . . . a simplicity in his manners that contrasts with the tone of that day, a pale and melancholy face.

He looks around him, "So this is it? . . . Everywhere ostentation and prodigality" (*Les Mississipiens,* p. 203).

In the course of the play Freeman protects the daughter of his former love by preventing another commercially advantageous marriage of that daughter to one of her father's business associates. Freeman's visit also redeems the girl's mother by inspiring her to reexamine her own conscience, with the result that she leaves her husband to live quietly and simply in the country. Freeman makes her husband return money fraudulently acquired from a group of investors called the "Mississipiens," money they had mistakenly given to him for nonexistent mines in Louisiana. Having done what he could to further spiritual freedom in his home-land, George Freeman goes back to America to continue his work there.

And George Sand put drama and theatre aside and went back to work on novels and articles written on behalf of her various friends, socialist philosophers, worker poets, and musicians. For several years she limited her theatre-related activities. Between *Cosima*'s failure in 1840 and the opening season of her own private theatre in late 1846 Sand wrote only four articles and a short dialogue which specifically pertain to drama and theatre. But these works are of critical importance to understanding Sand's shift of focus and objective during the period of intense theatrical activity which commenced at the end of the 1840s. One of the articles (1840) pleads for the preservation of Italian opera in Paris. A second (1844) explains in some detail what is wrong with contemporary theatre. And the third (1845) and fourth (1846) contrast Hamlet, the prince of romantic individualism, with Debureau, the proletarian Pierrot, a contrast that con-firms Sand's change of theatrical focus from the romantic individual to the collective voice.

Sand spent less time with her theatre friends, Dorval and Bocage, and more time with a growing circle of musicians and socialists. Some-times these last two categories did not mix well; Chopin held fast to his aristocratic snobbery and scorned Sand's more common socialist friends to the end. But at other times the combination proved fruitful. In 1840 Sand helped arrange a marriage between the famous opera singer Pauline Garcia (Malibran's younger sister), and another of her friends, the repub-lican radical writer and translator, Louis Viardot. That marriage was founded on spiritual and intellectual compatibility, but not on love, ap-parently.[43] Pauline Garcia Viardot's sensational tours to Moscow, Vienna, London and other European capitals inspired Sand's masterpiece, the novel *Consuelo* (1842–43), in which Chopin's mystical character appears opposite Musset's more libertine one to form a fictional triangle with the Pauline-Consuelo figure in their musical voyage from Venice to Bohemia. This work amply demonstrates Sand's general appreciation of music and particularly folk music.

On behalf of Pauline and Louis Viardot, Sand published an article, "Le Théâtre-Italien et Mlle Pauline Garcia," in the *Revue des Deux Mondes* (1 February 1840), in which she expresses alarm at the possibility of losing the Théâtre-Italien's performers and art. Louis Viardot was director of the theatre, Pauline a leading performer, and the art native Italian opera. If Paris should lose Pauline Garcia, by forcing her to gain her living in the opera houses of other European cities (which is what happened), by losing her the public misses not only the beauty of her singing and the intelligence of her acting, but the instruction and education she gives in her faithful reproduction of a composer's original intentions. "She enters into the spirit of the composers, she is one with their thought. . . . She never changes their idea or substitutes her own spirit" (p. 587). Sand, we recall from "De Madame Dorval," encouraged improvisation of words in an actor's performance, but evidently not musical improvisation in an opera singer's. Perhaps Sand held a musical score in higher esteem than a play script, and respected composers more than playwrights. Sand's regard for the theatre was at its nadir.

Sand explains her disenchantment with the theatre, the kinds of plays she disdains but which the public applauds, in a preface to her friend Leroux's translation of Goethe's *Werther* (1844). Sand credits Pierre Leroux with having cured her of romantic skepticism by initiating her into his larger mission of "ardent charity, fraternity, equality, humanity in one word."[44]

In her preface Sand asks the basic question, who is to blame for the bad theatre productions? The audience is at fault because it demands an abundance of surprises and intense excitement in its theatrical experience. The playwright is at fault for failing to give the public subjects with more integrity. The actor is at fault for compromising truthful characterization in order to make extravagant effects. Sand proceeds to analyze in some detail how each of these three guilty parties has contributed to the demise of good theatre.

Sand views the audience as a gross and gluttonous public:

> that insatiable need for fake emotions, entangled situations, for unexpected events . . . by which the burned out and spoiled public wants to be held breathless . . . the more he's given, the faster he absorbs that exciting nourishment, which doesn't really nourish him at all . . . his sympathy disseminated over too many characters, his emotion too quickly exhausted.

To satisfy this public's horrendous appetite, the playwrights have exceeded all limits. Their plays are pointless and chaotic, "profusion without order, flight without restraint." In appealing to the public's senses, the playwright has neglected its soul:

> You have put all his emotions in his eyes and ears. His soul is not attracted to your subject, because your subject doesn't hold together, doesn't have enough *ensemble* and homogeneity. So you are forced to make it more complicated, since your public doesn't want a minute to go by without surprise and excitement.

The actor has erred as much as the public and playwright: "The art of the actor has arrived, like all the rest, at that prodigality of effects which blunts all the senses all at once . . . and neutralizes the principal effect."

In order to satisfy the audience's need for constant excitement, to compensate for the play's lack of integrity, the actor consumes and distorts his talents:

> He gives his entrance everything he has, pushing himself to the limit. He spits his voice, hurls his gestures. He too has the fever, or he pretends to have it, in order to maintain the fever in the audience. But what's left to him after an hour of that fake power? Spent, he can no longer attain the true emotion which would command the audience's emotion. You can't give what you don't have anymore. The dramatic artist forced to identify with the character he represents is soon constrained to fall back on the same business he's already used, pushing it to the point of absurdity. He is no more than a madman who lacks inspiration, who cries and strains if he is at the opera, who twists and grimaces if he is on any other stage, who rails and cannot any longer express himself except by exclamation points. . . . No, no, all that is not true art; it's a false route, a squandering of marvelous faculties, it's an orgy of powers whose abuse is infinitely regrettable.

With all three, public and playwright and performer, contributing their cheap tricks to a chaotic theatre, who is at fault ultimately? "Puerile question," answers Sand, "it's a fault of history." Looking around her she sees "luxury everywhere, well-being nowhere. Wealth has strangled the beautiful."[45] Thus she echoes George Freeman in *Mississipiens*.

From Sand's denunciation of classically constrained acting in her story "La Marquise," one might think her more indulgent toward romantic excesses on the stage. Not so. Sand based her admiration of the Bocage-like actor Lelio in "La Marquise," and of Marie Dorval, on their simple and natural manner, their honest emotions, their truthfulness to the character. Sand derived no satisfaction from actors who would rant and rail and tear a passion to tatters in empty bravado, the worst excesses of the romantic revolution.

Sand makes one specific recommendation in her *Werther* Preface for theatre reform. She advises the playwright to integrate his subject matter: "The primary events should occur in a natural and necessary progression concentrated on a principal character in a dominant situation." This statement concisely summarizes our modern concept of a play's "through-line," a progression of character conflicts which leads toward one dominant objective of the play. Sand's emphasis that the progression be natural as well as necessary puts her ahead of Scribe's well-made play, which relied almost entirely on the necessity to move the plot along.

Within a few months of her Preface to *Werther* Sand wrote a one-act play which demonstrates precisely her counsel that a play's primary events should occur in a natural progression concentrated on a principal character in a dominant situation. Entitled *Père Va-tout-seul,* or *Father Go-It-Alone,* the principal character, a vagabond beggar eighty years old, is stopped on the country road by a gendarme who tries to escort the old man to a poorhouse, the dominant situation. The sequence of events occurs naturally: the nice young gendarme politely asks the old man to come along with him to the "depot for beggars"; the crusty old man refuses, declaring that those newfangled houses for the poor are really prisons. An argument ensues. The gendarme insists that the new law be obeyed— no more beggars permitted on the roads; and if Father Go-It-Alone resists going to the poor house, the gendarme will have to arrest him for breaking the law. Sand has placed her gendarme on horseback, which creates visual emphasis on the superior position of the man in uniform towering over the old beggar tramping along the dusty road. The old man, incensed and impassioned, paints a vivid picture of his humble origins, his love of the countryside, and his hospitable friends all over the province who give him bread and shelter when he needs it. But nothing moves the gendarme, who is impatient to get back to work and accuses the old man of avoiding doing honest labor. Looking up at the erect young man in his crisp new uniform and polished boots, the delapidated tramp answers:

> Yes, I hate work because work for the unhappy poor is hateful. It's something which uses up our strengths and gives us no means to repair them with. It's for those who have no other skill than the strength in their arms. If you only knew what that is, young man! if you only knew that the more a man is poor, sick and weak . . . the more is demanded of him and the less he is paid. . . . For the poor, work is the worst of resources.[46]

Their argument attracts other passersby: the curate, the mayor, and some peasants, who all take sides for or against the old beggar's plight. The mayor, a superbly crafted portrait of a small-town politician, declaims on behalf of his richer constituency how they worry about the safety of their property, women and children, when bums and beggars are allowed to roam freely over the countryside. The timid but kindly preacher at first encourages the old man to go along with the policeman, but then comes up with a plan that preserves the old man's liberty yet at the same time obeys the new law. He asks the peasants if they would mind giving the old man board and room one night every couple of weeks. They heartily agree to do so, but then wonder how this is in any way different from what they have been doing for the beggar all along. Well, yes, answers the preacher, now they do it without the old man having to ask for it. He becomes both their guest and their host.

Sand's play pleads for solidarity. If everyone in the community takes a measure of responsibility for those in need who are near at hand, there would be no call for distant and impersonal state-run institutions.[47] Sand wants the people to have the power to decide their own fate. Her socialism is an early form of syndicalism. When Sand wrote *Father Go-It-Alone* in 1844 Europe was experiencing a severe economic depression. The sight of a beggar at every crossroads haunted Sand and her contemporaries. The gap widened between the fortunes of the bourgeois capitalists (bankers and industrialists) and the urban and rural workers.[48] The beggar of the play typifies the losing side of the inequity. Fear of some beggars, who occasionally formed roving bands of thieves, drove state officials to take measures against all beggars, forceably housing them in "shelters for the poor." Sand objected to all beggars being treated as criminals: ". . . to consider as a *brigand* a man who asks for bread. But in accepting the idea that man is *solidaire* with man, there can be no other thought than destroying this horrible social inequality."[49] Her play gives an instructive example of how to destroy this social inequality. This extraordinary little piece, far in advance of its time, a dramatic fable on social reform, never reached the stage. It appeared in a journal in 1845.[50]

A touring production from England of Shakespeare's *Hamlet* helped to alleviate George Sand's disgust with contemporary Parisian theatre productions. After seeing the performance on 13 January 1845, Sand wrote to the famous British actor William Macready, praising his performance in the role of Hamlet:

> I had never seen *Hamlet* played before. . . . You made me forget the Hamlet of my imagination and see Shakespeare's . . . that multiple type more original and more complete than I had imagined. . . . It's you who made me feel and understand him for the very first time (*Corr.* 6:776–77).

Macready reminded the French public of their own Bocage. The critic Gautier shared Sand's enthusiasm for this British Bocage, especially for his energy, violent gestures, and staccato diction. Gautier admired the members of the English troupe in general for their stage concentration, for giving their attention to one another rather than to the audience. But Nerval complained that Macready made Hamlet's madness too real—precisely what appealed to Sand.[51]

William Macready played a significant role in reawakening Sand's lapsed hopes for the professional theatre. He paid a personal visit to Sand on 20 January 1845. Sand found him stimulating: "I was enchanted to hear a competent man speak on Shakespeare" (*Corr.* 6:783). That conversation on Shakespeare and Macready's acting in *Hamlet* inspired Sand to write an essay, "Hamlet," published a month later, in February 1845. Later, Sand dedicated her novel about actors, *Le Château des désertes*, to Macready. The British actor's dedication to creating truthful characters, and the meticulous care he devoted to developing his roles, agree with Sand's views on acting discussed above.[52]

Sand's essay, "Hamlet," does not talk about acting specifically, but concentrates instead on the subtext or inner life of the role. In other words, the essay is a character analysis. Persuaded that Hamlet is indeed mad, his world unwholesome, Sand feels profound pity for the character, but at the same time retreats in terror from his path towards madness and destruction. Hamlet's madness, says Sand, is not the repulsive kind that makes us avert our eyes in horror. Nor is it Ophelia's kind of madness which "hasn't the power to interest us more than an instant after her reason has abandoned her," her delirium being irreversible and her agony entirely personal.[53] Hamlet's madness maintains a state of reason that functions in "absolute forgetfulness of the heart's rendings." Born to love, being by nature amorous, poetic and tender, Hamlet is compelled to hate by knowledge of the world. The shock to his sytem caused by his awareness of evil has paralyzed the sensitive, feeling side of Hamlet's nature. Sand gives two stage pictures as examples of this paralysis: the first, his obliviousness to the loving and feeling Ophelia who kneels near him while he soliloquizes "To be or not to be"; the second, Hamlet philosophizing over Yorick's skull about Alexander's destiny and the meaninglessness of glory, totally forgetful of the murder of Polonius he has recently committed, and the lover he has driven to madness and suicide. Sand claims that this deadening of Hamlet's heart has unhinged his intelligence so that it loses itself in abstractions. Hamlet's reason and feeling have separated so that they operate independently of one another:

> Isn't man incomplete when he can think and feel only separately, in turns? . . . Who can tell us you aren't mad? Because if you weren't you'd be odious. To the contrary, we sense that you no longer have control over yourself, that your violence and cruelty make us suffer more than yourself ("Hamlet," pp. 68–69).

Sand feels pity and compassion for Hamlet because she sees the potential for his kind of madness in all of us:

> Your profound agony is ours; it's in all of us; it's all too human and real. It is the drying up in you of all the sources of life, love, confidence, candor, and generosity. It's that deplorable *adieu* that you are forced to say to peace and conscience, to all instincts of tenderness. It's that necessity to become murky, haughty, violent, ironic, vindictive, and cruel ("Hamlet," p. 70).

None of us could have held up against such insurmountable evil: "Who amongst us, when he contemplates the extent of evil to which the earth is liveried, who would be stronger, more just, and more patient than you?" ("Hamlet," p. 71). We can pity Hamlet all the more because our world is equally terrifying:

Weep . . . tremble . . . kill and murder, destroy and disappear, that's the lot of humankind. . . . From Adam to you, Hamlet, from your days to ours, the voice of the earth is an eternal sob which loses itself in the eternal silence of the skies ("Hamlet," pp. 71–72).

In spite of this doleful conclusion to her essay, Sand resists this bleak vision of the world and humanity. The essay serves more as a warning, to herself as much as to her reader, that what we play at we are in danger of becoming. Thus she chastises Hamlet, "One doesn't play with madness with impunity. . . . Your choice to play the fool attests that you are dominated by that preoccupation" ("Hamlet," p. 67).

"Hamlet" represents Sand's closing chapter in her preoccupation with the isolated, romantic individual. Up to this point the most sympathetic characters of Sand's plays and articles (Lelio, Aldo, Mario, Gabriel, Helene, Cosima, and George Freeman) have been those who are alienated, cut off from the people around them, alone in their quest for the ideal, knowing but perhaps a brief moment of happiness in love, and then dying or emigrating. But after her compassionate look at the isolated and melancholy Hamlet, Sand turns her back on brooding individualism, on her *drames du monde intérieur,* and proceeds to make her sympathetic characters the ones who can work and get along well with others. Those individuals who refuse to do so are cast out.

"Debureau" opens Sand's perspective onto a smaller stage in a tight little auditorium filled with the smelly, sickly working classes of Parisian suburbs. Sand wrote her encomium on the popular mime artist when he announced he would be retiring. The article came out in February 1846; Debureau died a few months later. Sand's short piece praises the artist, his use of the theater space, and his public. The artist's creation of Pierrot, a servant to Cassandre, never deigns to argue on his own behalf: "he would go to battle only to acquit his conscience; and the conscience of Pierrot is as big as his floppy doublet."[54] He is an optimist, certain that "by the denouement everything will have turned out for the best." This modern proletarian Pierrot acts much as Brecht's Azdak does in *Caucasian Chalk Circle* a century later. Sand reports how Pierrot's behavior may be slapstick, but its implications have a larger scope: "He's equitable; when he administers his admirable kicks, it's with the impartiality of an enlightened judge and the grace of a marquis." The plot line may be ridiculous, the situation scabrous, but Pierrot's role is to be cavalier, gallant, polite, insouciant. Sand admires Debureau's artistry which is always "self-possessed and self-contained, never neglecting or exceeding any effect." "How many bombastic and brawling tragedians would not be well counseled to study Pierrot's taste, measure and precision" ("Debureau,"

p. 220). His "sobriety of effects and accuracy of intentions" reaches the apogee of the art.

The stage space at the Funambules was scarcely separated from the audience, making the artist and his spectators one homogeneous group. Sand describes Debureau's adoring and respectful public, made up of "the people," an intelligent race, thin, small, prematurely aged, in bad health, suffering the miseries of poverty, bad climate, noxious housing, deplorable conditions of existence.

> Yet there's also a kind of febrile energy, mocking insouciance, nervous energy which resists sickness and death. Push them and they'll be heroic defenders of their barricades. Their type, their ideal of detached insouciance, of sudden perspicacity and sangfroid is Pierrot Debureau ("Debureau," pp. 217–18).

Just as Sand idealized her romanticist heroes, she would idealize her proletarian ones, in the belief that theatre should show the best examples of our aspirations in any class of society or occupation, not the worst of our deprivations.

A comparison of Sand's "Hamlet" and her "Debureau" clearly illustrates a major shift taking place in Sand's theatrical vision. Shakespeare's character of Hamlet contrasts markedly with Deburcau's Pierrot, the former a prince of royal blood and the latter a prince of the proletariat. Gautier called the mime artist Debureau the "Shakespeare of the Funambules" and his creation of Pierrot the Hamlet of that theatre.[55] Sand perceives Hamlet as the idol of romantic individualists, and Debureau's Pierrot as the favorite of the working class. Hamlet, a nearly ideal individual, disintegrates in stages during the course of his internal conflict, or *drame du monde intérieur*: from melancholy to isolation, to violence, to madness, and finally to destruction. Debureau's Pierrot, a mute servant who acts on his masters' behalf rather than his own, integrates, "knits up" the lowly individual into a larger order, a group, for solidarity and social progress. Hamlet's world is grand and tragic; Debureau's intimate and domestic. Sand's taste in theatre now moves from the former pole to the latter. She recognized this shift when she resumed playwriting after the 1848 Revolution, when she tells how she wants to write plays about real people, not idealized romantic heroes:

> I no longer like that severity and tension of heroes who live only in legends, because I don't believe in them anymore. . . . I am more touched by the true than the beautiful, and by the good than by the grand. I am more touched in direct proportion to my getting older and to my measuring the abyss of human weakness (*Corr.* 9:222).

2

Revolution and a People's Theatre

The Revolution of 1848 and Second Republic of France suddenly raised and then almost as quickly dashed the hopes of socialist democrats such as George Sand. For a brief time censorship was abolished, resulting in freer speech and experimentation in the theatre. But the euphoria for liberal politicians and artists which began in February did not last beyond the end of spring, when more conservative politicians took power. Essentially the Republic died when, in December 1851, Napoleon III staged a coup d'etat, and a year later had himself declared emperor.

Revolutionary changes in Sand's personal and professional life coincided with the 1848 Revolution. Just as the political revolution of 1830 had marked the breakup of Sand's marriage and the beginning of her professional writing career, so, too, the 1848 Revolution marked the end of Sand's eight-year companionship with Chopin, and the beginning of a quarter-century career as a professional playwright.

Sand's most creative and productive period of writing plays for the public stage coincided with the life of the Second Republic of France. During this time Sand completed eight full-length plays, and partially wrote at least two others. Of this total of ten or more plays, seven reached the public stage, representing almost half of her professional dramatic output between 1848 and 1872, and, even more importantly, constituting her most innovative efforts. She helped to create an entirely new genre, the realistic folk play. She made a serious attempt to revive respect for the commedia dell'arte. She progressed in her goal to give *ensemble* and strong psychological development to her dramatic characters. She contributed to the rise of realism in staging techniques. And she tried to get her socialist sympathies past the government censors in order to attract and educate a "people's audience" in anticipation of creating a "people's theatre."

Our current use of the term "people's theatre" stems from Romain Rolland's essay of that title first published 1900–1903. Rolland falls in line with a series of predecessors, Rousseau to Michelet, who theorize that a theatre for the people should feature legendary and national heroes.[1] Rolland attributes the concept primarily to Jules Michelet, who wrote about a people's theatre in 1848 in a lecture collected with others and published under the title (not Michelet's) *L'Etudiant*. In his tenth lecture, 17 February 1848, Michelet proposes national revolutionary heroes for subject matter in a new people's theatre, and the recreation of folk customs and festivals. George Sand had recreated folk festivals in her novels and would do so shortly in folk plays destined for Paris stages, specifically *Claudie* and *Pressoir*. But, as we have seen already in Chapter 1, Sand mistrusted hero worship, for she saw in it the dangers of egotism and chauvinism. Instead she celebrated the ensemble, the *groupe solidaire*.[2]

A great admirer of Rousseau, George Sand nevertheless could not accept his idea of the "noble savage," that man left alone is by instinct good, that society corrupts him. Instead, she advanced the idea that man's natural state is in a social context:

> There could not have been a golden age in Rousseau's primitive forest, if man didn't live there in complete solidarity with his brothers. Man is neither good nor bad in isolation. In such a state he doesn't exist as man.

Sand says living as an individual and living with others must be one and the same thing in a simultaneous ebb and flow of reciprocity:

> Give and receive, work and play, produce and consume, follow and lead . . . love and be loved, respect and earn respect, these are the simultaneous acts of the individual and general life which refuses division and distinction in the metaphysical formula.[3]

For Sand, the individual becomes fully human only when he lives with others and exerts himself on their behalf. That belief forms the basis of all of Sand's dramas and theatre work, and particularly the plays she hoped would attract the proletariat into the theatres of Paris.

When news of the Revolution reached Nohant in February 1848, Sand wasted no time in hurrying up to Paris to give whatever support she could to the republicans. She volunteered to serve the new revolutionary government as Information Minister, and proceeded to write several "Bulletins to the People," pamphlets which on the one hand encouraged "solidarity" for the workers, and on the other warned the aristocracy and bourgeoisie to raise their social consciences above selfish material gain— or else. These firebrand messages rankled a conservative theatre historian even in the 1860s, as he remembered how Sand's "Bulletins" had frightened the bourgeoisie into taking reactionary measures when they returned to power.[4]

Sand wielded her revolutionary pen to defend not only the new Republic, but also a new, and, she hoped, better, theatrical art. Writing for the left-wing journal *La Cause du Peuple,* Sand accuses playwrights of the previous twenty years of having committed dramatic parricide by devoting their energies to constructing well-made plays of intrigue, "the decadence and death of art." In her review of Augier's *L'Aventurière* (April 1848), which premiered at the Comédie Française, or Théâtre de la République as it had been renamed, Sand sees some hope for the future of theatre. Since Augier's "simple and sage" action takes place in a family's home and develops in an uncomplicated and naïve manner, it fulfills Sand's requirement that art be true to life. She commends Augier for characters who attitudes can be seen to change:

> The progression of interest isn't born by a sequence of changes in the anterior situation of the characters, but in a sequence of modifications in their ideas, in their affections, in one word in their moral being.[5]

Sand claims that this new theatrical art will appeal to their new public— "the people," who are themselves artists by intuition if not by training. She says that the artist should never believe "that anything can be too beautiful or too serious for them."[6]

Sand's own *beau geste* for the people of the Republic was the performance of her one-act play *Le Roi attend.* The people's audience which assembled at the Théâtre de la République on 6 April 1848, admitted free of charge, resembled the Funambules' public more than the upper-middle-class wives and dandies customarily found at the Comédie Française. This people's audience behaved much better than the audience for Sand's *Cosima* had. She exults:

> Never have our great artists found a public more sympathetic and more intelligent, not one orange peel in the loges, no conversation during Corneille's verses or Molière's prose. . . . The people are more delicate and more gentlemanly than all the gentlemen and dandies of yesterday.[7]

The evening's celebration of the new Republic began with Sand's one-act play and then proceeded to Corneille's *Horace* and Molière's *Le Malade imaginaire* and finished with new and old patriotic songs.

Sand describes her *Roi attend* as "a sort of pastiche in which the author expresses her own good intentions by attaching them to some of the most famous dramatic masters."[8] First the Muse of the Republic, played by Rachel (Elisabeth Rachel Félix, 1821-58), speaks, and then Molière, in a situation reminiscent of *L'Impromptu de Versailles,* in which he and his company of actors hurriedly try to put together a play for the waiting king. In the second part of Sand's one-act play, a masque-like procession of famous playwrights appears on the stage. Molière's troupe of actors has exited to perform, and the exhausted playwright lapses into a deep sleep. We see his dream: Aeschylus, Sophocles, Euripides, Shakespeare, Voltaire, and Beaumarchais, one by one, arrive on a cloud, accompanied by music, and speak to Molière about "liberty, equality, the rich and the poor." Rachel, the Muse, narrates. In the third part of *Le Roi attend* Molière wakes up to find himself in 1848 France. His actor friend Laforet tells him to hurry up, the king is waiting. The king? Where is he? Molière advances to the edge of the stage and peers out over the audience looking for the king. Then he salutes: "I can see the king very well now, but he's not Louis XIV, his name is 'the people'! the sovereign people. A word as great as eternity."[9] Gautier reports that this salute was greeted by a tumultuous applause. In his review of the event, Gautier thought Sand's speeches were "beautiful, lyrical . . . of that ample and large style familiar to George Sand."[10] Later, in the Revolution's sad aftermath, Sand would remember this happy experience, and it encouraged her to write more plays about and for "the people."

With the failure of Sand's political allies to win support and stay in power, Sand returned to Nohant in May of 1848. Revolutionary idealism ended in bloodshed in June, after which the months dragged on and the political and economic climate grew even more gloomy. Eventually many of Sand's leftist friends and lovers, such as Louis Blanc, were imprisoned or sent into exile. Some were spared more severe prison sentences and even execution because Sand interceded on their behalf. Because of her own avowed socialism, Sand felt herself in enough danger that in the spring of 1852 she made plans to emigrate to Switzerland (*Corr.* 11:64). However, the respect Napoleon III had for Sand as one of France's literary treasures prevented her enemies from persecuting her.

Determined to create something soothing and healing, Sand roused her flagging spirits and wrote a simple tale about Berrichon country folk. Writing this new novel, Sand characterized herself as a shepherd returning to her sheep.[11] Immediately popular when first published in December 1848, *La Petite Fadette* remains a favorite among Sand's novels, which number more than a hundred.[12]

Encouraged by actors at the Comédie Française, Sand adapted an earlier rustic novel, *François le Champi* (1847), into a play in the fall of 1848. She sent her first manuscript of *Champi,* the play, to Augustine Brohan, an actress at the national theatre who had performed in *Le Roi attend.* Brohan proceeded as Sand's agent, but she could not persuade the new management at the Comédie Française to give *Champi* a hearing. The theatre directors, newly appointed by a conservative government, must have looked askance at a play by a famous socialist. So, early in

1849 Sand sent a copy of *Champi* to her old actor-director friend, Pierre Bocage. When Bocage was appointed director of the Odéon on 1 April 1849, Sand acquired not only a sympathetic director, but a suitable theatre for *Champi* as well.

Sand knew that her play was suited to the Odéon audiences. The theatre's location on the left bank in a poor student quarter, far away from fashionable boulevards, meant that the first audiences to attend her play's performances would be composed for the most part of workers and students:

> We'll play it simply in front of a public of students and provincials who will look and listen without prejudice, and when the thing is swallowed with a little emotion by the grocer or big schoolboy, there won't be any longer a hue and holler when I'm seen in the theatre (*Corr.* 9.132).

In her last statement Sand doubtless recalls the group that hissed and whistled at her *Cosima* production in 1840. She didn't know it yet, but *Champi* would be her vindication.

Playwright Sand and director Bocage signed the contract for *François le Champi* on 1 July 1849 (*Corr.* 9:205). It gave Sand author's rights, as determined by the Society of Dramatic Authors, including royalties of about eight or nine percent of the total net revenues for the duration of the play's first run. (A revival would give less.) Sand then sent to Bocage her revised playscript of *Champi,* and asked him to indicate the changes he might like her to make; but she requested he not cut any speeches which gave depth to the characters:

> I don't hold fast to a single word or phrase in the play. Only try not to cut anything . . . that essentially marks the characters. In general in the theatre long passages are feared too much.[13] They're right not to want them, but in cutting them they create characters that no one knows, no one understands, and who seem to desire as if by chance. It's a default of all modern theatre (*Corr.* 9:208).

In the same letter Sand warned Bocage not to give the piece a lot of advance publicity, saying "my name raises storms" of protest; she did not know why. She advised him to play it simply, and if the play is worth anything, "it will go along its own little road. That would encourage me and we could try to fly higher next time. Don't go to any expense, the thing has no need, being matter-of-fact and commonplace itself" (*Corr.* 9:209). Obviously Sand could appreciate the merits of her new genre of dramatic literature without exaggeration. But she had less confidence when it came to her reception with Paris theatre audiences.

Champi did not reach the stage until the end of 1849, and in the intervening months Sand began to lose heart. Living in seclusion in her Berrichon country manor, cut off from the bustle of Paris politics and theatre life for over a year, Sand writes in August 1849: "Sadness renders one mute. . . . The most sincere writers are the most taciturn." Yet she must do something: "It's a duty to continue to work by whatever means." But her work needs a collective voice for inspiration, the sounds of real human voices:

> One can't live and feel in isolation. One isn't an instrument that plays all alone. Even if one is only a hand organ, there has to be a hand to turn it. That hand, that external force, the wind that vibrates Scottish harps, that's the collective sentiment, it's human life that communicates itself to the instrument, to the artist (*Corr.* 9:242–43).

In another letter accompanying her revised script of *Champi* sent to Bocage, Sand sadly recounts her efforts to comfort and console the people around her in the countryside who are suffering a cholera epidemic. "Poor humanity! And the poor doctors who hardly know what they're doing" (*Corr.* 9:263). Once the epidemic was over and Sand's spirits were rejuvenated by the commencement of another season of Nohant theatre productions (see Chapter 4), she gave full attention to the details of her *Champi*'s upcoming production in Paris.

Writing the play's text constituted only the first stage of Sand's work for the professional theatre. Music, casting, costumes and scenic properties for a play's production all originated with Sand, though they were not always carried out as she would have wished. It should be noted that theatre practice in this period of history in France usually required the playwright to act as director of his own play production. It was within the legal rights of the playwright to cast all of the parts and arrange all of the stage movement to his or her satisfaction.[14] Sand preferred to relinquish those rights in order to have a strong director, actor-manager such as Bocage to protect her from tedious rehearsals and bickering actors. The *Cosima* experience had discouraged Sand from performing these functions again. However, late in her professional theatre career, in 1870 for her production of *L'Autre,* Sand demonstrated that she had sufficient ability to take full direction of all rehearsals and production details when the Odéon's directors proved unequal to the task. (See Chapter 3.)

Sand sent her musical score for *Champi* to Bocage on October 5. *Champi*'s first published edition indicates the contribution Sand made to the production:

> The music is indispensable. It is composed of old Berrichon airs, gathered by the author, orchestrated and arranged to accompany scenes by M. Ancessy . . . orchestra conductor for the Odéon (*Corr.* 9:277n).

But Sand was less than satisfied with Ancessy's arrangements of her music:

> Ancessy chose well some of the motifs for the play, but squandered the rest, some superb motifs, for atrocious square dances where everything was disfigured in terms of sense and rhythm, like hair in a bowl of soup (*Corr.* 9:829).

On October 9 Sand sent Bocage designs for the costumes and for the one unit set (*Corr.* 9:281). When casting commenced toward the end of October, Sand wrote her recommendations for the kind of actress she wanted to play Madeleine, the leading female role:

> I would like an actress whose amorous passion exists underneath her maternity. Beautiful enough to be lovable, but not so much as to be loved at first sight, because to the contrary, that love for her must brood in the unconscious. So it's necessary that the woman have all the charms of a woman, those which give serene goodheartedness, but none of the seduction of a young girl (*Corr.* 9:313).

To assure that the costumes would be authentic, Sand sent to Bocage in November not only accurate illustrations executed by her son Maurice, but actual Berrichon headdresses for the actresses to wear in performance, with specific instructions on how to wear them:

> The coiffes must be supported by a *pique* underneath; an example is enclosed. Between the *pique* underneath and the coiffe must be a kerchief of the same form in white silk or black for mourning, pink or pale blue satin for dress-up. All of the coiffes are larger than the *piques* underneath; you adjust them with pins or basting thread. Don't put them on without paying attention to the manner in which they are attached. All of the character is in the manner of adjusting the frill or flap. Adding ribbons is not authentic, but, I believe, in the theatre will clarify character (*Corr.* 9:338).

Sand goes on to explain how the wearing of the coiffe contributes to characterization. Ribbons would be appropriate for Mariette to wear, since she is a young, flirtatious and self-centered girl. Ribbons would not be appropriate for Madeleine, who is a more reflective and older woman in delicate health. Wearing the flaps turned down indicates a widow, so would be suitable for Madeleine. As for furniture and props, Sand advises Bocage that any old solid wood furniture might be used by Berrichon country folk. But he is to pay special attention to Madeleine's wheelchair, which should be made of wood and leather (or cane) with big cloth cushions, an armchair on wheels, with the footstool attached and able to roll with the chair. "You cannot roll a person about on the stage with her feet just hanging down, it seems to me" (*Corr.* 9:337–38). All of these production details regarding music, casting, costumes, props, and furniture demonstrate Sand's strong sense of staging a play as well as writing one.

On 23 November 1849, George Sand's *François le Champi* opened at the Odéon Theatre in Paris. Its enormous success was not foreseen by Sand, who didn't travel up to Paris to see the opening, but hid in Nohant. However, soon afterwards, enthusiastic letters and reviews poured south to her château hideaway. Now that her return to the theatre had been greeted so favorably, Sand could breathe a little more easily. So in December she and her family traveled north to Paris to see a performance. They did not have to hurry, because the play's first run lasted until April 1850, almost one hundred and forty performances, a spectacular number for the period.

After seeing the production Sand complained to Bocage that the actor playing François, Charles Clarence, lacked the intelligence and creative spirit for the role: "that spirit which alone makes a true artist is truly lacking in him" (*Corr.* 9:411). Sand's admonition was prophetic: *Champi* was the high point of Clarence's acting career. But the actress Marie Laurent who played the role of Madeleine in *Champi* received Sand's highest praise. Laurent felt the role rather than "played" it: "Madame Laurent created the type of an honest and generous mother, at the same time austere and tender. Never has there been anyone who plays less at a role and feels it more."[15]

With *Champi*'s cast of seven, Sand created the potential for true ensemble acting, in which every character has his own development and integrity. Sand underlines this principle of *ensemble* in the Preface to the play, where she gives the greatest praise to the smallest part, the role of the servant Catherine:

> Biron made a leading role out of a little role. She is oafish and she is graceful, heavy and light, gruff and sensitive. That madonna's head and queen's body are not unrealistic in the trappings of a servant. . . . Calypso leading the cows. You see that in the country, and this time in the theatre.

In more general terms, Sand found the acting in *Champi* a bit too energetic but recognized that the opposite would have been boring. Over the next half century *François le Champi* would be revived many times. The play was a favorite not only of the audiences but of the actors. After seeing a "marvelous" revival of *Champi* at the Odéon in 1869, George Sand wrote to her son Maurice: "The actors are particularly partial to this piece, because all of the roles are developed, and, they say, they always find in their roles something more to do."[16] Sarah Bernhardt played her first major role, the part of Mariette, in that 1869 revival.[17] And another of the actors wrote to Sand asking for her advice, because he did not want to follow the theatrical traditions in creating his role. Sand ex-

2. *François le Champi* at the Odéon Theatre.
   Illustration of some of the cast and the Act I set for the première production, 1849–50.
   Courtesy of Bibliothèque Municipale, Châteauroux.

plains to Maurice, "he wants to follow the text and not the tradition, because *le Champi* has passed into the state of being a classic."

As France's first realistic folk play *François le Champi* appealed to audiences for a variety of reasons. A simple tale forms the plot outline: Champi the foundling (*champi* means foundling in Berrichon patois) returns to his foster home after a few years away on a distant farm working and growing up. He returns to his adoptive mother, Madeleine, who is recently widowed, convalescent, and burdened with debts. In the course of the play François, now about twenty years old, discovers that he is in love with Madeleine, who is perhaps thirty. This controversial aspect of the play appealed in an intimately personal way to the son-in-law of the late Marie Dorval. René Luguet had been Dorval's lover in the early 1840s, before he married her daughter Caroline. Luguet pours out his emotional response to a performance of *Champi* in a letter to Sand:

> Never have I felt such an emotion! That devoted boy, faithful guardian of the poor persecuted woman's existence. Happy son that could save his Madeleine! . . . How I cried, my handkerchief between my teeth. . . . It was she and I! . . . two souls who had need one for the other.[18]

Luguet's sister, Marie Laurent, we recall played Madeleine. At the end of the play François proposes marriage to Madeleine, and she laconically accepts, thus fulfilling Luguet's and the audience's oedipal fantasies.

The whole affair of François and Madeleine appalled Proudhon, who took a highly moralistic point of view. First Sand offends him by representing a bastard child as a model of filial devotion. Second, this bastard marries his own adoptive mother, "in spite of the cry from the conscience which protests against that spiritual incest."[19] Proudhon fails to mention the details of François' and Madeleine's characterizations. Madeleine had been unhappily married to an alcoholic who abused and beat her. François' first arrival as a child of eight or so exacerbated an already unhappy marriage, for the husband was jealous of the boy. This exposition, and more, takes place in the novel, not on the stage. The play begins with the return of François, grown, healthy and robust, willing to get Madeleine's flour mill back in operation to help her out of debt. He revives her health and her spirits. Emile Zola calls *Champi* a "psychological study," ripe for analysis. He credits Sand for her generous and tolerant treatment of a delicate subject, and for her refusal to see immorality where others saw incest. Zola only wishes Sand had made Madeleine less passive, for he would have liked to see the older woman fall in love with François, gradually, at the same time he falls in love with her.[20]

Sand created for the play a new character which does not exist in the novel, the peasant Bonnin, a simple, loutish, yet cagey young man. Bonnin's shrewish and selfish Aunt Sévère manipulates Bonnin, but in the end he stands up for himself against her and finally speaks some sense. The critics loved this new invention, "a happy creation,"[21] "adorable," but who, according to Delacroix, reformed a bit too abruptly, "not very peasant-like, and even less human."[22] Bonnin falls in love with Madeleine's sister-in-law, the young, pert, coquettish Mariette (the part Sarah Bernhardt would play).

Most of Gautier's interest in the premiere performance of *Champi* riveted on the realistic visual elements of the production. The set, a rustic interior for all three acts, varied the view outside the windows so that the season changed from winter to spring between Acts I and II. The illusion was complete; Gautier thought he was looking at an authentic thatched cottage from the Berrichon countryside, transported onto the stage. The huge fireplace, the rifles crossed and hanging over the mantle, the red and blue painted crockery propped on cupboard shelves—not a realistic detail escaped him. And the costumes "are of a rare fidelity and exactitude."

Sand's innovative use of peasant dialect impressed the critics. Gautier reports:

> Antiquated expressions, gaulish locutions, patois are employed with art . . . to read a long play written in peasant language must be tiring, to listen to it is a pleasure. Madame Sand, who has lived a long time in the country in free familiarity with the country folk, possesses the basis of that language, and imitates it with a rare perfection, both the malicious joviality and the naïve eloquence.[23]

Sand did not write the dialogue entirely in Berrichon patois, or it would have been incomprehensible to Parisian audiences. Instead, she did what J.M. Synge would later do for his Irish peasants; she utilized Berrichon expressions and rhythms to suggest Berrichon patois:

> I have gathered the old forms of the language that one speaks still in the provinces *d'oïl,* with the exception of some expressions born of country people's fantasy, good naïve French. That is the merit of the play (*Corr.* 9:372; December 1849).

But the playwright expressed some disappointment with the manner in which her dialogue was spoken by the actors, she wanted them to speak in a more "natural" rather than "academic" way. The actors enunciated too clearly, without making enough liaisons and elisions. Not even well-educated country folk would speak that clearly and distinctly. Deshayes, the actor playing Bonnin, was the exception. He spoke like a real Berrichon *paysan* (*Corr.* 9:814).

Sarcey and Zola, commenting a generation after Sand wrote *Champi*, both disliked her use of peasant language, but for different reasons. In his manuscript for a public lecture given at the Porte Saint-Martin Theatre on 20 February 1876, Sarcey discusses the merits of *Champi*. He commends Sand's extraordinary assimilation of the life, customs and manners of the peasants. But he thinks that the countryside and its inhabitants have changed more in the twenty years since *Champi* was written than in the previous six centuries. And while Sand's peasant language, "half peasant and half civilized," accomplishes the combination with "exquisite grace," Sarcey disagrees with Sand that peasants can speak so eloquently. He exclaims how limited peasant vocabulary appears to him; for example, grief-stricken peasants can only utter "Mon Dieu," over and over again.[24] Zola, writing at the end of the nineteenth century, finds *Champi*'s language an "intolerable pretention of naïveté," "mannered," "a dupery." But he praises *Champi* as the first play to demonstrate his principle that a dramatic performance can succeed without recourse to "coups de théâtre," and Zola admires Sand's plays in general for their simplicity and "natural development of characters and sentiments." He imagines that *Champi* must have been a "delicious repose for the public in the middle of the complicated abominations of romantic melodrama."[25]

Indeed, *François le Champi* was a "delicious repose" for audiences in 1849. As Sand's contemporary, the critic Sauvage, wrote in *Le Moniteur Universel* on 4 December 1849:

> The dialogue offers an interesting study of peasant language, a study that may be unique, pushed to the point of truthfulness, without obscurity and without affectation. That style surrounds one with scents of greenery and the countryside, and what new interest it gives to the most ordinary of things.

François le Champi's long run, financial success, and public acclaim encouraged Sand to continue to write plays for the professional theatre. She could imagine numerous character types she would like to dramatize and rehabilitate:

> We have on the stage clown hoboes. We don't have real poor people. . . . We have histrionics and Keans. We don't have true actors. So many occupations and situations, that I know, that I feel, but which have only furnished melodramatic or burlesque tableaux. I want to take these classes into their own settings, without either glorifying them or belittling them. With certain types that are made into grotesque caricatures, I want to make them cry without having to sob, laugh without bursting. . . . I've resolved to rehabilitate certain classes of the society. . . . All or nothing in making the struggle. I don't want the middle ground.[26]

Having rehabilitated a Berrichon bastard child in *François le Champi*, in her next full-length play, first called *Lelio* and then *Marielle*, Sand turns her attention to the professional actor and his troupe of improvisational players of seventeenth-century commedia dell'arte. She does not want to see any more "histrionics and Keans" on the stage, she wants to redeem "true actors."

George Sand first wrote *Lelio* as a scenario for her Nohant players to improvise. Half written and half improvised, *Lelio*'s first performance took place on the Nohant stage from 7 to 10 February 1850. The results of that effort excited Sand: "The actors played it seriously with emotion . . . a prodigious success, they all cried while playing" (*Corr.* 9:455). Having proof that the subject could succeed on stage, Sand wrote to a scholar friend asking for a variety of seventeenth-century play collections and biographies. That letter to Henri Martin (20 February 1850) has only recently been uncovered and published.

> I have in my head a subject for the theatre, a subject which pleases and impassions me. . . . To get it going I need some books, I want to immerse myself in the style and color of the times, which have more rapport with our Berrichon than one might think. . . . It's in the seventeenth century, between the end of Louis XIII and the beginning of Louis XIV. I have here Pascal, the Memoires of Cardinal de Retz, maître Adam, Scarron. I want to look at some others, at Regnier, Larivey, Alexandre Hardy, Jean de la Taille, Mairet, Voiture, Sarrazin, Chapelain, Desmarets, etc. I need the most characteristic.[27]

Martin sent her plays by Regnier, Cyrano de Bergerac (yet unknown for the most part), Rotrou, Hardy, Tristan, Racan, Scudéry, Salvator Rosa, and others. Sand thanks him and answers: "When I've leafed through them for eight days, I'll take on the form and modify it to a suitable point like a ragout which transforms itself in the cooking" (*Corr.* 9:452–54). So in April 1850 Sand leafed through the books with the result that she found Desmarets' *Aspasie* the only "beautiful thing" in the lot, a play she then recommended to Bocage for a revival (*Corr.* 9:536–37).

In addition to the style and color of the seventeenth century Sand needed specific details on the lives of commedia actors:

> I must have some details on the *comédie italienne*. I'm already well up on this point, since on the Nohant stage we have amused ourselves by resuscitating that old lost art, la commedia dell'arte . . . But exact notions on the customs and lifestyle of those mimes and improvisateurs, under the reign of Louis XIII and the Regency of Anne, are difficult enough to assemble, what one finds is sparse, incomplete and vague. If you can find me the *Vie de Scaramouche* by Mezzetin, I think that will help *(Lettres inédites)*.

She further explains to Martin that she doesn't intend to reproduce actual history or write a historical drama per se, but wants to place her subject,

3. George Sand and Others in *Marielle*.
Top left: George Sand as Fabio in *Lelio/Marielle*, performed at Nohant 10 February 1850, in *Recueil* 1:126.
Top right: Maurice Sand as Pierrot, *Recueil* 1:172.
Bottom left: Alexandre Manceau as Lelio/Marielle, *Recueil* 1:124.
Bottom right: Manceau as Lelio/Marielle in Scaramouche costume, *Recueil* 1:123.
Phot. Bibliothèque Nationale, Paris.

an original investigation into acting and staging techniques characteristic of seventeenth-century commedia dell'arte, in a milieu that is "possible and likewise probable." By the end of April Sand had finished her research and a full outline of *Marielle,* removing artificiality and any special effects from her model:

> You have no idea the work I've done. I've given as much labor to keeping out stage effects as others give to bring them in. It is absolutely necessary to make it *simple.* It was easy with the *paysans*; with other types it's very difficult (Sand to Bocage, 20 April 1850; *Corr.* 9:528).

She had done everything but write out the dialogue.

Since Sand wanted Bocage to direct *Marielle* at the Odéon and play the lead role, she did not want to undertake writing out all the dialogue in a somewhat archaic language until she has assurance from Bocage that he would like to do the play. She wrote to explain her intentions, to persuade him of the project's value, and to ask for his opinion:

> That epoch is . . . the moment when Corneille is a big and beautiful novelty, but when one still speaks the language of Hardy and Cyrano in the middle classes . . . a little more backwards than Corneille. . . . I want my characters to speak that language, not exact, because it is heavy. . . . There must be a translation just like the middle ground between Berrichon and French that I employed in *Champi.* . . . Besides, I've given a lot of study to that seventeenth-century language (*Corr.* 9:530–31).

Having described the language she intends to use, Sand questions whether or not she should leave her "odious" character a cardinal, or make him a prince. She wonders if the public might interpret the presence of a murky-minded cardinal as an example of her anticlerical sentiments, and thus confuse her specific purpose of focusing on actors, not clerics. But for historical color she prefers a cardinal. In the published version she makes him a prince.

In June 1850 Sand sent off a third draft of *Marielle* to Bocage, filling it with her "heart and tears." To judge by Sand's next letter to Bocage, his response to the script was less than enthusiastic. He wanted something "more spontaneous," "less studied," and thinks another "naïve peasant" play would suit the blasé Parisian public better than these commedia actors (*Corr.* 9:585). But Sand doesn't want to do two Berrichon peasant plays in a row:

> As an artist I like to always look in front of me, and not retrace my steps on the same road. . . . No matter if my play stays in the portfolio . . . a work is never lost . . . it makes progress in the author's brain. It's like an exercise . . . for which the presence of an audience is not essential: because the essential for me is not money or praise. It's me that I'm trying to satisfy (*Corr.* 9:586).

If Bocage thinks *Marielle* is too much of a risk in terms of investment, then, says Sand, he should not do it. However, the rest of Sand's letter attempts to build up Bocage's interest in the play. Marie Laurent (*Champi*'s Madeleine) would be a good choice to play the character of Sylvia, being the right age, not too young, and looking as if cut from the "cloth of a grande dame." Sand explains that Sylvia is based on the historical figure of Madame de Maintenon, on whom Sand has superimposed one quality judged lacking in the original model: heart. Sand rhetorically asks Bocage to imagine what that famous second wife of Louis XIV would have been like with her intelligence had she been capable of truly loving: "She would have had love for that poor old Scarron, that love which instead she reserved for Louis XIV. She would have finished in a convent rather than on the throne" (*Corr.* 9:587). So, no (in answer to Bocage), she does not want to make Sylvia younger, or else she would have to change the character from one end of the play to the other. The actor Clarence (who played François) would not be right for the part of Fabio in *Marielle,* because he is not young enough. And no, Deshayes would not fit the character of Marielle as Sand imagines him—Bocage would. "But," Sand lamely protests, "in sum, I have hardly thought about the actors, and I've resolved not to mix myself in that, absolutely."

Having done as much as she could on *Marielle*'s behalf for the moment, Sand took Bocage's advice and immediately got to work on a new rustic folk play. *Claudie,* roughed out in four days, was in rehearsal by the end of July 1850, on the little Nohant stage.

At mid-year 1850, poised between the fate of her two new dramas, Sand could not see that *Marielle*'s chance of being produced in a Parisian public theatre was going down, and *Claudie*'s coming up. She kept working and planning for both of them. In another long letter to Bocage, Sand devotes the first half to *Marielle* and the second to *Claudie,* giving a description of herself as an actor which adds historical interest to the letter.

First, regarding *Marielle,* Sand thinks Bocage is tormenting himself too much over the play. What does he think is so new in it, the language? There is certainly nothing new in the characters, except maybe that she has Pierrot played by a woman. Marielle, the aging actor who somewhat loses his senses when bereft of love, is not a new character to the stage. Sylvia resembles one of Corneille's women, a calm nature, faithful and devoted to her one love. Again Sand is forced to defend Marie Laurent as her choice to play Sylvia; she is not too old and is pretty enough to play the part, and Louis XIV period costumes will show her off. She goes on to protest that she has made no promises to any of the actors at the Odéon for any of the parts; she knows that things would turn out badly if she went against her director's wishes. She assures Bocage that his troupe of actors at the Odéon, even though they are not big names, actually because they are not, are appropriate for the roles in *Marielle*. Their status as simply hard-working actors would help to create an *ensemble* style of acting on stage:

> The big names, like Frédérick Lemaître or Bouffée, would not be content with a play in which there are other roles on the same level as theirs. As for me, my system is to make as many roles complete as there are characters. I will never write for one actor only. It's the death of art. Those big men would like to remake the play all for themselves, efface all that doesn't pertain to them, and find in each scene the effects made just for them, for their means of success, their manner of speaking (*Corr.* 9:631).

Sand's attitude about ensemble acting clearly puts her ahead of contemporary French theatre practice, which became increasingly a star system rather than an ensemble, until the reforms of the turn-of-the-century in the small theatres.

Sand gives a progress report on *Claudie* in the second half of her letter of 28 July 1850 to Bocage. The Nohant players are rehearsing the play in anticipation of Bocage's pending visit. Unless Bocage would like to walk through the part of Marielle reading from a script, they will not be able to do that play for him because they lack an actor. Sand herself will have to perform the role of Claudie, a young woman of about twenty. This amuses Sand, who, she says of herself, has absolutely no talent for acting, even though she is a good judge of acting. Since she stands like a mannequin on stage, she serves only as something for the others to use as a sounding board. And besides, she is forty-six years old, playing a young unwed mother. But it doesn't matter, she and her children (all young adults) will enjoy performing *Claudie* for Bocage in August, a play as "simple as a *bonjour*" (*Corr.* 9:632–33).

Unbeknownst to Sand, while she was writing this cheerful letter, on July 27 the government revoked Bocage's directorship of the Odéon, dealing a major blow to their professional theatre plans. Bocage had irritated the government by publically celebrating the one-year anniversary of the Republic in May, and admitting most of the audience to the Odéon's gala free of charge. Apparently when Bocage failed to pay a fine of two thousand francs he was fired (*Corr.* 9:641n). Once Sand received the bad news, she sent another letter to Bocage encouraging and assuring him that he was destined for bigger and better things. After all, he had two plays of hers on the way, and *Champi* already in his repertory. And they will be his as long as he wants them:

> I always believe that with you I can succeed in the theatre. Without you, if you abandon me, I would look elsewhere perhaps for my daily bread, but without relish, pleasure, or much hope, because I'd never know what to do (*Corr.* 9:642).

Bocage did travel down to Nohant to see the amateur production of *Claudie* with forty-six-year-old George playing twenty-year-old Claudie. The result: Bocage liked it and set out to find a suitable public theatre in Paris for a professional production.

Sand went to Paris in early September with a revised script of *Claudie* in hand to deliver to Bocage. Other theatre directors contacted her asking for plays: Lemoine-Montigny from the Gymnase and Arsène Houssaye from the Comédie Française, but Sand remained loyal to Bocage, certain he would find them a theatre. Sand describes Bocage as her coat of armor which protects her against the blows of the theatre world (*Corr.* 9:480). She gives Bocage credit for her first lessons in the theatre: "I owe the commencement of my understanding of theatre to him solely, to his conscience, to his ideas, which are those of a babbling genius, generally tiresome, but at moments strong and lucid" (*Corr.* 9:784).

All they needed was a theatre, a building they could rent from another director until Bocage secured his own directorship of a theatre again. Writing from Paris to her son Maurice in Nohant, Sand gives an update on their progress:

> Bocage rambles and bustles about like the devil to find a theatre. They are all at his disposition, all ruined, deserted, in debt, and so it's a question of finding the one least encumbered. He's been offered the Variétés, the Vaudeville, the Ambigue, the Gaîté, the Porte-Saint-Martin, the Théâtre Historique (*Corr.* 9:685).

Of these Sand prefers the Historique, founded by Alexandre Dumas in 1844, and known for its beautiful sets. She explains that "It's the best mounted . . . where the actors play best. The sets, accessories, and stage direction are so appealing and so true that the most improbable situations appear natural there" (*Corr.* 9:685). Bocage thinks he might be able to get the Ambigue, a space Sand finds frightful:

> It's a terrible theatre . . . the loges in the back are suffocating, where all the bad emanations of the auditorium are concentrated. But if the galleries are fine, and the public well disposed . . . well, after all, it is with the multitude that we wish to have our affair, little matter the rest (*Corr.* 9:716).

Next Bocage proposes the Beaumarchais, and Sand, who has returned to Nohant from Paris, patiently replies:

> I have no objection to the Beaumarchais. If we have good plays, and good actors, we'll be worth as much there . . . where the public is more educable, more naïve and more expansive than at the Comédie Française itself (*Corr.* 9:724).

But Bocage did not secure any of these theatres.

In spite of her patience and encouragement with Bocage, Sand was experiencing frustration and discouragement with her theatre plans, which she communicated privately to her good friend Mazzine:

> Theatre is my only study for the last year . . . it has reanimated me a little. It may be useless. The censorship which gives free license to revolting obscenities on the stage, may not permit one to preach honesty to the people (*Corr.* 9:709–10).

That was in September, and Sand must have been anticipating difficulties with the censors over some of the sentiments expressed in *Claudie*. She had cause to be concerned.

Finally Bocage secured the Porte-Saint-Martin, a beautiful space with seating for 1500, and famous in the romantic era for doing new and daring dramas. Bocage would direct the production of *Claudie* and play a principal role, Remy, Claudie's grandfather, the sympathetic octogenarian veteran-of-the-wars reduced to migrant farm work. Sand agreed to give Bocage half of her royalties, or about four percent of net revenues, to direct the show, leaving only four percent of net proceeds to Sand.

George Sand had financial worries. For *Champi*'s first run (November 1849–April 1850) Sand received total royalties of 21,000 francs, representing about eight percent of the theatre's net profits. The financial confusion which followed the political upheavals in 1848 left Sand 18,000 francs in debt (*Corr.* 9:807).[28] *Champi*'s returns enabled her to pay off her creditors. Financial success taught Sand that the theatre could be far more lucrative than publishing a novel. In addition to her eight percent author's share of the first run's net receipts, Sand could expect two or three thousand francs from the play's first publication, and about two hundred francs per month from performances in the provinces. A novel's publication, on the other hand, would pay Sand a total of three to five thousand francs for a first edition, depending on the length; publishers paid Sand one centime per letter (which helps to explain why she did not edit her novels more severely). Even with such a wide discrepancy between profits from plays and those from published fiction, Sand soon learned that spectacular gains from the theatre came rarely and were hard won. Any play, whether it turned out to be a financial success or failure, demanded much more time to deal with directors and other theatre personnel. And if the play closed after only a few performances, something Sand had experienced once before with *Cosima* and would again with others of her plays, her reimbursement for that work might be no more than a few thousand francs received for the play's first publication.

Over the course of the year 1850, when neither of her new plays was produced and she had no time to write a novel, Sand's financial situation worsened again. She owed Bocage 4000 francs and needed another 6000 by the end of the year (*Corr.* 9:807–8). Receipts from her two plays produced in 1851 would ease Sand's financial burden somewhat, but after 1851 she decided to follow a safer course and write novels too.

After *Claudie* finally found a home, casting and rehearsals got underway at the end of November 1850. The contract, signed on 30 November 1850, gave Sand the right to cast the parts and Bocage the responsibility for the *mise en scène,* or play's direction and production.

The less fortunate *Marielle* received a devastating defeat which left Sand desolate. When Sand first sent *Marielle* to Bocage in the spring of 1850, she had explicitly requested that he tell no one about the play, and, implicitly, certainly not show it to anyone, reasoning that she did not need anyone else's opinion but his: "Other opinions always influence me and often spoil what I would have done better all alone" (*Corr.* 9:556). Whether or not Bocage had heeded Sand's warning, the idea of the play was seized by two playwrights, Dennery and Fournier, and produced at the Gaîté on 9 November 1850. The play was assured of success with the famous actor Frédérick Lemaître in the title role of *Paillasse.* Miles away, reading reviews of the production in her château at Nohant, Sand, the unhappy creator of *Marielle,* complained to Bocage on November 20: "I've read the reviews of *Paillasse*; it's *Marielle.* It's all there, from one end to the other, not by similarity of facts and characters but similarity of situations." She despairs of *Marielle*'s ever reaching a public stage: "*Marielle* can do no more than return to the portfolio." Sand does not want to blame Bocage or anyone else for the leak, but she cannot help but express how disheartened she is by all the work she has done on the play—to this end:

> I'm not accusing anyone of an indiscretion, I believe that literary subjects are "in the air". . . . If they are good, so much the better for the one who treats its first. As for me, it's been over six months ago that I treated that subject. I worked at it with care, and there is much good in that work. Events have rendered it fruitless, so much the worse for me (*Corr.* 9:806–7).

Sand notes explicit parallels between the two plays in a subsequent letter to Bocage on November 24: like Marielle, "Paillasse has a noble wife who is kidnapped from him. He believes her lost forever and becomes desolate." Paillasse's son resembles Sand's Pierrot, and there are scenes of the commedia dell'arte, Arlequin, etc. (*Corr.* 9:812). Both plays have historical settings in which a troupe of commedia dell'arte actors tours the provinces. The name "Paillasse" refers to an actual character type, similar to Pulcinella, performed in late eighteenth-century France, just as "Lelio," Sand's first name for Marielle, had been a commedia character type played in both seventeenth- and eighteenth-century France. When Sand finally saw the production of *Paillasse* in January 1851, she called it an *ordure,* a trashy work disgustingly played by Lemaître, who made a parody of the original character type. That fact revived her hopes for *Marielle* a little: "tender and grave *Marielle*" would be their revenge (*Corr.* 10:49–50). But *Marielle* never did receive a public staging. A year later the play was published in the *Revue de Paris* in two installments, December 1851, and January 1852. Over a decade later the play appeared in a collection of Sand's plays entitled *Théâtre de Nohant.*

In his review of the first published version of *Marielle* (in *La Presse,* 6 January 1851), Théophile Gautier expresses how much greater his pleasure is in reading the play than he thinks it would be in seeing it performed, for his imagination is not contradicted by "gross reality." Classifying *Marielle* as a *spectacle dans un fauteuil,* or armchair drama, Gautier puts it in the same category as Shakespeare's *A Midsummer Night's Dream* and *As You Like It*—"impossible to stage." The critic's long and appreciative review of *Marielle* especially commends Sand's adept and penetrating characterization. All eight characters are fully realized and essential to the ensemble. He thinks that the treatment of the subject is "genial," but wonders if the rehabilitation of an actor is any longer necessary in the mid-nineteenth century, when the world can accept the idea that an actor is an honest man. But Gautier concedes that Sand has placed the action of her drama in an epoch when such "repulsions" were true. Gautier contrasts the style of *Marielle,* "an archaic simplicity," a "mélange of Molière and Sedaine," to Sand's more passionate language in her novels. Repeating his wish expressed a decade earlier in his review of *Cosima,* Gautier wishes Sand would let herself go and write lyrical passion again, be "carried away with movements of lyrical eloquence which are natural and not less real for having more color," rather than continue to write "patriarchal sobriety," as in *Marielle.*

It seems that Gautier makes two false assumptions: one, that Sand has written *Marielle* primarily as an armchair drama, when, as we have seen, she intended that it be produced by Bocage at the Odéon; and two, that Sand wanted to rehabilitate the actor, when she really wanted to rehabilitate or revive a genre of acting, the commedia dell'arte. Certainly Debureau's famous commedia character Pierrot needed no rehabilitation. But what of the others: Fiorelli's Scaramouche (Marielle); the swashbuckler Captain Fracasse (Ergaste); the gross, almost cynical Mezzetin (Florimond); the handsome young lover Leandre (Fabio); and the beautiful, beloved Isabelle (Sylvia)? Sand wants these commedia "masques" to be taken as seriously as Pierrot. She wants to see the three-dimensional human being behind the mask, not just for the pleasure of having an inside view into the private lives of seventeenth-century commedia actors, but with the stated purpose of appreciating the serious and sober artist behind the farcical buffoonery.

Early on in the play, Marielle expresses his concern that French theatre tastes are changing; a preference is growing for more formal, regularized written dramas rather than for their irregular, improvisational theatre. He asks what will happen to free speech on the stage should commedia disappear:

> When we no longer have the right to speak the truth about kings . . . to tickle them adroitly . . . those unhappy souls will hardly ever laugh. . . . Think about how our improvised babble escapes all censorship, and that no one can predict or prevent our satires. When we show the common people their own follies and vices under the guise of Brighella, Mezzetin . . . or Pierrot, they can take it and enjoy it. But when Pantalone, the Doctor and the Captain . . . are no longer permitted to personify the faults and malice of rich men, scholars or the military rank and file, the powerful will be inured . . . and the poor will have to endure their own satire all by themselves.[29]

This, of course, is Sand's gentle admonition of mid-nineteenth-century repression in France, rather than simply a historical documentation of the decline of commedia dell'arte in seventeenth-century France. Deburau could mock the common people at the Funambules; but what actors, what character types in what theatres were permitted to satirize the rich and the powerful? Sand regretted the banishment of Lemaître's Robert Macaire from the stage in the 1830s, a satirical characterization of cynicism and greed par excellence, another casualty of France's assiduous censorship.

That Gautier did not perceive Sand's larger historical picture and political commentary in *Marielle* is understandable from a critic who did not like his art polluted by social or political statements; Gautier was an advocate of "art for art's sake." Less understandable is how Gautier failed to see the potential for *Marielle* as a good performance piece; but he was certainly not alone, since Bocage obviously had similar reservations. Even today, in a commentary written in the 1970s, a scholar has judged *Marielle* too long to be adapted to the stage.[30] Actually it is not that long, and even if it were that would not deter most producers and directors from cutting and rearranging a script.

Sand's commedia dell'arte play has much to recommend it to the stage. The scenes cannot be fully appreciated without seeing and hearing them interpreted by actors. Two examples should help demonstrate this point, first, a single brief moment in the play, and second, a sequence of scenes.

At the end of the play, a deliriously happy Marielle (whose beloved Sylvia has been returned to him), sensing that he has lost his grip on reality, musters up enough strength and concentration to give young Fabio, his adopted son and an actor, some last instructions. Fabio has been chafing throughout the play because Marielle will not give him the good comic roles to play, such as Scaramouche. Instead, he has had to remain the young lover, which he feels does not stretch his talents enough. Marielle has already explained to Fabio in Act II that he cannot play the comic roles until he develops more grace and suppleness in his movements, until he will no longer care about making his movements pretty to look at. Now, in the last moment of the play, Marielle gives Fabio this advice: the more he can learn to hide art, the more beautiful it will appear to be.

> The actor must hide the technique of his playing, and never give his all to every bit of his part. Sobriety is the last word in knowing how to do it. Without sobriety you'll have absolutely no gradation in your part.

Marielle then performs an illustration of this gradation:

> For example, when I want to laugh in the pantomime, I keep myself from bursting out all of a sudden. I arrange the expression on my face. Look, you can see . . . I give the impression of being balanced between laughing and crying, as if my immobile face hurts to move. No one knows where I'm going . . . but I get there little by little (*Marielle*, pp. 392–93).

Sand's stage instruction then directs the actor playing Marielle to "burst out laughing, then sob, then let out a single cry, then fall down." Thus Sand shows how the character cannot contain himself in this simple demonstration of his craft. He gives out everything and falls dead. The excess of both joy and suffering splits Marielle asunder, just as it does King Lear in his last moment.

In a second example of *Marielle*'s performance potential, Sand creates a strongly evocative stage environment with nothing more than a table and chairs, a few hand props and the one-by-one sequential entrances of four characters onto a nearly naked stage, or *tréteau nu*. At the beginning of the sequence of scenes which entraps the play's villain into a confession, he enters the empty space alone. He is Desoeillets, the troupe's stage manager, who has stolen the cash box, and assisted the odious prince in kidnapping Sylvia. He carries into the darkness a basket and a lantern, advances to an actor's makeup table and lights two candles, then sets up his meager supper and bottle of wine on the table. He eats and thinks aloud how he has suffered like a dog simply to support his family. Florimond, the rancorous misanthrope, enters the gloom. This is not the first time that Desoeillets and Florimond have passed away a dreary evening in some serious, silent drinking; but they are not friends. Florimond says to Desoeillets that they may both be misanthropes but with a difference: "Sometimes I say angry things, but they never lead to mean actions; while you with your stinger always dipped in honey . . . you have a venomous bite" (*Marielle,* p. 376). Florimond sits with a bottle and drinks, then discovers that while he has started to get drunk, Desoeillets has only been pretending to drink out of his bottle, then surreptitiously hides it in the basket at his feet. Angered, Florimond grabs Desoeillets' bottle, pushes the villain against the wall, throws the wine at him and commands him to drink. The contemptuous vituperations Florimond hurls at Desoeillets are worthy of Macbeth's yelling at his servant, the "whey-faced loon." At this moment of nearly uncontrollable violence, a third character enters the dark and joins in the drinking bout. Ergaste, the good natured swaggerer, taps the shoulder of Florimond, who in turn releases Desoeillets, who in his turn falls back in his chair in a heap. Ergaste gives Florimond the signal to stop drinking, because he will need his help; so Florimond retreats to a corner and tries to shake himself out of his torpor. Fresh to the assault, Ergaste manipulates Desoeillets into drinking enough to get drunk, and then through a series of badgering questions and statements manages to trip up the villain into an unwitting admission of guilt. The three are then joined by young Fabio, falsely accused by Desoeillets, and the cumulative effect of unmasking the truth is accomplished. These scenes with their dark atmosphere of drunkenness, rancor and suppressed violence resemble the baiting of Parolles in Shakespeare's *All's Well That Ends Well.* However satisfying it may be to see the villain caught and bagged, the style of the hunt sours the victory. There is humor, almost macabre, but certainly not farcical buffoonery as Wentz claims in her analysis of this scene,[31] unless we qualify it as grotesque farce when a drunk throws wine at another, slams him against a wall, and then suddenly drops him when tapped on the shoulder. But that argument can only be settled satisfactorily by a director and actors interpreting the scene and producing it on the stage along with the rest of the play.

Sand's play about players makes use of theatre trappings for its settings. In the Prologue, the commedia troupe gathers in a hotel room in Turin, Italy, and rehearses a scene amidst suitcases, as it prepares to return to France for a theatre engagement. Act I, set on a mountain slope between Grenoble and Lyon, shows the troupe acquiring its Pierrot, an overworked farmhand orphan girl leading her geese across a meadow. Acts II and III are both set in an actual theatre, or rather the backstage of a theatre in Lyon, a space which serves the actors as both dressing room and greenroom in the wings. *Marielle*'s settings are but one example of Sand's symbolic landscape, which can be seen in many of her plays and novels: the artist climbs to the heights for inspiration and then descends to the valleys to give practical application to his art.

There are two plays-within-the-play in *Marielle*. The first, the rehearsal in the Prologue of "Marriage of Scaramouche" turns rehearsal into reality when Marielle (Scaramouche) and Sylvia (Isabelle) recognize their love for one another while playing it, and really do get married later in the play. The second occurs at the Lyon theatre in Act II, when the players perform for the Lyon audience on a stage we cannot see behind the curtained door leading from the troupe's dressing room foyer out onto their stage proper. We must imagine another stage and another audience through that door. Only through the eyes of the actors waiting in the wings, who peer through that curtained door, can we perceive what is happening on their stage. The effect is like a Roshomon play: since we cannot see how Marielle has fallen and hit his head against a table corner while performing for the Lyon audience, we first rely on what Florimond reports he is seeing, and he says that young Fabio deliberately pushed Marielle too hard so that he would fall into the table. But when Marielle, dazed and unhappy, comes offstage onto "our" stage, he denies the possibility that Fabio pushed him. At this point in the play we would likely choose to believe Florimond's interpretation; but later, reflecting back on the incident we would probably absolve Fabio of the deed. And so the viewpoints shift and multiply. The actors' lives on their stage blur into their offstage lives. The fact that Sand has drawn her characters from famous historical figures (Fiorelli and Molière for Marielle, and Madame de Maintenon and Madeleine Bejart for Sylvia) and mixed them with fictional figures (Florimond based on a cantankerous character in Scarron's *Roman comique*, and Fabio on Mignon in Goethe's *Wilhelm Meister*) gives *Marielle* additional interplay between fact and fiction, reality and illusion. Thus Sand's play on players, like *Hamlet*, employs theatricality to comment upon and even influence reality.

Sand's creation of Pierrot, a naïve and credulous adolescent filled with childlike wonder and simplicity, bridges theatricality and reality because she believes that what the actors are doing on stage is actually happening. She bursts into tears when Fabio gives her a stage slap. But Pierrot also has a keen talent for imitating all the different voices of members of the farm family who have been bossing her around for years, as she demonstrates on the mountain side when we first meet her. This su-

perior ability at playacting, at make-believe, does not contradict her in-
genuous naïveté, but complements it. Sand suggests that credulous playing
and playful believing are essential to superior acting. Pierrot has that
ability to superimpose the imaginary onto the real, while at the same time
pulling from reality what she needs to create an illusion. The training she
lacks to be an accomplished actor she will get from her association with
Marielle.

Sand did not want her commedia characters to be interpreted in the
same manner as Lemaître interpreted Paillasse, "a disgusting parody of
the original type." Her actors are not to be played as caricatures, but as
full-bodied, sympathetic, even sober and solemn characters, who lend
dignity to their station as improvisational actors of the commedia dell'arte.
Not until Pirandello would the kind of actors' play Sand had begun to
imagine actually be written and staged. And not until Copeau's Vieux
Colombier would the commedia dell'arte become fully rehabilitated. But
Sand helped show the way.

Relegated to the bookshelf, *Marielle* has never had a chance to prove
its worth on the stage. *Claudie,* written the same year (1850), fared better
and had an immediate impact on stage practice. *Claudie*'s stage innovations caused a stir of interest in Parisian audiences when it opened at the
Porte-Saint-Martin on 11 January 1851. In both subject and staging technique the play broke new ground.

Daring for its time, *Claudie*'s kind portrayal of an unwed mother, a
poor farm girl, sharply contrasts with its condemnation of the middle-
class young man who seduced and abandoned her. Claudie not only receives forgiveness, but eventually marries the most desirable man in the
countryside, and is reintegrated into respectable society. Sand's sympathetic treatment of this unwed mother in *Claudie* and of a bastard child
in *Champi* precedes the plays of Dumas fils, who is given credit for the
new treatment.[32]

Sand's staging ideas for *Claudie* produced as strong an impact on
theatre history as *Claudie*'s subject, for they gave impetus to the rise of
realism and naturalism on the French stage. First identified as a movement
or school in France during the 1850s, stage realism spread from Parisian
theatres to other countries.[33] One of those missionaries of theatre realism
who spread the new school abroad to England and America was Charles
Fechter. It was Fechter who played the romantic lead opposite Claudie in
the 1851 premiere. Fechter also played Duval in the premiere of *La Dame
aux camélias* in that play's premiere one year later. He then worked as an
actor-manager in London during the 1860s, and then in America during
the 1870s (dying in New York City). His contemporaries and later histo-

rians recognize Fechter as a primary source in the evolution of realistic acting and staging technique.[34]

Claudie has the same rustic simplicity and authentic detail as Sand's first folk play, *François le Champi*. Act I of *Claudie* is set in the yard of a Berrichon wheat farm; Acts II and III in the house of the farm's foreman, M. Fauveau. Claudie and her eighty-year-old grandfather, Remy, are hired hands, migrant farm workers who follow after the harvest wagon. What makes *Claudie* an advancement over its predecessor in terms of realistic staging is Sand's detailed treatment of hand tools and stage properties which give the characters realistic activities to perform on the stage, activities which contribute to characterization as effectively as does the dialogue. Otherwise, *Claudie*'s language and costuming derive from the same Berrichon traditions as *Champi*'s.

Much of *Claudie*'s realistic stage activity reenacts women's work. In the opening scenes the foreman's wife, Madame Fauveau, enters wearing an apron covered with flour; she has just left the kitchen and carries a basket of freshly baked bread.[35] When her son Sylvain arrives from harvesting in the fields, barechested, carrying his shirt over one shoulder and a pitchfork in his hand, Mme Fauveau silently takes the shirt, sits and sews on a button. That done, she gets up to wash vegetables in the trough near the well, upstage center. In a later act we see Mme Fauveau in her own kitchen cooking and serving supper. At the harvest festival her gift to Claudie is, appropriately, scissors and needles and thread.

Sand keeps Claudie even more busy than Madame Fauveau. After working all day harvesting wheat in the fields with the men, Claudie goes directly to the well and draws water (with some difficulty so that Sylvain comes to give her some assistance with the heavy bucket), and then washes dishes, silently, speaking not a word all the while. Dishes done, Claudie exits with a basket of laundry to sort and put away. Later, inside Mme Fauveau's house, we see Claudie standing over an ironing board, with a series of old-fashioned irons lined up by the fire. Claudie is the most silent and the most industrious of all the play's characters. Sand's good people work hard and speak little.

By contrast, the handsome, self-serving lad Ronciat, who five years previous to the action of the play, had seduced and abandoned Claudie, does nothing but talk on stage. Vain and egotistical, Ronciat makes promises he never intends to keep, and lies and slanders for the sake of appearances, his own. He proves himself useless to this hard-working and honest society. So, in the end, he is driven out, banished from the immediate countryside. Thus Sand purges the collective conscience: those who will not reform must leave.

Claudie and Ronciat represent the extremes, or opposite poles, in a tight ensemble of seven characters. Sylvain and his mother, Mme Fauveau, resemble the Claudie character in terms of being industrious, honest, and good-hearted. Monsieur Fauveau, a more miserly and begrudging temperament, the farm's foreman, and Madame Rose, the farm's attractive and coquettish bourgeois widow and owner of the farm, have a little more in common with Ronciat. Remy, the octogenarian grandfather, like a half-mad Tiresias, acts as a pivotal point for the others.

Sand's casting advice for *Claudie*'s roles, indicated in a letter to Bocage on 3 December 1850, emphasizes the importance of ensemble acting in this play:

> Have a good actor for Fauveau. The role is more important than one might believe, and the mother too. . . . The fatal mistake in an actor's art is to believe that one has success in proportion to how much is taken away from the others. It's the opposite which is true. If one plays well around Rachel, she will play ten times better, and she will have that much more success. And she will find upon each of her entrances a warm audience . . . instead of a tired out or cold public, which she is forced to reheat with each of her entrances, at great expense (*Corr.* 9:824–26).

To support her concept of ensemble acting, Sand created group activities in her play which could clarify interrelationships as well as comment upon individual characters. The harvest festival at the end of Act I provides the most spectacular example of this. The Berrichon peasants observe ancient pagan rites to celebrate the harvest. Remy, the harvest bard, dedicates the sheaves and the workers celebrate in dance and song. But just as in ancient agricultural ceremonies, symbolic of separating the chaff from the wheat, a scapegoat is driven out of the society, so, too, in Sand's play, the misfit Ronciat is identified among the celebrants and will have to be driven out to purge and cleanse the culture he pollutes.

A less obvious instance of group activity which comments upon interrelationships and individual characters in *Claudie* as effectively as the harvest celebration, though in less mythic and more mundanely realistic detail, occurs in the opening scene of the play. We see the foreman Fauveau sitting at a table counting out money to be paid to the farmhands who have just finished the annual wheat harvest. The hard labor of scything wheat in the fields generally falls to men only, but Claudie works side by side with her old grandfather in order to add her half-wages to their subsistence. It is evening and there will be the big festival to celebrate, but Claudie and Remy intend to start out on their long walk back to their hut some eleven miles away. Fauveau counts out an amount equal to one man's salary and gives it to both the woman and the old man as their payment. Sylvain protests; he has seen how hard they have worked in the fields. He wants them each to receive full salary. Fauveau, insensitive neither to his son's plea nor to his wish to please Madame Rose, the owner, by saving her a little more money, compromises by paying the two an amount equal to one and a half workers. Neither groveling, nor with overbearing pride, Claudie and Remy accept the payment, quietly, faithfully. In this one activity we see the conservative, middle-of-the-road nature of the foreman, who is neither mean nor generous,[36] the generous good nature of Sylvain, and the courageous forbearance of Claudie and Remy.

Intent upon making every detail of the stage production representative of the real environment and natural behavior of the provincial folk in Berry, Sand gives precise instructions in her script of *Claudie* and in her correspondence with Bocage. Sand's attention to detail can be appreciated in her concern about the harvest wagon.[37] Bocage wants his scenic artists to make oxen out of cardboard and place them in front of the wagon on stage. Sand retorts that such a device would make the audience laugh, and she does not want any laughter, particularly of that sort, because the ceremony is supposed to begin on a more solemn note. The best solution, she says, would be to have one or two of the hefty farm hands, such as Sylvain, pull the wagon on stage. But if Bocage is going to insist on painted cardboard animals, Sand suggests that just the heads be visible, as if the oxen were standing behind a low retaining wall, which would mask their bodies in a natural manner. She then gives directions on how the heads should be decorated to fit the Berrichon festival customs (*Corr.* 9:832–33, 842). But Bocage ignored the playwright's wishes and put large cardboard oxen on the stage. Sand was right; the audience laughed.[38]

In two published articles, both entitled "Manners and Customs of Berry," Sand describes how the regional festival should have been enacted:

> The *gerbaude* or harvest festival is an agricultural ceremony that the author . . . composed for the stage with great fidelity, but which the theatre did not know how to reproduce. . . . A mountain of sheaves solemnly arrives pulled by three pair of enormous oxen, all ornamented with flowers and fruits and beautiful children perched on the summit of the last sheaves. . . . The children are as blond as the sheaves, tawny like the oxen, like the earth covered with thatch, because everything is harmoniously colored in those hot days when even the sky is all gold and amber when the evening approaches.[39]

The ceremony ends with all the men raising their scythes and hats in a great shout, a sound which Sand compares to a battle but which is actually the triumphant cry of fellow laborers dedicating the last sheaf to the heap. Sand wants dance movements and musical accompaniment to reflect the temperament of Berrichon peasants rather than the Parisian taste for

theatrical effect. She warned Bocage that the festival should begin so-
berly—no songs, no dances until after old Remy has finished dedicating
the sheaves. She warned the orchestra leader at the Porte-Saint-Martin,
Monsieur Vaillard, that Berrichon folk music must be played slowly for
the dancers. In the first of her articles on Berrichon folk customs she
describes the dance:

> The dance is done softly by the women, accentuated by the men, very monotonous,
> going forward and backward. . . . It's almost impossible to dance it if one isn't born
> in Berry or transplanted there for a very long time. The difficulty, which isn't apparent
> at first, comes from the offhandedness of the fiddlers, who fly ahead a half measure
> when they please; then the dancer must pick up the step in the air to recover the
> measure. Natives do this instinctively without misstep.[40]

Bagpipes and drums join the fiddlers in the Berrichon orchestra. The
singing and movement should have a monotonous, rolling quality, true to
the natural environment:

> It's a country of hard and heavy earth, where large and strong oxen slowly pull the
> plow and the man. It's a solemn slowness. Even gaiety itself is melancholy. . . . In a
> village festival here everything is calm, nearly sad, the music and the dance; and the
> singers have the air of chanting vespers. Then there'll come a burst of madness . . .
> dancers and drunks do a furious allegro. That lasts an instant and then everything
> returns to calm as if nothing had happened. You'd do well to throw in such unexpected
> movements in the overture and the harvest festival. Such contrasts are not lacking in
> charm, and for those who have lived in this country they will ring true (Sand to
> Adolphe Vaillard, 11 December 1850; *Corr.* 9:838).

Sand did not want to sentimentalize or prettify provincial customs of
Berry; she was not writing pastoral poetry.[41] She wanted the authentic,
unadulterated dance, song, and manner of the Berrichon peasants, something the professional theatre was not willing yet to give her.

The disappointments Sand suffered during the staging of *Claudie*
were not limited to pictorial and musical misinterpretations. The government censors bickered with her over the references to "the poor people,"
or Ronciat as an example of "the bad rich."[42] Sand had to prune such
references out of her script before the censors would approve the play for
staging. She conceded, saying she would do anything but lie (*Corr.* 9:891).
But the censors' mutilations of *Claudie* so disgusted her that she lost all
interest in the play production (*Corr.* 10:35). As with *Champi*'s opening,
Sand avoided going to the opening night of *Claudie* by sequestering herself
in her Nohant château. Only after favorable reports of the play's reception
reached Sand did she travel up to Paris and attend the fifth performance.
She thought Bocage "beautiful and strong," but the others only sufficient

at most. The lead actress, Rachel's sister, Lia Felix, played a weak and lackluster Claudie; however, Sand approved of the cast's *ensemble* (*Corr.* 10:43).

The critics greeted *Claudie*'s premiere with more enthusiasm than Sand did. The critic for *L'Illustration* admired everything about it: "serene sentiments," "naïve characters," "strong and penetrating language," "splendid simplicity," Claudie's "eloquence and truth"; the whole experience was "ravishing." An illustration for the set in Acts II and III, the Fauveaus' house interior, accompanies this critic's review. The picture shows an austere but affluent interior, leaded windows and well-crafted woodwork along a staircase and small balcony, an indication of multilevels for acting space. The entire cast is illustrated, arranged in an ensemble focused on Claudie primarily, Sylvain secondarily, and Remy supervising (*L'Illustration,* 18 January 1851).

Both P. Busoni of the *Illustration* and Théophile Gautier of the *Presse* see an analogy between Sand's *Claudie* and ancient Greek and Roman literature. Busoni calls Sand a "*gerbe-mère*," or mother of the sheaves, a Demeter. Old Remy reminds Busoni of a character out of Virgil's *Georgics.* Gautier calls Claudie a "rustic Antigone," and Sylvain a "rustic Apollo."[43] Years later (in 1872), when the distinguished critic Hippolyte Taine wrote to Sand asking her to write plays again, he compares her talent to "the old Greek poets." "Only in those authors of a hundred tragedies" can Taine find "a vein as natural, as abundant, as sane . . . the flow as spontaneous and harmonious" as Sand's.[44]

Jules Janin applauds the "rare *ensemble*" of *Claudie*'s players, and places Sand in the first rank of playwrights. Nevertheless the play's ostensible immorality offends Janin:

> The antique morality, the old centuries in their severe wisdom and instruction, that law of honest people which says that a girl must be a chaste girl, that's what troubles me at this moment and what redoubles my attention, so much so that I want to see by what . . . sophistries the illustrious George Sand could enable Claudie to marry Sylvain (*Journal des Débats,* 13 January 1851).

Janin rejects Sand's rehabilitation of Claudie, the unwed and therefore unchaste mother. Janin rather perversely claims that Sylvain, who best personifies chastity and charm, "is the true *fille* in all this, and the true *garçon* that's Claudie!" Another critic who somewhat shares Janin's moral outrage finds it highly distasteful that Sand should at the same time place Claudie on stage with Ronciat, who has "possessed" her, along with Sylvain, who will possess her. This critic speculates that a more practised playwright would have killed off Ronciat before such an awkward triangle

4. *Claudie* 1851, at the Porte-Saint-Martin Theatre.
Nineteenth-century illustration of theatre in author's possession.
Second act set; Fechter to the left, Bocage center.
Courtesy of Bibliothèque Spoelberch de Lovenjoul (Institut de France) Chantilly.

of characters could possibly occur on the stage (*Le Moniteur Universel,* 20 January 1851).

In the longest review of *Claudie*'s first production (fifteen pages) Gustave Planche argues in favor of Sand's rehabilitating a fallen woman. He cites Mary Magdelene. Generally opposed to dogma in drama, even the dogma of charity and the thesis of divine law's superiority over human law, Planche credits Sand with having avoided writing a didactic argument or thesis play, by having made it a "simple and touching poem" instead. She has "hidden instruction under passion." In Planche's opinion the best conceived and most complete character in the play is Remy. The grandfather's inner struggle between his desire for vengeance on Ronciat and his care that Claudie may still love the scoundrel, he resolves through self-abnegation, patience and devotion to his granddaughter. Planche thinks that Ronciat accurately represents the vanity and egotism of the rich country lads who exist in the French provinces. And he defends Sand's right to offer up such a realistic portrayal rather than concede to stage convention, which had heretofore permitted only idyllic pastoral shepherds who no longer exist in real life and may never have. What Planche doesn't like about *Claudie* is its language, which he condemns as "monotonous and false." He hopes that in the future Sand will employ the language of her novels in her plays (but avoid adapting her novels to the stage). After giving Sand a lesson in stage construction (he would like her dramatic action to unfold more rapidly, and have "useless scenes" edited out altogether), Planche compares Sand to Sedaine, and finally concludes that *Claudie,* faults and all, heralds the end of cheap imitations of Shakespeare and Calderon and a return to analyses of passions.[45]

Reviewing a revival of *Claudie* in 1876, the critic Francisque Sarcey shares Planche's negative opinion that Sand writes with faulty construction. But, says Sarcey, Sand compensates with a great style which idealizes and aggrandizes her subjects. He can remember the first time he saw *Claudie,* around 1856, and how he wept at the end of the first act of that "majestic idyll." But he doesn't like the play's final speeches, which go too far beyond rehabilitating Claudie and make of her a veritable "apotheosis," something "excessive and unpleasant." If fifty or so lines were to be trimmed from the end, *Claudie* would be a "pure diamond."[46] Sarcey would have been pleased to see Sand's original ending to *Claudie* before Bocage changed it and expanded his role. The manuscript in Sand's own hand gives a last scene of only a few lines in which Remy has no long speeches, and Madame Rose, rather than Remy, brings Sylvain and Claudie together at the last moment. Bocage added the apotheosis, but nothing more than that and a couple of line changes. And with the talk in the 1870s about naturalism, Sarcey sees *Claudie* as the best example of naturalism because of its "marvelous poetry."[47]

5. Scenes from *Claudie* Illustrated by Maurice Sand.
Courtesy of Bibliothèque Spoelberch de Lovenjoul
(Institut de France), Chantilly.

In the 1890s Benoist agreed with Sarcey that *Claudie* is Sand's best play, but thought the piece flawed by lack of action and too much of the interest placed in sentiment and style. Benoist saw the play as more idealistic than realistic. Remy and Claudie he compared to Oedipus and Antigone.[48]

On the occasion of Sand's centennial birthday celebration in 1904, the Comédie Française produced *Claudie,* and Sand's biographer (Varvara Komarova), whose nom de plume was Vladimir Karénine, was in the audience. She describes (in the last of the four volumes of her Sand biography) how some in the audience had arrived at the performance predisposed to dislike the play; but by the end these "young snobs" were shouting "Bravo! Bravo!" with the rest of them. Karénine defends Sand's use of realistic language in *Claudie* against earlier detractors who thought it too simple and vulgar, by showing her similarity to Tolstoy, who came to use the same device as Sand in giving each character his own style and manner of locution. In this 1904 production the problem of the cardboard oxen was solved by eliminating the hay wagon altogether, and placing just one enormous sheaf of wheat in the middle of the stage for the harvest festival. The strongest impression *Claudie* left with Karénine had nothing to do with any debate on its morality; instead the experience struck her as a "hymn to work," a glorification of laborers. "Without that wheat, without those workers, there wouldn't have been any of us in the auditorium." In the last scene of the play, with the sound of evening vespers bells, Remy and Claudie and Sylvain kneel in prayer on the kitchen floor, forming a tableaux of "The Angelus." On seeing this Karénine remarks how reminiscent it is of Millet's famous painting of the Angelus. In fact Sand's Angelus, created during 1850 and 1851, precedes and perhaps influenced Millet's, which he painted in 1859.[49] When Karénine left the theatre she felt refreshed. *Claudie* had given the audience the courage to continue their work.[50]

In addition to critics' responses, Sand received many personal letters praising the production. Marie Dorval's son-in-law wrote again, saying *Claudie* was "a prayer to God," and would be the first book he'd want to read to his grandchildren (*Corr.* 10:44n). Succeeding generations of children have indeed listened to readings of Sand's rustic tales.[51] Until very recently George Sand's reputation as a writer rested primarily on her "children's books." The tender rehabilitation of Claudie, born in a period of national crisis, was last performed in another period of crisis, in 1942, during World War II.

6. Berrichon Melodies for *Claudie*, in George Sand's hand.
    Bibliothèque Spoelberch de Lovenjoul (Institut de France), Chantilly.

3

Professional Pragmatism

Claudie's production began 1851 with an artistic triumph but failed to materialize into the financial success Sand and Bocage had hoped for. They had counted on a hundred or more performances. But Sand herself terminated the first run after only forty-three, because the Porte-Saint-Martin managers had proposed cutting her half of the royalties from four to three percent, and then added the insult of alternating *Claudie* with a vaudeville comedy. So Sand exercised her option and closed the production in March 1851. It had paid for its production expenses and got Sand out of debt, but that was all.

The theatre audiences at Porte-Saint-Martin perturbed Sand as much as did the managers. She had written the play for "the people," but they didn't come: "The sad thing in all of this is that the people to whom this work is addressed don't have the time, the means, or the desire to go to the theatre" (*Corr.* 10:106). But the bourgeois class came to see *Claudie* and then complained about its "socialism." Sand attributes their dissatisfaction to another cause; her play is "a reproach" to their "guilty conscience" (*Corr.* 10:101, 106). She sadly acknowledges that the play does not change audience attitudes:

> The public is an animal without guts in real life. Every day it walks all over unfortunate people like Claudie and Remy. But show them on the stage and the public weeps. What a singular animal! too impressionable to be hated, too inconsequential to be loved (January 1851; *Corr.* 10:49–50).

Perhaps with her next play she could establish a "people's theatre."

But Sand had other problems with her theatre career. The Odéon management which had replaced Bocage sued Sand and Bocage for taking *Champi* with them and reviving it at another theatre. The Odéon claimed *Champi* as its property, citing the rules of the Society of Dramatic Authors which give to the theatre which originates a play's production playing rights for that play during an allotted period of time (six years, normally).

Sand's defense, that the rules of the Society did not yet apply to her when she produced *Champi* because she did not become a member until six months later, did not hold up in the courts. When the Odéon tried to collect damages, Bocage balked, and eventually Sand had to make amends with the Odéon management on her own.[1] Much of Sand's energy and time during 1851 and 1852 was taken up with this nettlesome business.

Convinced that if only Bocage could secure the directorship of a theatre all his own, they could create a great repertory together, Sand followed with interest the construction of a new theatre. Located not far from the boulevard theatres (on 29 rue du Château-d'Eau), the theatre under construction promised to be new and innovative in design. An inventor-designer named Barthelemy resolved to solve acoustical problems by designing the theatre with a circular stage, curved scenery and the audience seated in an auditorium shaped as half an ellipse. Barthelemy said, "I want to make the stone and cement sing" (*Corr.* 10:123n). Sand encouarged Bocage to try to secure the management of this new theatre space:

> The big business, my friend, is to take, to seize, to obtain, to hook this theatre under construction. . . . Deploy all of your energy so that this affair carries through the government council. . . . With such a theatre as this we would make our fortune, honestly, nobly. Don't let this one get away from you. I see there all your future and mine (*Corr.* 10:122–23).

Sand thinks the little theatre would be ideal for her experiments in commedia dell'arte: "If you take the little theatre we'll bring to it our special knowledge of Italian theatre of the seventeenth and eighteenth centuries and a famous repertory" (*Corr.* 10:168). But Bocage did not manage to obtain the theatre.[2]

When Sand again raised the question to Bocage of producing *Marielle,* he offered the counter proposal that she write the real historical drama of *Molière* rather than merely the suggestion of Molière in the character of Marielle. He wants "frankness, valor, greatness . . . and what charms me is the alliance of the two names: Molière and George Sand" (Bocage to Sand, 13 February 1851; *Corr.* 10:80n). The idea did not appeal to Sand at first: "It's a profanation to wish to arrange Molière's life, even to embellish it" (*Corr.* 10:81). If Bocage is interested, she has another peasant folk play for him, already half written, "a bad male Claudie in a rehabilitated village who is converted and pardoned by love" (*Corr.* 10:108). But Bocage wanted *Molière,* not the *Pressoir,* so Sand put aside the latter for two years and plunged into *Molière.* By mid-February 1851 Sand was passionately engaged in the project and by the end of the month she had established the types and situations for the play.

Begun as a reworking of *Marielle,* Sand reports that the final product has very little in common with the original; "not ten lines" are the same (*Corr.* 10:184). The sequence of settings for both *Marielle* and *Molière* remains somewhat similar: Acts I in the country when Pierrot or Pierrette is added to the company; Acts II in the actors' dressing room backstage before and during a performance. And most of the characters in *Marielle* have their historical equivalents in *Molière:* Fabio (Baron), Ergast (Brécourt), Florimond (Duparc), Sylvia (Madeleine Béjart), and of course Marielle (Molière). The cardinal or prince character who is never seen in *Marielle* becomes the Prince de Condé who *is* seen in *Molière.* But the most important change between the two plays in terms of characters is the addition of Armande Béjart, who, Sand claims, is a new type for the theatre (*Corr.* 10:108–9).

To Sand the most interesting things about famous people are the details of their intimate lives, what is least known about them. She prefers a version of Molière's life which deals with his spirit and heart rather than the exterior life of noble deeds (*Corr.* 10:147). "I like him best with his weaknesses, his faults, and his miseries; I find him greater this way than draped as a historic figure the way the world wants to see him" (*Corr.* 10:85). Sand chooses to ignore those versions of Molière's life which emphasize his cuckoldry, and instead selects a more "delicate" version which shows his young wife to be vain and flirtatious, but not unfaithful. In her earliest conception of Armande, Sand says she is a "cold flirt who is smart and who does not love Molière" (*Corr.* 10:147). Molière loves this ingrate and dies from chagrin as much as from illness. Armande loves no one. Intelligent and ambitious, proud, flirtatious only by design, mocking, vain, dry, ungrateful, Armande fascinates at the same time she repels. This complex creature whom Molière loves like a father, husband and lover, commands the audience's attention and interest as much as Molière's. Sand says that Molière would have lost interest in Armande and forgotten all about her if she had actually been a courtesan.[3] The playwright provides no clear explanation for why Armande is the way she is, other than her youth and native temperament, but steers our interest in the direction of watching what this type of woman can accomplish for good and ill. Armande inspires Molière, and she destroys him. Molière's friends and associates surround him and try to protect him from his mercurial wife, but only worsen his condition by depriving him of the object of his affections and thus leave him to his jealous fantasies.

Sand advises Bocage to have the vain Armande's costume covered with diamonds, ribbons, and pearls; and to have her older sister's, Madeleine's, be very simple by contrast (*Corr.* 10:176). In Act IV, scene 5 (the act cut from Bocage's production) Armande enters in the costume of

Elmire in *Tartuffe*. Annoyed with the plainness of her costume she complains to her old husband, "You can say what you like, but my costume is horrible and there won't be a bit of applause when I go out on the stage" (*Molière*, p. 411). Molière, preoccupied as he is with larger political questions and the future of his company, sees the humor in being required to attend to his wife's toilette: "You want to represent a bourgeoise in the costume of a princess, and a convalescent getting out of bed in the flowers and diamonds of someone returning from a ball!" Armande retorts that while it may not be realistic to be so attired, the purpose is to give pleasure, and no one will applaud what is disagreeable to look at. Molière must remind her that there should be more to applaud than her diamonds. Bocage needed the same reminder.

As the spring of 1851 progressed, Sand's enthusiasm for the production of *Molière* turned sour. Bocage kept asking for portions of the play to be rewritten. So Sand rewrote, arguing all the while that the first version had been the best. Technical aspects of getting the play mounted at the Gaîté were not going to Sand's satisfaction either. She had arranged for her friend, the composer Gounod, to adapt some of Lully's music for the production; but the orchestra leader at the Gaîté wanted to do so himself, and he prevailed with Hostein, the theatre's managing director. Sand wanted Fechter to play Baron—she had written the part with him in mind—but the theatre could not or would not engage him. Worst of all, Bocage went ahead and made what changes and arrangements he wished without always consulting Sand first. He even went so far as to cut out the entire fourth act of the original script, with its strong revelations of character for both Armande and Molière. While he cut away the script and cast lesser actors in the supporting roles, Sand warned Bocage that by diminishing the importance of the secondary characters he would diminish the principal figure at the same time. This was not the first time she had talked to him about *ensemble* playing. But Bocage needed reminding:

> The only good and true method is to conserve each character and give to all of them serious value. Molière is the soul of the play, the others are the body. But Molière cannot be soul and body all together. He loses his superiority if he has only dummies and dodos around him. He must have forces around him, if he is to exercise his own and make it understood (*Corr.* 10:195).

As the director of the production, Bocage would have had no argument with this advice; but as the actor playing Molière, Bocage might have had some difficulty following it. Sand kept writing letters to Bocage asking for information, giving suggestions and revisions, and receiving no replies.

And to add to her worries she had to contend with the censors again. They objected to Molière's making a toast to "the people," when he lifts his glass in salute to "the poor people of France who pay the fiddlers for all the festivals and the trumpets for all the wars" (*Corr.* 10:247n).

Sand's confidence in Bocage to conduct rehearsals and go through opening night without her never flagged in their productions of *Champi* and *Claudie*. But with *Molière* she felt she must go up to Paris in order to salvage her script, or at worst, see if she wanted to cancel the production altogether, which was her right (*Corr.* 10:246–47, 252–54). The opening would be late in the season, when the theatres along the boulevard begin to vacate for the summer, a further drawback for *Molière*'s success.

Molière opened on 10 May 1851, and closed on the 24th after only twelve performances, tepidly received by audiences and critics.[4] Bocage's production of *Molière* befuddled the critics. What is the point, they ask in their reviews. Busoni (*L'Illustration*, 17 May 1851) thinks Sand wants to rehabilitate Armande Béjart, or otherwise the play has no point at all, even though it is "charming and interesting." John Lemoinne writes in *Journal des Débats* (14 May 1851) that Sand is wrong to sanitize the character of Armande:

> Why has George Sand changed all that? Why instead of leaving Armande to be what she was, a daughter of the theatre, light and easy, Sand has made her into a simple flirt, out to satisfy her vanity more than her pleasure, making poor Molière die of jealousy—for nothing?

When Gautier said of *Marielle* that the actor no longer needs rehabilitation in the nineteenth century, he may have been correct about an actor, but obviously not about an actress, as Lemoinne's comment about "daughter of the theatre" proves. Lemoinne concludes that Sand's great talent for showing the "development of an internal battle of passions," the deeper psychological factors, makes for weak drama. Gautier, too, is troubled by Sand's lack of clarity in purpose and design. "The character of Armande is not designed with enough clarity."[5] If she's only a flirt, not actually unfaithful to Molière, then why is she humiliated and ostracized? Gautier's impression that Armande's character lacks clear definition may be due in part to the cuts made by Bocage or insufficient understanding on the part of the actress playing Armande. But whether they liked the character of Armande or not, these reviews show that the critics focused on that character, which is what Sand wanted.

In the Preface to *Molière*'s first edition (Bocage's production edition without the fourth act Sand reinstated for later publications), Sand defends her "intimate drama" against those critics who complain that it lacks dramatic action. She asks if dramatic action excludes analysis of sentiments and passions. She wants to know the characters, their nuances, their development, the motives for their actions. Reflection satisfies her more than suspense. She is convinced that her fault is not in the goal, but perhaps in the execution. She will do her best going her own way, but she is certainly not encouraging others to follow: "If the theatre were to become a school of patience and calm analysis we'd no longer have a theatre." The difficulty is to analyze rapidly, but in any case analysis must be made:

> Our fathers were not skeptics or arguers like us; their characters were more of one piece, they had beliefs and . . . resolutions that were not submitted to discussion. Today we all philosophize and discuss. A modern Othello would need to explain himself more to us for us to accept him.[6]

This need to have an opinion on everything and talk about it leads to contradictions and confusion, as Sand demonstrates in a second preface to *Molière*.[7] She quotes numerous statements from a variety of critics who reviewed the production. Taken together they constitute a mass of contradictions and useless judgments from which the playwright learns or gains nothing. Sand regrets that she must look for the truth about her own work all by herself, without aid of either well-wishers or enemies who wish either to encourage or correct her. She observes that the critics base their opinions on their reading, not on the experience of doing what they criticize; therefore their advice is of limited value to her and other playwrights.

Another big disillusionment for Sand as a result of the *Molière* production was, again, her failure to appeal to the masses, though this time, apparently, representatives of "the people" did attend, but did not like the play:

> The public of the boulevards, which I wished to instruct and treat well, the public at ten sous which must be the people and for whom I've sacrificed the high-paying public of the Théâtre Français, took no notice of my devotion. They like murders and poisonings better than literature with style and heart, . . . and it will take quite a lot to ameliorate that taste (Sand to Charles Poncy, 6 June 1851; *Corr.* 10:307–9).

Sand sadly noted that in the end only men of letters and the middle class came to see the final performances of *Molière*.

But in spite of any setbacks and disappointments, the energetic and ever optimistic Sand continued through to the end of 1851 giving herself over entirely to theatrical activity:

With the novel I stay on a modest and tranquil course. I have no desire to run that course . . . this devilish love of work, this new genre of work has so heated up my brain in spite of myself, that I dream only of the theatre and see my ideas only in that form now. . . . It's a feverish activity, but as along as it holds me, I must concede to my fantasy (*Corr.* 10:382).

After *Molière* and before the year was out, Sand went on to write three more full-length plays (*Gabriel, Nello* and *Le Mariage de Victorine*), and a novel in dialogue form *(Le Diable aux champs)*.

Sand described her adaptation of *Gabriel* (1839), which she renamed *Julia* at one point, as a cloak and dagger melodrama with "twelve beautiful scenes" of approximately five hours playing time (*Corr.* 10:397–99, 425–26, 523). She wryly commented that this new piece was already too old for the boulevard theatres, and yet too modern still for the Comédie Française. When Rachel at the Comédie got wind of the play, she expressed an interest in playing the lead. Sand would have none of it; she wanted a woman who could convincingly look and act like a real man on the stage, not like "a woman in disguise who shows her big behind to the public" (*Corr.* 10:427–28, 493). She had hoped to get Fechter for the part of Astolphe, and Amalia Fernand for Gabriel (Fernand had the same reputation as Marie Dorval for being a lesbian). Sand wanted her play to prove to the public that she could write a good melodrama, but *Gabriel* was never produced. The manuscript, which ended up in the hands of Paul Meurice (with whom Sand collaborated on two plays in the 1860s), has not been seen or heard of since,[8] and no copies exist.

Sand's plans in 1851 for her new play *Nello* met with similar obstacles. Based on a Hoffmann fantasy, the play's more intimate setting, small cast, and limited set requirements made Sand think that the Gymnase would be interested in it. But the Gymnase director thought it too socialist (*Corr.* 10:530). Then she tried the Vaudeville, where she hoped to cast Fechter in the role of Nello and René Luguet as Keller (*Corr.* 10:476), but those plans fell through too. Months after both plays were finished, Sand could not seem to interest any theatre in either *Gabriel* or *Nello*. She was bewildered:

I don't understand anything about theatre, and I ask myself if I should continue in such a craft. If I were a director of a theatre and someone read *Mercadet*[9] to me, I would not believe it playable and listenable; and if they presented *Nello,* I would be struck by its loving and poetic side. However, the directors are right since the public makes them right. . . . That public seems so strange to me that I'm now more disgusted with it than I was in the beginning (*Corr.* 10:541).

Sand's hopes for *Nello* revived when Frédérick Lemaître read the manuscript and said he would like to play Nello; but that came to nothing. In 1854 Bocage expressed an interest in playing *Nello* and worked with Sand on a completely revised script, but his indecision and delays prevented his playing the part. Instead the new version, called *Maître Favilla,* picked up by the Odéon, opened in 1855 with Rouvière in the principal role.

Another product of Sand's labors in 1851, a novel written in dialogue, *Le Diable aux champs,* did not reach the public until several years later, and then only in a modified form. Sand had begun this "comédie monstre" as a commentary on contemporary class structure in France, but when it was published in 1858 the social issues had largely disappeared. It makes the observation that post-1848 France has only two classes: those with money and those without. Ironically, Sand observes that her society is more fragmented in opinion and loyalites than under the old class structure. One of *Diable*'s characters (Maurice) reflects on what would happen if *Tartuffe* premiered in 1851, rather than in the seventeenth century. There would be not only the outraged bigots who would lobby to squelch the piece, but surely a group of supporters such as those whom Molière had to assure that the play would be played. Or would there? Sand finds too many interest groups in present-day society:

> I believe that *Tartuffe* would fall flat, not because of the passion stirred up against it, but because of the absence of a big enough group to support it. . . . Philosophers would find the moral too timid. The Republicans would not approve of the prince. . . . The Proudhonists wouldn't want the honest elegy to piety. The Saint-Simonians and Fourierists wouldn't want the elegy to marriage and the family. The writers would divide into ten factions for or against the style and the substance of the piece.[10]

The shadow of the theatre public obviously loomed large and ominous on Sand's horizon.

Sand addressed her next play, *Le Mariage de Victorine,* to the bourgeois tastes of the bourgeois audience. All she needs is a congenial bourgeois theatre. She cannot wait any longer for Bocage to find his own theatre, and she tells him frankly that his battles with theatre managers have crushed her plays. The directors have been dishonest, but Bocage has been too impatient (*Corr.* 10:278). She will have to pilot her little boat herself (*Corr.* 10:287). Pierre Hetzel, Sand's publisher, temporarily filled Bocage's shoes as her agent and theatre advisor during the summer and fall of 1851. Through Hetzel Sand secured the Gymnase for *Victorine.* The play was written in the spring, staged at Nohant in the summer, and produced in Paris in November 1851.

Victorine almost went to the Comédie Française, and Sand's observations on that possibility provide us with an inside look on how the national theatre of France operated, and how Sand perceived her own role in the actual process of putting a play into production. Because *Victorine* serves as a kind of sequel to Sedaine's *Le Philosophe sans savoir*, it seemed particularly suitable to the Comédie Française, which kept the Sedaine play in its repertory. Sand permitted Hetzel to proceed in negotiations with Arsène Houssaye, the new director of the national theatre, even though she had some reservations as to whether Hetzel and Houssaye, both young and theatrically inexperienced, could handle all the casting and directing responsibilities. Sand cautions Hetzel that the *mise-en-scène* is a specialty that has to be learned, and neither of them has been trained to it. Besides, she does not like the style of direction she has seen on the Comédie Française stage, which produces "sugared interpretations" that are "artificial," "cold as ice," and "without enough *vraisemblance* or freedom" (*Corr.* 10:292–96, 301). And the actors at the national theatre, with the exception of Regnier and Geffroy, are too proud, ungiving of themselves:

> They don't trouble themselves to rehearse. . . . The actors there have a kind of polished impertinence . . . I've never seen anywhere else. Elsewhere I've found the actors warm, conscientious, affectionate. At the Français the ladies and gentlemen are all charming . . . but at every occasion they'll tell you, in the most gracious manner . . . that they are doing you a great favor to act in your play. . . . They rehearse badly, in fact they don't rehearse at all. . . . I've never seen a real rehearsal at the Théâtre Français, unless the author shouts ferociously, and I'm too well raised to be ferocious (*Corr.* 10:292–96).

Sand needs the rehearsal process in order to see how her play works and what needs revising: "to understand, judge and complete my plays I must see and hear them." If Houssaye promises to supervise the rehearsals and make sure the actors work, so that Sand does not have to be there all the time and "listen to the actors talk about their personal affairs during rehearsals," she will present *Victorine* to the theatre's committee for a reading and a vote. But she must be the only one permitted to make any changes or cuts in the script (Sand to Hetzel, 3 June 1851; *Corr.* 10:292–96).

But a change of policy at the Comédie Française decided Sand against submitting *Victorine* there after all. A new play had previously needed a committee vote of approval before it could be produced, a committee basically made up of the theatre's actors. And though Sand recognized some difficulties with the system, such as conflict of personalities, she preferred that the committee remain mostly made up of these "intelligent artists." But the government had a different plan, and proceeded to reconstitute the committee so that its new membership became a majority of government appointees. Sand did not want a group of government bureaucrats deciding the fate of her plays (*Corr.* 10:317–18). Not that she objected to any particular individual appointed, but she could not accept the fact that they would be representatives of the government rather than free agents, and thus be unable to distinguish between artistically and politically motivated choices. "The liberty, the dignity of an author must in no way suffer an administrative veto" (*Corr.* 10:343).

So instead of the Comédie Française, Sand told Hetzel to go to the Gymnase with *Victorine* and negotiate with its manager, Lemoine-Montigny. The Gymnase, or "House of Scribe," as it had been called during the first half of the nineteenth century, had *not* been one of Sand's favorite theatres. Back in 1839 when she made her first tentative steps into the world of the professional theatre, she encouraged Bocage to move from the Gymnase, where he had found himself temporarily, on to a bigger theatre, "because with the little concision that the heavens have endowed me with, there's little probability that I could ever restrain myself to the close quarters of the Gymnase" (*Corr.* 4:626–27). When Lemoine-Montigny first approached Sand for a play in March 1850 (he wanted her to adapt *Fadette* for his stage), she refused, and confessed to a correspondent that she could not stand the actors there (*Corr.* 9:481). Now, with Hetzel already negotiating on Sand's behalf, she expresses the same reservations: "After the Français, I can see only the Gymnase for my piece. I don't like Rose Cheri or Bressant, but I know that they have the qualities required by that theatre and its public" (*Corr.* 10:321–34). Sand was definitely not interested in the "ten sous" public this time.

She consented to the Gymnase on certain conditions. The play must open in the fall, the good season, not in the summer when the public has departed for the country. She wanted the contract to permit her to have another of her plays appearing at another theatre simultaneously (generally forbidden by contracts). The play must be able to leave the Gymnase after three years rather than the customary six; and if the director Lemoine-Montigny should leave the Gymnase at any time, the play would revert back to Sand (*Corr.* 10:397–99). Some of these demands were met in the contract signed 31 July 1851.

To Sand's great relief, when she attended the last week of rehearsals in November she found that the theatrical operation at the Gymnase more than met her expectations. Lemoine-Montigny, whom she had never met before, proved a congenial director, and his wife Rose Cheri an able and conscientious actress in the principal role of Victorine:

> The director, the actors, the whole world here is charming. They work admirably, conscientiously and furiously. In sum, at this theatre I find not the least hint of disagreement. . . . Decidedly, it's going better without *père* Bocage than with him! (*Corr.* 10:559).

The Gymnase gave Sand a congenial and appropriate environment for her more intimate and realistic dramas, nine from 1851 to 1862. The smallness of the theatre and the simplicity of the acting style enhanced psychological nuance in Sand's characters. Stage realism is said to have begun with Lemoine-Montigny at the Gymnase. The playwright Sardou reported, or perhaps speculated, that before Lemoine-Montigny's reforms in the 1850s, the actors ranged themselves on the stage side by side at the edge of the footlights, and instead of speaking to one another they spoke directly to the audience. "Struck with this absurdity, Montigny put a table in the middle of the stage with chairs around the table; and the other actors sat and spoke naturally, looking at one another as one does in reality."[11] Dumas fils also credited Montigny with being the first theatre director to give his actors realistic stage business: characters changed their chair positions while speaking, and ladies knitted during their dialogue.[12] After the success of Dumas fils' *La Dame aux camélias* (1852), his first play, most of his subsequent plays were staged at the Gymnase. The theatre which was named "House of Scribe" for the first half of the nineteenth century could have been called "House of Dumas fils" for the second.

But Sardou and Dumas fils appear to have overlooked the staging work of Sand and Bocage, and others like them whose experiments in realistic techniques precede those of the Gymnase. As we have seen in *Claudie,* Sand did more with her characters than move chairs and knit on stage. Indeed, as early as 1840, Sand's Cosima worked at her spinning wheel on stage. But the Gymnase did make progress in firmly establishing stage realism. In her description of the set for Dumas fils' *Demi-monde* (June 1855), Sand relates how real the illusion could appear on the stage of the Gymnase. *Demi-monde* was

> staged with a richness and careful study unprecedented in the theatre. You will see great progress, the set for the salon hung with real damask, authentic stuffed furniture, and real accessories as in real home life. Montigny is on the right track in that regard; and the audience, without really being aware of it, submits to the illusion, which certainly adds to the success of some plays, even the good ones (*Corr.* 13:173).

But Montigny, whom Sand addressed as "mon général," committed his Gymnase operation to a bourgeois audience which wanted middle-of-the-road fare, nothing too extreme. As Sand said, "they don't want to laugh too much, and they only want to cry a little" (*Corr.* 11:197). To Sand this audience was a "constipated public" (*Corr.* 11:236). Another contemporary, Jules Barbey d'Aurevilly, described the Gymnase and its public as, "always that predominant class which has no more literary spirit than political spirit."[13]

Opening night of *Victorine* at the Gymnase was well received, and so Sand and the Gymnase company looked forward to a long and prosperous run. But on 2 December 1851, Paris awoke to soldiers in the streets making their rounds of arrests and plastering proclamations on the walls— Napoleon III's coup d'etat was underway. On December 4, a day of much gunfire in the streets, Sand left Paris for Nohant. Calm was restored and on December 9 the theatres reopened. But, because of the sickness of one of the actors, *Victorine* did not resume again until December 17.

Writing to Lemoine-Montigny from Nohant, Sand speculates on future class struggle to this manager of the arch-bourgeois Gymnase: "It will not be the socialists who will trouble us now. . . . It is the capitalists, the middle class who are to be feared . . . the danger is not in ideas, but in appetites and needs" (*Corr.* 10:608). To Hetzel, less bourgeois and a politically radical publisher, Sand communicates a more chastened view:

> France will never be a republic so long as the proletariat and the bourgeoisie believe they have different interests. . . . Providing for the sufficient comforts of the proletariat, which is both consumer and producer, will make for the prosperity and security of the bourgeoisie. . . . It's so simple and so logical, this reciprocity of interests, and in a few years time peace will be made between the two classes (*Corr.* 10:613–14).

Her condition for this optimism was that the Emperor Napoleon III would assure jobs and education for "the people." But the emperor's new government was not as conciliatory to the political left as Sand had believed it would be. Massive arrests, deportations, and even executions got underway in January 1852. Hetzel had to seek political asylum in Belgium, and Sand again found herself without a manager-agent for her professional theatre career.

Napoleon's Second Empire, which officially began in December 1852, supported and was supported by the haute bourgeoisie; capitalism and materialism shaped the culture, and the interests of the lower classes were largely ignored. Sand had to accept the fact that her audiences would be bourgeois, and her plays after 1851 address themselves to that audience.

Sand's attitude toward the theatre public had always been ambivalent. At best theatre audiences bewildered her, and at worst they disgusted her. But as an avid theatregoer herself for over fifty years (1820s to 1870s), Sand's ambivalence extended to the kinds of plays she as an audience member would like to see. By 1848 plays had become excessively melodramatic, too full of intrigue and excitement; Sand therefore wanted to see and create more soothing, calm, and psychologically interesting plays. She communicated that goal in 1850:

> We have a higher goal than vanity or money. We wish to give to the people plays that moralize, console, make us more tender, a sort of antidote to that dramatic literature

which, however, I myself like, that is thrilling, brilliant, passionate, but that speaks to our coarser nervous fibers and not to the more delicate fibers of the heart (to Bocage, *Corr.* 9:841).

So, as a writer, if not always as an audience member, Sand hoped to create plays that would be good for the audience, not cater to their lower instincts by providing what they might think they want. But Sand had to learn by experience that audiences support what they think they want, not what a playwright thinks is good for them. A dozen years after writing *Le Roi attend* in 1848, to celebrate the people's Revolution, when Sand proclaimed sincerely, *"Le roi, c'est le peuple!"* in 1860 she ironically observes: "The public is king. It doesn't want modification, persuasion, or amelioration. Do what pleases it. . . . But like all tyrants, the public very quickly grows tired of its courtesans" (*Corr.* 15:645).

Generally, Sand found Parisian audiences too bourgeois, too rich and too blasé. She would have preferred that the proletariat, "the people" attend. But the audiences for *Champi, Claudie* and *Molière* taught her that the people would not or could not come to the theatre. So instead of consoling and instructing the proletariat as she had intended, Sand irritated middle-class audiences with her "socialist hymns," egalitarian folk heroes, and satirized bourgeois characters. She had already alienated that class with her novels: "I've wounded the bourgeoisie which reads my books, and I haven't instructed the people as I had intended because they cannot read me" (*Corr.* 10:142–43). But with the new regime Sand began to treat the bourgeoisie more sympathetically or at least not as harshly.

Writing for the middle class meant narrowing the range of characters to family, friends, and business associates, placing them in the confines of a bourgeois sitting room or tended garden, and letting them talk about making money and good marriages. There would be no more of *Claudie*'s brave new proletarian world, with its golden wheat, smell of freshly baked bread, sounds of bagpipes, fiddles, and folk songs. Embittered artists such as Baudelaire and the Goncourts accused Sand of having capitulated to bourgeois tastes. She did, but not entirely. Her plays after 1851 attempt to educate and gently satirize that bourgeois audience.

The lower-class Victorine, daughter of a clerk, marries the boss's son and into a family of successful and kindly businessmen. Fulgence, assistant to Victorine's father, intends to marry her himself. But he is a jealous and egotistical skeptic and misfit. When Sand wrote the sequel to Sedaine's *Philosophe sans savoir* she added Fulgence to the original cast of characters. She probably created Fulgence to serve as a contrast to the kindly bourgeois characters of the play, for he demonstrates the faults of the petty bourgeoisie. But Sarcey later describes him as the "personification of the bitter proletariat" (*Quarante ans,* 4:210).

Sand made one more attempt at a sort of folk play, one about towns-people rather than *paysans*. *Le Pressoir* probably began as her "male Claudie" in 1851. It was produced at the Gymnase in 1853. The charac-ters, village craftspeople, or town workers, carpenters and woodcutters, live in wine country. They have built a new "pressoir," or wine press, to be dedicated at the end of the play in time for the grape harvest. The set resembles a classical stage with one household on each side, the stage-right house tidy and prosperous, the stage-left run-down and dilapidated. This visual contrast represents the opposition in the two main male char-acters. The young man who is generous and self-sacrificing lives in the tidy house. His rival, who is selfish and egotistical, lives in the run-down house. In the final scenes of the play, during the dedication ceremony of the press, when the town officials and syndicated workers gather to cel-ebrate their solidarity, the egotist violently lashes out at his rival with an axe, but is overpowered, rehabilitated, and reconciled with his society. Two supporting characters, Suzanne Bienvenu and her fiancé, Noel Plan-tier, foreshadow Chekhovian country humor. Suzanne, by far the more intelligent of the pair, bosses her simpleton boyfriend around mercilessly, but Noel takes it with good heart and nature. Noel's speech pattern, a leitmotif of misprounuaciations, resembles the squeaky shoes of Yepikho-dov, "Two and Twenty Troubles," in *The Cherry Orchard*. The play in-structs the audience on how to distinguish between real and false love: the first is generous and self-abnegating; the second may be passionate, but is jealous and egotistical.

Sand also made another effort to revive the comedia dell'arte in one more play destined for the public stage, *Les Vacances de Pandolphe*, which opened at the Gymnase in 1852. While the opening scene creates an amusing picture of a celibate middle-class professor, Pandolphe, on va-cation at his Alpine cottage sitting under his linden tree ("my tree," "my house," "my garden") bantering with his clever and upwardly mobile servants, the rest of the play bogs down in a rather too heavy-handed attack on the greedy, materialistic gentry and its courtesans. A claque in the audience, shocked by the piece, whistled and hissed. The critics were aghast that Sand could have imagined that this play would make anybody laugh (*Corr.* 10:789–90, 11:329–31).

Sand defended *Pandolphe* and *Pressoir* as kindly portraits of the bour-geois class, but that may have been stretching the point. Pandolphe, the likeable law professor, stands apart from a gang of bourgeois vultures who cheat and lie to get the loot left in a will. And the craftspeople of *Pressoir* can hardly be considered bourgeois in Sand's context, for they are la-borers, the people. After *Pandolphe* and *Pressoir*, Sand wrote no more commedia or folk plays for the public stage. The simplicity and naïveté of these two genres particularly suited Sand's talent for creating fable-like metaphors and moralities; but they were not suited to contemporary bourgeois taste.

Sand herself needed a change from writing tender little consoling pieces. She wanted to revive some excitement by returning to romantic plays. In a long letter to the Odéon's new director, Gustave Vaez, Sand discusses the need for a theatre where romantic melodrama can be revived. She mourns the debasement of good romantic drama:

> Not long ago there was a romantic school created by Hugo and Dumas, well supported by others immediately following, and then spoiled by small-fry imitators. It was those bad imitations which killed the genre. One became weary of crimes and misfortunes.[14]

She tells Vaez that the success of her *Champi* was mainly due to the public's weariness with romantic excesses: "One of the first, I made a protest, albeit gently, with my little *Champi*. My success was due to that lassitude with great drama more than the play itself." However, Sand now thinks that the pendulum has swung too far in this opposite direction, that treasures from the old school are too easily forgotten by a sheepish audience:

> We've returned to the tender, that's all very well, but we've abandoned the big and the strong; and the Shakespearean school with its restorers Hugo, Dumas, and company, is forgotten and disdained by this infantile audience which goes too quickly where it is pushed.

Soon the same thing will happen to this "new school":

> Already the imitations of Sedaine have invaded the theatre and the defaults of the genre (those which are the easiest to imitate) will one of these days bore and repel this same public which won't want sad things anymore, and which will perceive soon enough how the tender can turn into silliness.

She rhetorically asks Vaez if there is not anything worth reviving in that old school which, while it lacked taste, measure, and sobriety, nevertheless impassioned them for twenty years. Should its faults be replaced by the faults of this new genre? In the romantic school there were too many stabbings, assassinations, poisonings, but does that means that "everything must finish at the present by marriages and little songs?" She worries that all the big theatres are going to become like the Gymnase, when it should be up to some of them to resuscitate the grandeurs of the past.

> To work for the little troupe of Montigny, powdered and charming as it is, that's amusing without a doubt, but it's only one facet of art, and I won't hide from you the fact that I'd rather try to revive serious drama—it alone permits lyricism.

She fears the decline or even loss of lyrical language from the stage if realism dominates: "Style will disappear if we aren't careful . . . seeking the natural (which is necessary in matters of reality), prose will come to exist no more as a language." She says she will try to buttress the temple of romantic lyricism, but to do so she needs a theatre director who believes in the artistic value of the effort.

Sand wrote a play adaptation of her romantic novel *Mauprat* (1837) in order to fill the need for romantic lyricism. When it was suggested she submit it to the Gymnase, Sand balked:

> Don't talk about *Mauprat* for the Gymnase—it doesn't go with them no matter what they might say about it. It's necessary to work *expressly* for the Gymnase, to have subject matter that fits their proportions and especially wait for what they ask for. . . . Montigny gives up too easily on the plays that are not guaranteed successes, by saying to himself that the prudent man runs no risks (to Hetzel, April 1852; *Corr.* 11:35).

Sand needed another theatre, grander and richer than the Gymnase, to stage her romantic melodrama *Mauprat.*[15]

A change in the management at the Odéon again signaled good news for Sand's plans to write more romantic dramas. Gustave Vaez, known for his libretti to Donizetti's operas, took charge as one of three Odéon directors in the spring of 1852. Sand envisioned making the Odéon the center of her theatrical operations. As France's "Second National Theatre" the Odéon was much more congenial to playwrights than France's first national theatre, the Comédie Française. Sand reports that the Odéon "isn't a theatre like the others, it doesn't run after money. It's large and full . . . a state-supported theatre to encourage young literary and dramatic forces, to educate and produce authors and actors" (January 1854; *Corr.* 12:236).

Vaez remained in the triumvirate of directors at the Odéon long enough to stage two of Sand's more romantic plays, *Mauprat* in 1853, and *Maître Favilla* in 1855. But soon after the latter he left to become director of the Opéra. In the 1860s a more conservative Odéon management produced two of Sand's more domestic dramas, *Villemer* in 1864, and *L'Autre*, starring Sarah Bernhardt, in 1870.

Mauprat had a large measure of success in reviving public taste for romantic melodrama, and was itself revived many times on the Odéon stage. But it was the only one of Sand's old-fashioned melodramas to reach the stage. Her work on *Gabriel/Julia* came to nothing when another of the Odéon directors, Alphonse Royer, vetoed the production, saying the play was "too sad." While the critics did not rave about *Mauprat*, their response was generally favorable. Everyone remembered the novel and how much they had enjoyed reading it when it was first published in 1837. Edouard Thierry (*Le Moniteur Universel,* 6 December 1853) commended Sand's "rare industry" in making the drama almost an entirely separate work from the novel, having given it a complete theatrical action which does not exist in the novel. Gautier (*La Presse,* 8 December 1853), to the contrary, observed that a sufficient amount of the novel's satanic and desperate poesy and Anne-Radcliffe-like cliff-hanging excitement transferred over to the play to assure its success. But Janin complained that the play performance ran far too long. (Dumas père reported that the play lasted until one fifteen in the morning, so certainly Janin had a point.) Janin wearied of too many bandits on stage, and only one woman in "the middle of all that noise and smoke." He regretted that the genius who wrote *Indiana* and *Valentine* would stoop to write a melodrama for the boulevard public (*Journal des Débats,* 5 December 1853). The reviewer Pontmartin in *Revue des Deux Mondes* agreed with Janin that Sand had lowered herself too much in writing a melodrama, and that the novel *Mauprat* lost its literary qualities in the play production. Pontmartin faulted Sand for disdaining contemporary society in her dramas, for escaping into rustic folk drama, commedia dell'arte, and now historic melodrama (1 January 1854). Critics in the succeeding generation who witnessed revivals of *Mauprat* reaffirmed a general disappointment in Sand's play adaptation of a novel they had enjoyed reading more; what was touching and moving in the novel appeared laughable on the stage.[16]

Alexandre Dumas père, the master of romantic melodrama, rather liked Sand's dramatic version of *Mauprat,* and made some interesting remarks which compare Sand's approach to playwriting to his own. From a practical point of view Dumas thought the stage at the Odéon too large for scenes of four or fewer characters, which often occur in Sand's play. The thirty-five-foot-wide proscenium opening should have been masked for those intimate scenes. He also suggests that the Mendelssohn music composed for the castle siege in Goethe's *Goetz von Berlichingen* would enhance the siege scene in *Mauprat.* The difference between himself and Sand as playwrights, Dumas says, starts with their focus; he focuses on the action, she on the characters. His action creates the characters, while her characters create the action. He sculpts for the stage, she paints. His characters move and agitate; Sand's dream, think, and philosophize.[17]

Some of Sand's success in creating strong dramatic characters must have been due in part to her underdefining rather than overdefining the roles. She wrote with an eye to the actor, with respect for what an intelligent and artistic actor could do with the role. This is evident in a letter Sand sent to the actor Barré, who was playing a supporting role in *Mau-*

prat. Barré had written to Sand asking her for advice on how to develop his character of Patience. Sand responds:

> I'll not give you any other counsel than this: look for it and create it in your own nature. Character details are in the novel and in the play. But the *type* is left to the creation of the artist. That's a law that I always impose upon myself in writing for the theatre, because I believe that the actor must bring the results of his originality to the ensemble. If he's not intelligent he'll make a type that's untruthful or displeasing. But when he understands as you do, he can successfully make a character different in aspect from the description the author gives. You have in your playing the good nature, the roundess, the soundness of intentions, the honesty and simplicity of means (*Corr.* 12:118).

Whether or not Sand's advice had an effect on how Barré played Patience, his character was a favorite with the critics and the audience.

Gossip behind the scenes at the Odéon leaked to Sand that the popular playwright Ponsard had successfully lobbied with the critics to give *Mauprat* only a lukewarm reception in order that the Odéon close her play sooner and give one of his plays a revival earlier in the season. Odéon personnel kept Sand posted on the results, which apparently went in favor of Ponsard. Sand's play was pulled at the end of January 1854, after only two months into the first run, even though the box office receipts were still on the upswing (*Corr.* 12:210, 280n).

With *Flaminio* (1854), Sand returns to another example of good bourgeois characters; she pits an artist (the Italian bohemian Flaminio) against haute bourgeois interests. Sand does mask some of her bourgeois characters in this play with titles such as "princess." In *Flaminio* there are both good and bad bourgeois types. Flaminio himself is transformed into a prospering architect-engineer who builds monuments of industry rather than the puppets of former days. Sand created a comic English lady in *Flaminio,* whose attempts to speak French with her anglicisms and heavy English accent are an early example of their kind on the French stage, but which eventually became a staple.

Maître Favilla (1855), a play hotly contested by Janin and Sand, is a tight three-act structure with a simple plot and small ensemble cast, set in a country house. A critical review more favorably disposed towards *Favilla* than Janin's reports that this "simple piece, a shadow of a dream, poetic and charming," is as "elevated and vast as the genius of its author." "Kreisler in *Contes d'Hoffmann* could not have been more fantastic than this Maître Favilla" (Philippe Busoni, *L'Illustration,* 29 September 1855). There is no doubt that Sand had Hoffmannesque fantasies in mind as she wrote *Favilla.* But the play bears some resemblance to Molière's *Tartuffe,* and is even more strikingly similar to Sand's successor Chekhov's *Cherry*

7. Scenes from *Mauprat*, 1853.
   Courtesy of Bibliothèque Spoelberch de Lovenjoul (Institut de France), Chantilly.

Orchard. Keller, the bourgeois merchant who knows the cost of every-thing and the value of nothing, combines the hyprocrisy and lust of Tar-tuffe with the calculation and profit-motive of Lopakhin in *Cherry Orchard*. As a Tartuffe, Keller tries to seduce Favilla's virtuous wife; as Lopakhin he tries to secure the country estate and manage it in the new, impersonal, profitable manner. There is even an old Firs-like family servant in *Favilla* named Frantz. Favilla, a foolish and lovable old musician, receives the audience's sympathies, even though his claims on the estate appear ridic-ulous, just as Madame Ranefskia is both sympathetic and ridiculous in Chekhov's drama of changing social structure in the Russian countryside.

Sand dedicated *Maître Favilla* to the actor Rouvière, who played the principal role. She had seen him play Hamlet, and observed that he soared like an eagle in the tempest, and now as Favilla he gracefully circles the puffy clouds. He makes "the *romanesque* appear natural . . . the *roman-esque* illusion real."[18] In his obituary of Rouvière, Baudelaire remembers the actor's portrayal of Favilla and how it had surprised everyone: "Rou-vière had always played bitter, ferocious . . . natures. In *Favilla* he played a paternal . . . lovable . . . role . . . coming from a little known side of his nature, a love of utopia, revolutionary idylls, cult of Jean Jacques Rousseau."[19] Critics such as Janin and Baudelaire understood what Sand was doing in *Favilla*, creating a "revolutionary idyll"; it was just that the former did not like it and the latter did.

With Jules Janin we have a particularly instructive case of how Sand's relations with drama critics could be somewhat problematical. Sand held most of the Parisian critics in generally low esteem. Early in the fall of 1853 when her crisp contemporary play *Le Démon du foyer* played to full houses at the Gymnase, Sand complained to the director Montigny about official critical response. She does not mind attacks on a play's form, content, or performance qualities. But she does mind attacks on her as a person; critics treat her as an "impertinent, proud fool." She's forty-eight years old, a successful novelist, trying to establish a new career as a playwright, and the critics will not give her a chance (*Corr.* 12:338–39). Perhaps if she wooed the critics with gifts and favors as other playwrights do, they would not abuse her the way they do (*Corr.* 12:620–21). Sand declares that dramatic criticism as a school of ideas, a body of instruction, does not exist:

> Criticism does not exist. There are some critics who have a lot of talent, but a school of criticism no longer exists. They don't agree on the for or the against of anything. They go about cutting down or building up merely by chance, they go as the world goes. . . . They are ingenious, they have style, but for all that there isn't a shadow of instruction. Nothing holds together in what they say. It's not their fault, nothing holds together in humanity anymore (to Champfleury, January 1854; *Corr.* 12:267).

The only critic for whom Sand ever expressed much admiration was Gustave Planche. She didn't agree with him, but she liked his critical stance:

> I didn't share his principles of exclusivity in art . . . but agree with him that it's better to have a faith, a dogma, than to judge by chance, by fantasy or the impression of the moment. . . . He said to be a critic one needs to have a logical ensemble of opinions, well reasoned (*Corr.* 15:103).

Sand recommended to other writers that they ignore the critics, rather than argue with them or cater to them. Since the critic is not an artist, and can judge art only from the point of view of his opinions, it is best not to engage in debate with him. For while critics may be conservative in their opinions today, tomorrow they might be revolutionary, "and not any more artistic for that probably" (July 1854; *Corr.* 12:498–99). With passing time and more stage experience Sand's opinion of critics did not improve. She came to see the theatre as a cavern, where the cave dwellers live only off the flesh of others (*Corr.* 12:478). Or it is a battleground where the playwright must be his sole defender:

> To make theatre happen you need an army of directors, artists, friends, all of whom abandon ship with the first wave of cold response from the audience, the first hostile review. The army will abandon you and plead with you not to recommence. . . . I'd rather renounce such a battle where I don't know who my enemies are or with whom I am fighting (January 1860; *Corr.* 15:645).

Sand cannot understand why all the critics are "enraged" against her (*Corr.* 15:571). Neither can others. Victor Hugo writes to Hetzel about those who attack Sand: "There is now a sort of gross hatred and sacrilege mounted everywhere against that generous and noble spirit. I don't understand that animosity of man against a woman" (*Corr.* 12:576n).

Jules Janin was the leader of the critics violently opposed to Sand's theatre career, or rather more opposed to a socialist like Sand succeeding in a theatre career. Even though she reproached herself for it later, a particular review written by Janin so provoked Sand that she wrote a long letter of rebuttal. She wanted the editor of *La Presse,* Emile Girardin, to publish it, but he refused, using as his excuse the fact that Janin had spoken kind words about his wife (playwright Delphine Gay) at her funeral. Sand never sent the letter to anyone or ever had it published in her lifetime; but she saved a copy for later readers. As it addresses itself not only to the role of drama critics, but also to the state of her own social conscience, a full account of its contents may be useful.

The review that so irked Sand was Janin's of *Maître Favilla,* which premiered at the Odéon in September 1855. He describes *Favilla,* one of

Sand's major dramatic achievements, as "a little thing . . . an absurd fable . . . with an impossible hero—a madman," "an apotheosis of a violin," "a biased condemnation of the bourgeoisie," "realism." The lead actor, Rouvière, playing Favilla, Janin sarcastically anoints as "king of the realists" (*Journal des Débats,* 24 September 1855).

In Sand's letter of response, she chastises Janin for criticizing what he is incapable of understanding. He has gone outside a discussion of the dramatic work and its performance, and expressed an opinion on what he supposes are Sand's personal sentiments, sentiments which Sand says are not there. He has accused her of hating the bourgeoisie. Her plays contradict this accusation: *Victorine*'s bourgeois characters are noble, good, and sincere; the principal character in *Pandolphe* is a lovable, pure, and simple bourgeois law professor; and in *Flaminio* the grand bourgeois and in *Pressoir* the petit bourgeois characters are all sympathetically drawn. For the first time, she has pitted an artist character against a bourgeois character in *Maître Favilla.* The bourgeois merchant Keller has faults which are greater than the fact that he is bourgeois—he is a hypocrite and ridiculous. And the artist Favilla is a sympathetic, but impossible, old fool. But is Keller that bad, asks Sand. She answers sarcastically:

> What a great crime to make the old linen merchant unappreciative of music, unable to distinguish an honest wife from a bohemian, hesitant to marry his only son to a penniless young woman. There indeed is a condemnation of the bourgeois which is cruel, acerbic, bitter, systematic.[20]

Sand refuses to accept Janin's reproach that *Favilla* demonstrates a "systematic hatred" of the bourgeoisie.

Why asks Sand, has Janin renounced his destiny, "which is to see, to understand, to love the theatre?" Isn't he the one who first discovered and advertised the clown Debureau? Sand tells him to get on with his business, and leave Sand's personal morality out of it. "You make pronouncements on the content, when you should only on the form." For while Janin's criticism of theatrical form can be "masterful, brilliant, erudite, exquisite," he is not a philosopher, and to be a complete critic one must be able to philosophize a little, says Sand. Instead, Janin creates his criticisms with the emotions and spleen of an artist.

Janin has aged too much at his reading lamp to understand people any longer: "Open your eyes to the present society." Things have changed. The old class distinctions no longer exist. "Look up from your books." "According to you the rich are the wise and the poor the foolish," whereas actually at present, "it's *luck* alone which decides the destiny of becoming rich."

That honest bourgeois who counts out each evening the modest profits of his day's work, who doesn't play at the stock market, who doesn't hazard the grand schemes of big industry is no longer called the bourgeois. He's the people, and the only difference between him and the artisan is the amount of activity, invention, and ambition.

The laborer, peasant, shopkeeper, artist, her characters Flaminio, Fulgence, Keller, Favilla—all of them are "the people." Among them, "the only aristocracy is in intelligence and virtue."

Sand says that the realist (in Janin's negative sense) par excellence is speculation: "queen of vicissitudes," "enemy of the ideal," "who pushes men into a feverish fight for success, and disdains the contemplations of the artist, the erudition of the critic, the systems of the philosopher, and the aspirations of the . . . moralist, equally." That race of speculators "invading the moral and physical forces of our epoch," does not constitute a separate class; it is made up of all walks of life. All it needs to know is banking, financial calculations, how to play the game, "because the big game has become the soul of modern society." But the optimist Sand sees progress toward socialism, toward a "solidarity of interests." "Speculators are becoming more intelligent, and they are profiting by economic, social and political work."

"Our job," Sand concludes in her comments to Janin, "is to fight against an excess of prosaism . . . to save some pearls, or at least some flowers, from being carried off in the storm."

This letter to a powerful critic shows how Sand the socialist resents being attacked and accused of hating the bourgeoisie. Sand's comments at the end of the Second Republic in 1851 have already shown that she had decided to redirect her dramas, to put aside her goal to console and instruct the proletariat, which she discovered could not afford to attend the theatre, and instead turn her attention to educating the bourgeoisie. She certainly did not want to alienate her audiences by offending them, so she tried hard to soften her satirical portraits of the bourgeoisie. Janin had picked up a copy of an earlier version of *Favilla* (published in Brussels by Hetzel), begun in 1851 under the title *Nello,* which shows a much harder and stronger satire of the bourgeois merchant Keller. As Sand points out in her letter, Janin was wrong to drag that version into the discussion, since the later version in *Maître Favilla* was not nearly so severe a portrait.

While *Favilla* played at the Odéon during the fall of 1855, Sand wrote *Françoise,* another gentle satire of a *"bourgeois gentilhomme."* Sand wrote the role Françoise for her good friend, the much admired actress Madame Arnould-Plessy, a member of the Comédie Française troupe. But after a reading before the committee, the national theatre turned down *Françoise,* and so the play went to the Gymnase, where it opened in April 1856. And

Sand wrote an adaptation of *As You Like It* for the Comédie Française in which Arnould-Plessy played the heroine—not Rosalind, but Celia; and Rouvière the hero—Jacques!

In *Françoise* Sand shows how contemporary materialism and ego satisfaction conflict with higher values and virtues. She wants the audience to see the need for raising moral and intellectual well-being to the level of material well-being. In a gadabout, dandy character, Henri, Sand develops the "combat of a young man taken with the lively temptations of the century . . . often lovable and good, his conduct is not voluntarily bad . . . but his remorse is sterile and his heart impotent."[21] People in the play describe Henri as "more seductive than solid"; "worst of all, he's an egoist!" Henri wants to marry Françoise, an ideal, tender, charming, virtuous young woman who lives modestly in the Berrichon town of Bourges helping her father in his doctoral research. It's "an ideal Protestant household" says critic Saint-Victor (*La Presse*, 6 April 1856). And Françoise wants to marry Henri. But as another title of the play says, "He who loses gains." Françoise loses Henri to another, richer woman, who saves her from an unhappier fate, that of being married to Henri herself. Instead of Françoise, Henri will marry the daughter of two masterfully satirized parvenus, Monsieur and Madame Dubuisson, former innkeepers. M. Dubuisson is now the "biggest banker in Berry," and his wife the most determined of social climbers. Their daughter Cleonice, "the prettiest *enfant terrible*, the joy of the comedy, petulant, badly raised, graceful, genteel," captures Henri in a "golden caprice," says Saint-Victor. This critic concludes that the play succeeds by "subtle sentiments, beautiful thoughts, and insinuation, like so many of Sand's plays." Gautier particularly likes Sand's innovative characterization of Henri, who is a protagonist but not a hero, "odious under a light appearance" (*Le Moniteur Universel*, 7 April 1856). Gautier thinks this character, "drawn by the hand of a master," is entirely new to the theatre. M. Dubuisson, with the ruddy face of a peasant and ridiculously extravagant clothes, reminds Gautier of a "rural Shylock." But Jules Janin has not a kind word for Sand's new play, nor for that matter, for all the others, which he condemns in the same review as "insipid things," "myths," "miserable parodies of comedy and drama" (*Journal des Débats*, 7 April 1856).

But Sand's next effort, her adaptation of *As You Like It* at the Comédie Française in April 1856, Janin says he likes better than *Favilla* or *Françoise*, and thinks Sand has condensed five acts into three rather neatly (*Journal des Débats*, 21 April 1856). Gautier likes Rouvière's Jacques and Arnould-Plessy's Celia, the two lead roles. Everyone lauds Sand's *Comme il vous plaira* for being the first time Shakespeare's *As You Like It* has been attempted in French on a Parisian stage. The Comédie Française spared no expense in creating lavish sets and costumes for this historic event. But beyond its historical significance, Sand's *Comme il vous plaira* must have been a disappointment, for she turns Shakespeare's expansive play of light and shadow in the Forest of Arden into an ordered, logical, and somber rehabilitation of the melancholy Jacques. It is Celia who loves and reforms this misanthrope. We hardly see or hear of Rosalind and Orlando. Sand had no intention of slavishly imitating Shakespeare; she expressly wanted to create an equilibrium between the school of sensible realism and lyrical idealism.[22] And to her contemporaries she achieved that goal. As one observer puts it, she did not adapt the play to amuse the public, but to give "greatest value" and "highest taste" to this "regal literature."[23] Victor Hugo's young Belgian editor, Albert Lacroix, brought out a book in 1856 which applauds Sand's development of the Jacques character, "that Alceste of the Renaissance." Lacroix recognizes a theme of Rousseau's in Sand's adaptation, that of showing the opposition between a man who has been corrupted by society and one who has recovered his generosity and enthusiasm in solitude.[24] But Charles Dickens, who was in the audience, did not like the adaptation at all.[25]

In spite of Sand's efforts to preserve stage lyricism and romanticism, imagination and idealism, realism was in the vanguard. She could stem the tide only if she extended the limits of realism. By refusing to limit the term to the mundane she could accept realism. Sand's correspondence with France's "father" of realism, Champfleury, apparently helped him to clarify the characteristics of the new movement. Responding in January 1854 to Champfleury's request for Berrichon folk songs, Sand tells him that "all this talk about new artistic battles is much ado about nothing—mistaking a rag for a gauntlet" (*Corr.* 12:263–68). In June of that year Sand wrote another long letter to Champfleury in which she poses the debate between realism and romanticism in a manner similar to Stendhal's for the classicists and romanticists in his 1823 essay, *Racine et Shakespeare.* Sand cautions:

> If you consider yourself as a defender of the principle: art arranges nothing and is no more than the accurate reproduction of reality, I will respond to you: very well, but on the condition that it will be a true artist in charge of seeing and transcribing. We always feel the spirit which moves his hand and makes it skillful.

Sand's romanticist addresses her realist:

> You've pushed the ideal out of the door . . . you only analyze facts. You don't look for the beautiful or the rare, you don't believe in the exceptional, you admit to no fiction, finally you don't clothe your models or your style, you call a cat a cat and you make of art a *Daguerreotype.*

The realist responds:

> I don't analyze, I show; I don't reveal, I prove. . . . I have no need to ornament.
> . . . And the story of a cat well understood and well said is worth more than one of
> a star badly interpreted. Finally I make nature as beautiful as nature is (*Corr.* 12:481–85).

Thus Sand defends the realist without condemning romanticism. In her
"school" there is room for both.

In Champfleury's published manifesto of realism, called "Du Réalisme: Lettre à Madame Sand," (1855), Champfleury gives Wagner as an
example of realism in music, Courbet in painting, and George Sand in
drama. "Critics say your dramas of the country are tainted with realism.
They reduce the country folk to *paysans*."[26]

Sand responds to Champfleury's essay with her own, "Le Réalisme,"
published in *Courrier de Paris,* September 1857:

> Monsieur Champfleury, we hear, has broken with the past . . . he hasn't. . . . He has
> been sufficiently original for a student of Balzac. . . . They [the realists] are looking
> for the *natural,* and they've started all over again, a little late, a campaign against bad
> classicism already vanquished and buried.

She says that before anyone ever heard of realists, the romanticists, and
before them Molière, had won the campaign for the natural against the
artificial. A major drawback of realism as Sand sees it is exclusivity: "The
realists have taken on quite a task . . . in wishing to diminish all that isn't
suited to their will." She uses Shakespeare as an example of a great spirit
and the opposite of exclusivity: "Shakespeare, who is the great Pan of
literature, sang in all the modes, from the obscene to the sublime." All
theory should be left aside; artists should do what they can do best: "For
my part, I believe that one should gild and bejewel when one knows how
to do it well; likewise, one should be simple when one knows how. The
one is not any easier than the other." As an example of realism she particularly admired, Sand gives Flaubert's *Madame Bovary,* "with the painting of the bad, M. Flaubert knew how to make a beautiful book" (rpt. in
Questions d'art, pp. 287–94).

Many years later when Sand and Flaubert had become close friends,
she expressed to him her desire to write another essay on realism, with
specific reference to Zola's novels, which she thinks are strong and of
great value. But they do not change her way of seeing, which is:

> that art must be the search for truth, and that the truth is not a picture of the bad. It
> must be a picture of both the good and the bad. . . . Life is not filled with monsters,
> society is not formed only of scoundrels and wretches. . . . Imbeciles dominate, it's

true, but there's a public conscience which weighs upon them and obliges them to respect the law. It's all very well to show these rascals but only if you show their counterparts; otherwise the naïve reader, which is the reader in general, becomes sad and appalled, and denies you in order to avoid despair.[27]

Sand never wrote that essay. Two months later she was dead.

Following Sand's 1857 essay on realism her professional playwriting career continued with *Marguerite de Sainte-Gemme* in 1859 at the Gymnase. Though it paints an amusing and realistic picture of middle-class marital affection and squabbles, the play as a whole reflects Sand's half-hearted interest in writing for the public stage at this time.

Sand's efforts to apply psychological realism to the one-act play form proved to be more satisfying. The form had existed for a long time mainly as an amusing teaser, entr'acte, or epilogue to an evening's full-length play. The genre had been taken seriously by Marivaux, Goethe, and Musset, all of whom served as examples for Sand. She gave the form more sobriety by surrounding her psychologically developed characters with realistic stage settings and stage business. Sand's first professionally staged effort, *Lucie,* failed dismally when it was performed at the Gymnase in 1856. Working and reworking the piece for Montigny's troupe, Sand wrote to the director:

Why must a one-act play be gay? But, you tell me, all of them are. That's all the more reason to try one which isn't. There's more novelty in making a serious little drama about a family in one set than to make a joke last an hour. And if it saddens the audience, they cannot complain that it lasted too long (*Corr.* 12:298).

Sand adapted *Lucie* from a Goethe piece, "Brother and Sister." Her next original one-act play to be staged publically achieved a notable success.

Le Pavé, meaning "the paving stone," was the title of Sand's one-act play which opened at the Gymnase on 18 March 1862. Since the piece was conceived as a short story in dialogue form intended only for private performance at the little Nohant theatre, Sand was surprised when Parisian public theatres wished to produce it. Both Montigny of the Gymnase and Rounat of the Odéon requested the piece from Sand after reading the version published in *Revue des Deux Mondes* (15 August 1861). Since Montigny had asked for it first, in fairness, Sand gave it to the Gymnase. She sent Montigny a second script based on the Nohant performances of the play, more detailed in stage directions and set requirements than the published version. She agreed with Montigny to change the male neighbor role into a female role (*Corr.* 16:657). There are only four characters in the play: a seventeen-year-old serving girl, Louise (played by Marie Delaporte, who had "deliciously" played Cleonice Dubisson in the original production of *Françoise* six years before *Pavé*); a twenty-three-year-old country boy valet, Coquelet (played by Pierre Berton, son of François Berton, who had played Henri in *Françoise*); the neighbor (played by Cheri-Lesueur, who was Madame Dubuisson in *Françoise*); and Durand, a forty-five-year-old naturalist-mineralogist (played by Lafont). Sand reports to her son Maurice on opening night that Durand and the neighbor got off to a cold start, but later when Coquelet entered everything changed and it warmed up (*Corr.* 16:854). Sand was so taken with the young actor Pierre Berton that she later based a novel, *Pierre qui roule* (1869), on him. He, in turn, was grateful to Sand for giving him his start in professional acting with the part of Coquelet.[28]

Pierre Berton particularly pleased Sand because he interpreted the country boy valet as a *naïf,* not a *niais,* or silly fool (*Corr.* 16:657). Sand did not want her one-act to be played as a farce with laughable and ridiculous characters.[29] She intended *Pavé* to represent life in the country, "more serious and simple," in contrast to life in Paris.[30]

The play takes place in Durand's country cottage, where he keeps all his mineral and rock specimens and tools. Sand draws an affectionate picture of an absentminded amateur scientist, happy-go-lucky, childlike and self-satisfied in his modest creature comforts and settled way of life. Durand's servant Louise takes good care of him and shows a remarkable intelligence and aptitude for research, which helps Durand in his "work." Coquelet, Durand's valet, has the rough manners, uneducated air, and good heart of a country-bred servant boy. Since he befriended Louise when they were young children and all the others teased Louise, she describes him as her "consolation." These three characters seem at first to accept without complaint their stations in life. But a neighbor who intends to marry off her widowed niece to Durand upsets the established order of this little household. The prospect of marriage disturbs the amateur scientist; he wonders what would happen to Louise. Then Coquelet provokes Durand even further by telling him proudly (but falsely, Coquelet thinks) that Louise wants to marry this simple valet. Durand's fury at the possible match of Louise and Coquelet makes him realize that he would like to marry Louise himself. So he fires Coquelet and sends him away. Louise, who really does love Coquelet and now sees that she does want to marry him, begs Durand to bring Coquelet back. There is a threat that Durand may use his gun if he catches sight of Coquelet. But when Louise expresses sincere preference for Coquelet's good nature over someone, anyone, with more intelligence and education, Durand, in a moment of poignant awareness that he is too old now for youthful love and idealism, submits to his fate and goes next door to tell his old neighbor that he will have dinner with the niece after all.

Durand's transformation from the contented, childlike celibate we see at the beginning of the play, to this dry, aloof, cold, and sad forty-five-year-old man at the end, evokes a truly touching picture of aging and disillusionment. The subtle shifts in Louise's attitude toward Durand, from the devotion of a daughter-servant, to a growing awareness that Durand's feelings for her may be more than paternal, to a mature recognition that she loves her young playmate and will have to hurt Durand, demonstrate how effectively and efficiently Sand mastered the craft of giving psychological depth to characters within the compact confines of a one-act play form. She proves that psychological change can make a strong dramatic action, even in a short time and a small space.

George Sand's serious, natural, full, psychological one-act dramas such as *Le Pavé* precede by almost thirty years Zola's, Strindberg's, and Antoine's experiments in the form. Another of Sand's one-acts, *Le Lis du Japon*, followed in 1866, produced at the Vaudeville. A stylish dialogue that blends Marivaux, Carmontel, and Musset, combined with an O'Henry-like story line, it gives the impression of being both a naturalist and a symbolist play. The innovative setting shows an artist's basement studio, where we see outside through the windows only the pedestrians' lower legs and feet. The artist, who paints flowers for a living, is being evicted from his studio, so, in a last grand gesture, he cuts from its roots a rare and expensive Japanese lily and presents it to his upper-class landlady, whom he secretly loves. Sand's last one-act play to be professionally produced in Paris, *Un Bienfait n'est jamais perdu*, a proverb in swift and bright repartee that Sand found in an old carton of manuscripts and revived, played at the little Théâtre de Cluny in 1872. It was Sand's last play premiere.

In 1864 Sand's full-length play adaptation of her novel *Marquis de Villemer* made the biggest sensation yet of any of her plays, and proved to be her greatest commercial success, with the one possible exception of *François le Champi*. Today's reader of *Villemer* may find it difficult to ascertain just why this one should have been so much more popular than all the others. The characters are well drawn, the story line charming, the romantic intrigue engaging; but then these qualities apply equally to many others of Sand's pieces. The timing of *Villemer*'s appearance was critical. Sand had just published an attack on the church clergy in her novel *Mademoiselle la Quintinie* (1863), which, while it scandalized one faction of society, roused support from another, particularly the more free-spirited students of the Odéon quartier where *Villemer* was staged in 1864. Huge crowds of these students and other supporters gathered around the Odéon and stood outside when there was no more room inside, to cheer their heroine

8. Crowd gathers around Odéon Theatre, morning of *Marquis de Villemer* Premiere in 1864. Courtesy of Bibliothèque Municipale, Châteauroux.

George Sand, a sixty-year-old novelist and playwright who regarded this display of devotion with quizzical amusement. In a letter to her son and daughter-in-law, Sand describes the tumultuous audience reception given her on opening night:

> At ten o'clock in the morning the students assembled in the Place de l'Odéon, and, throughout the piece, a compact mass which had not been able to gain admittance filled the neighborhood. . . . The event has kept the Latin Quarter in a perfect uproar all day; all day long I received batches of students, who came with their school cards in their hats to ask me for orders, and to protest against the clerical party by giving me their names. . . . Inside the theatre, each scene was received throughout with shouts and stamping of feet, in spite of the presence of the whole imperial family. In fact everybody applauded, the emperor like the rest. . . . Tonight quiet is now restored, the traffic resumed, and I am going to bed.[31]

Sand adapted both *Villemer* and *L'Autre* from her novels; the novel *Marquis de Villemer* first appeared in 1860, and *L'Autre* was adapted from *Confessions d'une jeune fille*, published in 1864. Likewise, two other Sand plays produced after 1851 were adapted from novels: *Mauprat*, the novel published in 1837 and the play produced in 1853; and *Flaminio*, and the novel *Teverino* in 1845 and the play in 1854. She wrote to the director of the Gymnase, where nine of her plays were produced, "Look through my novels and find one that appears most convenient to your stage and I will take the time to adapt the play" (February 1853; *Corr.* 11:580). After 1852 only two of Sand's full-length plays were originally conceived as plays, *Françoise* and *Marguerite de Sainte-Gemme*.[32] The period of feverish dreaming and thinking in dramatic form had subsided. By adapting her successful novels to the stage, Sand could rely on her reading public to become her playgoers.

L'Autre was George Sand's last full-length play premiere, staged at the Odéon in 1870. While the Odéon remained Sand's favorite theatre in which to work (she located the acting troupe of her novel *La Pierre qui roule*, 1869, on the stage and in the wings of the Odéon), she had further disagreeable experiences there caused by ineffective directors and temperamental actors. In 1870, at sixty-six years of age, Sand was forced to exercise full command over the rehearsals for *L'Autre* for the duration of the play's preparation because the two Odéon directors, Chilly and Duquesnel, were incompetent and had no respect from the actors.[33] As Sand reports in a letter to her son, "The direction is so hesitant, so incapable that no one works when I turn my back."[34] Chilly told her they could not go on without her. So she had to think of everything, the props, the lights, the furniture, and the costumes. And there is always someone absent or sick at rehearsals. Mlle Page, who plays the supporting female role, is "furious" because she did not get the lead. Sand describes her as someone you would not want to touch with pincers. Sarah Bernhardt, who plays the lead (her first lead role), is "silly" but a "charming character."[35] At least Sand could use the rehearsal period to revise her script, as was her custom.

This last full-length play dramatizes the conflict of a young realist-pragmatist, almost an egotistical cynic, with a romantic-idealist. Sarah Bernhardt played the young female goad who brings these two men to a new awareness, that each has within himself the opposite type. The goad forgives and rehabilitates, Sand's dramatic watchwords to the end. *L'Autre* succeeded with the public and earned Sand 12,000 francs before it was forced to close by the 1870 Revolution's barricades and gunshots in the streets. Sand had already retreated to Nohant. Another revolution marked a major change in Sand's theatre career, just as the 1830 and 1848 revolutions had done. But this one also marked the end of a career.

Perhaps the most significant contribution Sand made to nineteenth-century theatre history during this period of professional pragmatism was her cogent analysis of the debate between realism and romanticism. Add to that her work in creating new bourgeois character types, and in applying realism and psychological development to the one-act play form, and we can see that in balance this closing period of Sand's professional theatre career ends on a good note albeit in a minor key.

9. Theatre of Nohant with Garden Stage Set and Audience,
   in *Recueil* 1:195.
   Phot. Bibliothèque Nationale, Paris.

4

A Theatre of One's Own

George Sand's little theatre of Nohant preceded Jacques Copeau's Vieux Colombier by sixty-seven years. Copeau ruminates on Sand's contribution to the experimental theatre movement in one of his unpublished notebooks on comedia dell'arte: "Bring back the experiment at Nohant related by George Sand. . . . That little theatre of Nohant, as described by Sand, must have been infinitely more lively than the majority of our professional theatres."[1] And lively it was for several seasons, from 8 December 1846, when the Nohant troupe opened with an improvisational performance of Sand's scenario *Le Druide peu délicat,* to 31 August 1863, when Sand's last Nohant script, *Daphnis et Chloë,* was performed. During those seventeen busy years Sand wrote and produced (and sometimes acted in or directed) over seventy partially scripted scenarios and as many as twenty-five fully scripted plays.[2]

Situated at the geographic center of France in the province of Berry, George Sand's country estate stretches out along a promontory which rises almost imperceptibly from the River Indre, less than a mile away to the west. The Berrichon countryside, with its gently undulating sheep pastures, crisscrossed by tree hedges and muddy ditches, resembles parts of Scotland or Ireland. The resemblance is more than geographic, for Berrichon folk instruments include the bagpipe, and the kin of those Celts who danced around Merlin's stones on the British Isles kept vigil over their own sacred stones in Sand's Berry.[3]

George Sand's château dominates the little village of Nohant, a handful of farmhouses and a small old church. Stables and farm buildings, a formal park and orchards, and income-producing grazing and farm lands comprised the formal Nohant estate. The château, a conservative eighteenth-century mansion of three floors, derives its status as "château" from the medieval turreted castle it replaced in 1767.

Sand's grandmother, Aurore Dupin, purchased the Nohant château in 1793 with what remained of her once considerable fortune. Berry's docile and slow-to-change life style provided for the harried aristocrat a peaceful retreat from the troubles of the French Revolution she left behind in Paris. The bucolic setting would likewise be an oasis for George, the granddaughter, seeking some peace and quiet after several tumultuous years in Paris and abroad.

The house was relatively new, forty-one years old, when four-year-old Aurore Dupin came to live with her grandmother in 1808. Sand inherited the estate when her grandmother died in 1821, and held onto it despite her husband's efforts to claim the property during their legal separation proceedings in the 1830s. In terms of furniture and interior decor Sand changed very little in the château, preferring to retain the ambience of her childhood memories, with the omnipresent portraits of her ancestors overseeing the salon. George Sand's own granddaughter, Aurore Lauth-Sand, the last private owner of the Nohant château, deeded the property to the French government before her death in 1961. She preserved the château as George Sand left it upon her death in 1876. So, for almost two hundred years, 1793 to 1961, the Nohant château was dominated by a succession of three women primarily, all named Aurore, grandmother to granddaughter. These fortunate circumstances permit us to see the mansion much as it must have looked when the grandmother purchased the property in 1793 and as George Sand lived in it for three-quarters of the nineteenth century.

The mansion's most prominent occupant described her house in a rather modest manner:

> The house is sound, airy . . . moderately spacious for a country house, and infinitely too small to be a château. But such as it is, it serves our needs . . . our preoccupations: we have found means to make two artist studios [one originally built for her friend Delacroix], an engraver's studio, a small library and a little theatre, with a vestibule and a storage room for the sets. The theatre is the only thing a little curious about our house.[4]

The curiosity of building a theatre in a private house was not new to Sand's family. George's great-grandmother, Marie de Verrières (the mother of George's grandmother, Aurore Dupin), an elegant and wealthy courtesan, together with her beautiful courtesan sister Geneviève, played in their own private country and Paris house theatres. Marivaux wrote the play *Deux Aspasies du siècle* especially for the Verrières sisters to perform in the vast theatre space of their sumptuous Paris mansion, which contained fourteen loges (seven of them masked to conceal women who wished not to be seen). Here professional actors from the Comédie Française and dancers from the Opéra mixed with amateur performers, a mélange similar to Sand's troupe at Nohant in the 1850s, over a hundred years later.[5]

But Sand's private theatrics began on a more intimate and modest scale than her great-grandmother's. During an exceptionally cold December in the winter of 1846, snowed-in and melancholy, George and her family cheered themselves by improvising pantomimes. While Chopin played at the piano the players danced in front of a crackling fire in the salon's fireplace. Thirty years later in an essay she wrote just before her death, Sand recalls those first musical pantomimes:

> It started with the pantomime . . . the invention of Chopin. He improvised at the piano while the young people mimed the scenes and danced comic ballets. I leave it to you to imagine how those admirable and charming improvisations intoxicated the heads and made delirious the legs of our dancers. He conducted them . . . according to his fantasy . . . from light to severe, from burlesque to solemn, from gracious to passionate.[6]

Chopin left Nohant in 1846, never to return. But the troupe continued to play, moving from dance and pantomime to improvised scenarios.

Sand's first scenario to be performed at Nohant, *Le Druide peu délicat,* provoked spontaneous and hilarious buffoonery. Sand describes that first performance in an "Avant-propos" to her son's published history of commedia dell'arte characters.[7] Actors donned "mad and bizarre" costumes: for the Druide "an old white drape trimmed with red, gloves of green linen, and blue eyeglasses," and for the hero "a pointed hat surmounted by a parrot's feather, his body squeezed into a sort of jumper made of violet silk; he holds a guitar without strings." A green folding screen represented the forest, and three cushions stood for stones, the Druide's sacred dolmens. While the young hero improvised a "romance of great energy," the "public," Sand's pet dog Marquis, bolted onto the stage barking. Just at that moment the wicked Druide arrived, and, taking advantage of Marquis' unforeseen entrance, simulated an animal sacrifice on a sacred stone, the biggest of the three cushions. The young hero rushed to the dog's defense, for, as he recounted to the others, this was not really a dog, but the "genie of the forest concealed in a canine form." During the ensuing battle between the hero and the Druide the stringless guitar flew across the stage with a clatter, and only the quick entrance of a fast-thinking druid priestess brought the combat to an end. Eventually everyone gave in to fatigue and retired from the stage. The lamp died down and the little dog went back to sleep in front of the fireplace to the sound of the piano.

Sand's original manuscript for *Le Druide* exists in the extensive collection given to the Bibliothèque Historique de la Ville de Paris (B.H.V.P.) by Sand's granddaughter Aurore. Actually there are two manuscripts for this particular piece, one for each of the two known performances: the first on 8 December 1846, and the second on 15 August 1850 for Bocage's visit to the Nohant château. The playlet must have been a favorite of the troupe's, since it was revived four years after the first performance for an illustrious visitor. One of the two manuscripts (033 B) gives the original cast: George's son Maurice (twenty-three years old at the time) played both the king and the Druide; Eugène Lambert, Maurice's comrade and fellow art student from Delacroix's studio, played the romantic lead, a bandit; Fernand de Preaulx, the fiancé of George's daughter Solange (he was only temporarily a member of the Nohant troupe as Solange Sand changed her mind a few months later and married the mad sculptor Clesinger), played a drum major; and Augustine Brault, or "Titine," an adoptive daughter of George's who at the time had a crush on Maurice, played the princess. George played the piano. Sand's scenario in two acts begins with the princess of Granada, who loves the bandit, being forced by her father the king to marry the man of *his* choice, the drum major in his guard. After the application of sleeping potion to the drum major, and a combat in which the princess threatens the traitorous Druide with an axe, the king capitulates and permits his daughter to marry her bandit. The Druide is killed and the drum major reconciled.[8]

The day after the little theatre of Nohant officially opened, Sand shared the happy results with her friend Emmanuel Arago in a letter, 9 December 1846:

> We started our carnival yesterday with magnificent *travestissements*. I wrote the piece during dessert, roles were learned during coffee. Costuming at ten took the longest and was the most amusing part of it all. The play was performed at midnight, followed by a supper, and to bed by two. . . . Anyone arriving in the midst of all this would think he was dreaming, or had chanced upon a madhouse (*Corr.* 7:556–62).

In the Nohant Theatre season's first nine days (December 8 to 17) Sand wrote and produced nine scenarios. She and the company then took two weeks during Christmas to prepare for their big production of *Don Juan* on New Year's Eve, and the next push in January of twelve more scenarios. On December 30 Sand wrote a long letter to her editor, Hetzel, describing how her life had been taken over and regulated by this new theatrical activity (*Corr.* 7:569–76):

> Imagine this, to fill up our long winter evenings my five children act in plays. Every day I'm forced to make a new play for them, to be author, actor, director, costumer, stagehand, design and properties assistant, to call rehearsals, to direct the movement, to be prompter and the orchestra at the piano when I'm not on stage.

She recounts how they rummage in the attic for materials with which to make sets and costumes; that the results are ingenious and authentic:

> With a screen, old curtains, foliage from evergreen trees, rags fished out of the attic, gold and silver paper, we come to make scenery, costumes, flats—all portable, installed in the salon where it's warm, and put in place in ten minutes. . . . Unlike stylish actors, we don't compromise with the bizarre fashions of the past. With flax we make wigs of the most disheveled style, with paper, extravagant ruffs, having all the chic of ancient portraits.

She goes on to explain the actors' preparation. They spend very little time in rehearsal. Sand presents her scenario at dinner, "an outline of very elementary dialogue." The players read through it two or three times and choose which roles they wish to play, though Sand has designed the roles with specific players in mind: "Each takes the role he wants. I make the choice easy by making the roles fit the spirit and taste of each." Sand will not tolerate a star system in her troupe:

> I'm never troubled by the pretensions of lead actors who ordinarily wish to take the whole stage for themselves and forbid such star effects to all the others on stage. In my plays, there are no star effects for any one player, or else I put them in for all of them.

The actors may even change Sand's original intentions if they wish:

> Everyone looks into the character of his own role. It's also permissible to interpret [the character] other than the author [has done], when one has a better idea than his; to take seriously what he has made comic and comic what he had wished to be serious.

Having made these decisions the troupe exits from the dinner table, gets into its costumes and reports back to the salon promptly at eight. In the light of the chandelier they marvel at the brilliance of one another's costumes, then put up the set and properties and perform. The mirror over the fireplace, the crackling fire, and Sand's pet dog Marquis constitute the only audience:

> The fireplace represents the audience, and offers a big crackling fire which always laughs and sometimes hisses without annoying anyone. . . . The public [Marquis] gets so excited he jumps onto the stage and commits a thousand follies with the young principals.

For their subject matter Sand draws from a variety of sources:

> We resuscitate the commedia dell'arte, Cassandre, Pierrot, the capitaine Fracasse, the handsome Leandre, Colombine, Isabelle, etc. With this cast of characters, permitting the most fantastic and diverting anachronisms, there is no play we cannot make up. Sometimes we parade the principal heroes of this troupe into the world of Hoffmann. . . . Sometimes Fracasse goes astray *chez les druides,* and he's threatened with being slaughtered on a dolmen, other times . . . [he] meets up with the heroes of tales of Perrault.

Thomiris reine des Amazons, performed on December 11, serves as an example of Sand's "fantastic and diverting anachronisms." The twelve-page manuscript (B.H.V.P. 054) divides the action into three acts and mixes Greek Amazons with the Celtic Merlin-the-magician and commedia dell'arte characters. Scapin and Fracasse (played by Lambert and Maurice respectively) find themselves in an enchanted forest. They try to survive on bitter fruits. Melancholy and dejected they sit under a tree, unaware that Thomiris, Queen of the Amazons (played by Solange), and Bradamante, an actual Celtic warrior queen (played by "Titine") are perched in the tree ready to spring on their prey. Clad in tiger skins, the warrior women cast a net over the two unsuspecting commedia characters. Thomiris calls upon Merlin to work a magic spell: she wants him to stop the beautiful singing of Scapin and Fracasse because as long as they sing her sisters will not cook and eat them. So Merlin (Fernand) enters, makes some magic circles and incantations, and departs. Evidently the singing stops, and the two queens march their prisoners to the Amazon camp. But Bradamante, still charmed by the men, pleads for their release with Thomiris. The queen of the Amazons, however, is heartless and immovable. Scapin perceives their fate when he sees the large rotisserie. A kind of Midsummer Night's madness ensues, with Merlin casting a spell on one then another of the foursome, making them fall in and out of love with one another, until in the end they are all reconciled and dance the finale.

The sixth scenario in Sand's first series, *La Belle au bois dormant,*[9] shows a marked increase in scripted dialogue. This *féerie pastorale* in three acts opened December 13. It is another of the "fantastic and diverting anachronisms" in which Sand combines pastoral with fairy tale, Daphnis and Chloë with Sleeping Beauty. The play's point of attack occurs late in the action: Sleeping Beauty, or "La Belle" has been asleep for one hundred years in a grotto. Daphnis guards his sheep on the hillside near the grotto. A fairy comes to tell him that if he can restrain himself from falling in love until nightfall she will make him the richest man on earth. He satisfies himself that the challenge will be easily met, since he loves only his sheep. Prince Charming arrives looking for the dwelling place of La Belle; he is full of remorse since it was his unfaithfulness to La Belle which consigned her to the long sleep. He must find her now that the time is up, and if he can persuade her of his reform and faithfulness, they will be reunited. He swears to Daphnis that he is cured of his roving eye, that is, until the shepherdess Chloë enters. Prince Charming tries to seduce Chloë, and chases her around the stage. But Chloë's love for Daphnis is true, and she rushes to the shepherd for safety. Alone, an amusing and tight repartee between Daphnis and Chloë shows Daphnis fighting not to fall in love with Chloë, and in the end submitting to his true feelings for Chloë, throwing to the winds the fairy's promise of future wealth. Meanwhile the princess awakes, reveals that she no longer loves Prince Charming, and pledges her heart to another who shares her grotto. Then rival fairies cast spells on all of them: La Belle and her true love are put to sleep again, Daphnis and Chloë are likewise punished with a sleep, Prince Charming's nose is made inordinately long, and a comical servant is made to believe that every time he tries to speak someone kicks him from behind. In the end these spells are lifted and the rightful lovers permitted to live happily together.

In plot, use of music, and pantomime, *La Belle* resembles the medieval French musical comedy *Robin et Marion,* written by Adam de la Halle in the late thirteenth century. Daphnis and Chloë, like Robin and Marion, are from simple, good-hearted, down-to-earth country stock. Sand's Prince Charming like Adam's knight lusts after the little shepherdess, suggesting a social satire similar to Beaumarchais' in *The Marriage of Figaro* (in which the Count Almaviva tries to oust proletarian barber Figaro from the affections of the lower-class but highly desirable Suzanne). Sand's last Nohant scenario, *Daphnis et Chloë* (1863), returns to these pastoral lovers; but until a manuscript or copy of this last piece turns up one can only speculate on whether it was based on the earlier *Belle au bois dormant.* But even some of Sand's more realistic, less farcical, scripted Nohant plays, such as *Le Pavé* (1861), tell the same story of lower-class playmates who become lovers when threatened by an upper-class intruder.

A New Year's Eve performance of Sand's scenario *Don Juan* ushered in 1847 at Nohant. While the script for this piece has yet to be located, the experience of that performance receives full documentation in Sand's novel *Le Château des Désertes,* written three months later at the end of Nohant's first theatre season. Intended as a meditation on dramatic and theatrical art, Sand dedicated the work to her English actor friend, William Macready. The book was finally published in time for Macready's retirement in 1851.

The novel's action revolves around the physical and psychological journey of a young painter, a French artist. He begins his journey geographically, traveling to Vienna and Italy before a long sojourn in the French Alps. Sand uses the landscape in *Château des Désertes* in the same symbolic manner as in some of her other novels and plays: climbing to heights represents a clear-eyed search for self-knowledge and truth, while descending to the plains may be either a muddled and confused wandering into false ways or simply practical reality, mundane day-to-day existence.

In Vienna the young painter meets Boccaferri (read Bocage and Macready), a hard-drinking and discouraged older actor. Boccaferri's daughter Cecilia, a scholarly, intelligent, reflective artist, performs on the professional stage only to support herself and her father, whereas a family friend of the Boccaferris, Celio Floriani, a vain young actor-singer, performs in pursuit of fame and riches. Boccaferri explains to the painter the difference between the true artist and the false, between Cecilia's performance and Celio's: "An artist who looks for success without conscience is a courtesan. An artist who loves art for its own sake is calmer; for he does not depend on others' praise or blame in order to make progress."[10] All four of these principal characters will grow and change with experience in a private theatre in the Château des Désertes.

The painter must also learn the difference between true and false love. In Turin, Italy, he has a love affair with a false woman, almost a courtesan, without conscience. In this gateway city he must choose between following the false woman to Milan, farther down into the practical and self-serving plains, or go alone up into the mountains in search of a true woman, a calm artist. He chooses to risk the Turin-Briançon road up to the heights of the French Alps, and just outside of Briançon (which claims to be "the highest European city") the painter comes upon the Château des Désertes, snowbound and mysterious, wherein true artists and friends perform in a secret and private theatre.

The novel's improvisation of *Don Juan* begins. Unbeknownst to the other actors, the young painter has been surreptitiously mustered into the cast to play the statue. Upon entering the château he is led blindfolded to a dressing room and shown his suit of armor: "a mélange of ancient and rococo, as used in the panoplies of our last centuries."[11] To his surprise, the helmet, breast plate, arm and shin guards are all made of cardboard, but so well modeled and painted in relief that "two steps away the illusion is complete." The coat is made of glued cloth, which, with its inflexible pleats and folds, could not have resembled sculpture any better. A mask completes the costume, representing an austere and aggrieved old commander, the "man of stone" in *Don Juan*. The whites of the eyes painted on the mask, doubled by the gaze coming from within, give the character "something horrifying."

Having put on his armor, the man of stone is again led through dark corridors to a graveyard, where he is shown his tomb and pedestal covered with real ivy. Through the mask he dimly perceives real yew trees around him and moonlight shining through cypress branches. A second look reveals that the yews are supported by stones, and the moonlight is a candle in a blue bowl shining on a sky of dark cloth. The tombs around him are cardboard painted to look like marble. In front of him is a big curtain of green velvet, but otherwise nothing resembles a theatre. That is, nothing is arranged to create scenic effects for an audience placed on any one side. And there is no backstage for the actors. The lighting all comes from above. The floorboards are hidden under a great green rug, to imitate moss. Behind him is raised a false wall made to look like a real cemetery wall. Here one has not gone after the conventional scenery of artificial distances, which create an illusion of perspective only to those members of the audience seated in the center of the orchestra.

When the curtain opens with the chorus singing from Mozart's *Don Giovanni,* the statue sees in front of him a pretty little hall lit by three chandeliers hanging from a vaulted ceiling, and two rows of loges decorated in Louis XIV style. There are no footlights. The actors arrive; none of them knows that there is a real person inside the statue. Don Juan is in a Louis XIII costume of such historical veracity that "the statue" has the impression he is looking at a family portrait. The costume is not the actor's own fantasy of what the costume should look like, but actual garments of that epoch, or so it would seem. The beautiful Anna looks like a Velazquez painting. Ancient extravagance has not been modified to suit the less exaggerated tastes of a nineteenth-century bourgeois public. Inside the statue, the painter exclaims to himself, "For me, a painter, what good fortune."

The acting space is so well disposed for the liberty of the actors' movements that they do not give the impression that they are acting in a play at all, but rather persuade one that they are the real characters in the drama. The voice and movement of the statue so startle the actors that they respond with genuine fear, contributing immensely to the realism and dynamism of the scene.[12]

After the performance Boccaferri's actors gather around him in the orchestra pit, their greenroom, sitting in chairs at a big table loaded with books and papers and placed next to a grand piano. This is where the actors meet between acts to discuss the proceedings, and then again after the performance to evaluate their work. The director pays careful attention not to interrupt the actors while they work on stage, but saves his comments for the entr'actes and afterwards when he takes on the role of "enlightened public."

On this occasion Boccaferri explains to the new cast member the company's staging and acting techniques. He attributes the innovations of their staging to the size of the stage:

> It's true we employ rather naïve means in our decorations; the charm of them would be lost in a big theatre. We can place real trees and stones all the way to the back of the stage because it is so small, and because the big theatre's means of creating perspective are not possible for us.

The scenic innovations in Sand's château theatre were years ahead of professional theatre practice: natural arrangement of stage objects in an intimate space, permitting free movement of the actors (as opposed to placement of set and furniture to the advantage of an audience on one side, requiring the actors to position themselves in more static arrangements); stage lighting from above, eliminating the use of distorting footlights; and an attention to detail in costumes and properties which has the effect of stimulating the *actor's imagination* and sense of illusion. Sand's actors must believe in their environment in order to create believable characters.

Boccaferri then instructs the French artist in the tenets of his acting school. He explains how the scenario of *Don Juan* grew out of the actor's need to interpret rather than translate a character role. Their Don Juan is a synthesis of at least three Don Juans: Molière's, Mozart's, and Hoffmann's.

> We are here to interpret more than to translate. Molière's Don Juan is a marquis, Mozart's a demon, and Hoffmann's a fallen angel. Molière gives more character development and Mozart the wonderful scene with Donna Anna. So it's up to the actors to combine and create (*Château des Désertes*, pp. 128–29).

An actor who is called upon to combine and create a new character on stage must be a complex and deep person in real life:

> What is an actor?—a man of heart and intelligence would be forcibly a good actor if the rules of the art were better observed. He must be able to develop on the stage the soul and genius that he has in his real life (*Château des Désertes*, p. 110).

Boccaferri proceeds to impart specific instructions on how an actor goes about developing his soul and genius on the stage: first, by intelligent reflection and concentration, and second by ensemble acting. Actors must stay in character throughout a performance, even when they are not on stage, and between scenes. They may be able to rest their body and voice, but not their intelligence, which must continue to work, to survey recent emotions and prepare for the next scene:

> The theatre must be the image of life; just as in real life man recollects in solitude in order to understand the events which press upon him and to find good counsel and the power to govern his life, so must the actor meditate on the action of the drama and on the character he represents. Between each scene he must look for the developments that his role calls for (*Château des Désertes*, p. 119).

This objective to "look for the developments that an actor's role calls for," to draw on inner resources of intelligence and imagination in order to create a believable character, an image of life, challenges a modern critic's objection that Sand's actors are limited to playing themselves, to playing only what they are already.[13] On the contrary, Sand's actors strive to expand themselves by playing a diversity of roles; they want to keep growing both as artists and as real people.[14]

Boccaferri stresses the importance of giving support to the other actors on stage. When not speaking, an actor must listen attentively to the actor who is, for "even if a tirade is well chosen and well spoken with true inspiration on the part of an actor, it cannot work if it is not listened to conscientiously and attentively by the other actors" (*Château des Désertes*, p. 112). Like Sand, Boccaferri is adamantly opposed to the star system of acting:

> Everyone helps one another . . . it's a big error to believe that an actor for being more brilliant makes his interlocutor more pale—a pernicious theory of individualism which reigns in the theatre more now than ever before. The theatre is the collective work par excellence. He who is cold and freezes his neighbor communicates contagion with desperate promptitude to all the others. But if the actor is full of passion and emotion, instead of being isolated, he is seconded and warmed by his entourage (*Château des Désertes*, p. 121).

Boccaferri appeals to his troupe to be brothers in art, to have mutual affection for one another, "A bad comrade is a bad actor. . . . For one to be good and true it's necessary for everyone to be" (*Château des Désertes*, p. 122).

Back at her own theatre in the Château of Nohant, Sand expresses apprehension that actors who give in to vanity and egotism spoil their art. In a letter of 30 December 1846 to Hetzel she exults that her children's improvisations are "better sometimes than anything I've ever seen on any stage." But she doesn't want to tell them that, because "if self-pride came to stick its dirty nose in our pleasure, everything would be spoiled" (*Corr.* 7:569).

Late in life (1876), Sand recalled that the greatest value derived from her château theatre was the education it gave to her children, or young adults:

> I remember well how in former days our improvised playing had prompt and good effects in clarifying our children's ideas, in unclogging their speech, and in constraining them to follow closely a line of logic even in the feverish excitement of their playing. I believe that this is a good school for the young, not a base of instruction sufficient by itself, but the best of exercises for training the self to enlarge itself, to wish to learn more in order to manifest more.[15]

So Sand's actual château theatre at Nohant, which began as a diversion, very soon turned into a school to educate her family, to train the self to enlarge itself. Sand's ideal château theatre in Boccaferri's Château des

Désertes serves as a proving ground for aspiring artists to exit from the stage the better for the experience than when they entered,[16] a chance for them to develop their art away from the demands of a professional theatre which requires that they flatter and cater to a corrupt society. The theatre of the Château des Désertes provides actors with a halfway house between the real world and the purely imaginary ideal.[17]

Soon the little theatre of Nohant would make Sand's novel a reality. It went dark on the eve of the 1848 Revolution, and remained so for most of that year. The former troupe dispersed, giving rise to an entirely new form of Nohant Theatre production: puppets.[18] In their desire to cheer up George Sand, the disheartened revolutionary, Maurice Sand and Eugène Lambert devised an entertainment of hand puppets performed on top of a high-backed chair. Over the years Maurice's puppet theatre evolved into an elaborate operation with a space of its own in both the Château of Nohant and his apartments in Paris. The 1952 inventory of Maurice's puppet collection numbered 139, some of which still may be seen in glass cases placed in the audience seating area of Nohant's theatre. Maurice and his friends carved the wooden heads and hands, and George designed and sewed their costumes. Fourteen of Maurice's puppet plays were published in 1890, a year after the author's death. Five of these puppet plays have been translated into English.[19]

When the "big" little theatre of Nohant resumed productions in the autumn of 1849, Sand applied her abundant energies to reviving commedia dell'arte. With characteristic enthusiasm she divulges her dreams to Bocage in a letter written in October 1849. The art of improvisational commedia depends on getting the right kind of actors and then training them:

> It would be a very curious and original thing to be able to revive this primitive art. . . . As for me, I'd go 300 leagues to see something like the ancient Lelios, those grand masters who improvised such beautiful scenes. . . . You can no longer find such actors already made. They must be produced. That would be a school to establish [this and following quotations in *Corr.* 9:299–303].

Actors must be liberated from the confines of speaking a playwright's language, fixed and stilted in its academic jargon:

> You can find people who are capable of becoming such actors, who could speak for themselves. . . . It's annoying that all those who have the gift of improvisation are forced to moulder in the jargon of the palace [Académie Française]. What tears, what terrors, would be produced by an actor given the chance to find all by himself his own soul's cry, his speech of indignation or sadness. Everything else would seem cold and icy after that.

Sand recognizes in Bocage the inspiration and intelligence conducive to a commedia actor:

> I've seen you interrupt your part in order to speak directly to the audience. A lot of people blame you for that. I, to the contrary, like such spirit. . . . It seems to me that had you played during Richelieu's time you would have been an *improvisateur* of the first rank because you need to go out beyond your role and be a person simultaneously with being an artist.

Sand approaches twentieth-century Brechtian acting theory in this last thought, that an actor might "need to go out beyond his role," to be a person separate from the character, a commentator on the character at the same time he creates it.

Sand based her dream of reviving commedia and training improvisational actors on extensive research into sixteenth- and seventeenth-century dramatic literature and firsthand observations of commedia performances. Adding a pragmatic note to her idealism, Sand relates that while commedia actors in former days could not maintain a consistently high level of performance in their improvisations, their flashes of inspiration were vastly superior to anything written by a playwright:

> The Italian improvisational actors had their faults as contemporary writers relate; how they got confused, repeated themselves or cut things too short. Some scenes were totally lacking in any appeal, but the audience would wait indulgently, knowing that at one moment or another the actor's inspiration would return and make up to them the damages. And in effect, when that inspiration came it was incomparable, and impassioned the audience more than the greatest interpreters of the greatest writers could ever do.

Sand wishes she had the means and influence to establish a theatre for such actors: "If I were a prince, I'd launch such a theatre and not rest until that primitive art was resuscitated in a little corner for my pleasure" (*Corr.* 9:299–303).

By mid-season (1849–50), with a dozen more of Sand's scenarios mounted on the Nohant stage, Sand began to think that perhaps she could indeed resuscitate that primitive art in her little corner. Her players "have restored at Nohant an art lost in France," she says. She is pleased and inspired: "I have learned more with these big and little actors of Nohant than in all that I have seen played at Paris for the last twenty years. Why and how, I cannot tell, but it's like that" (*Corr.* 9:419–20).

This second major Nohant theatre season, devoted almost exclusively to experimentation in commedia dell'arte, clarified the procedure her actors followed in preparing and mounting an improvisational scenario. She outlines this procedure in a November 1850 letter to her aristocratic cousin, René Vallet de Villeneuve, then owner and resident of the Loire Valley Château Chenonceaux. Because the letter so masterfully captures the spirit as well as the operational details of the Nohant Theatre it is quoted at some length without interruption:

> Like you we're making a theatre at home, smaller and without such a beautiful room as yours has, but with as much fire. . . . Our scenes of human life take all sorts of forms, ballet, pantomime, *drame,* comedy. Since we've been doing it for four years we've become very strong. For a long time we played without a public, then admitted twenty or so old friends and naïve Berrichon servants who don't expect a written play with actors' parts learned by heart. The short three-page scenario has each scene indicated in three lines. We've arrived at a surprising ensemble. Two rehearsals to get down our entrances and exits, the blocking, and the character, which is up to each individual to develop in terms of nuance and distinctive manner [*guise*], but which must correspond to the action. It's an excellent literary study for my young people. They learn to express themselves better . . . and sometimes, when they are onstage they find a natural and spontaneous eloquence that the pen never encounters. They learn by heart the plays I intend for the public theatre. . . .
>
> Each player writes a sketch of his own role and has it in his hand while waiting in the wings. The general scenario is posted backstage, which each player consults in his turn. No break in concentration is permissible. It's necessary always to be watchful of the action, who must enter or exit and at what point. Memorization work is reduced to knowing the order of a dozen scenes per act, and for each scene the dozen or so short phrases, or exclamations, that serve as landmarks. For those who have only two or three scenes per act, the work is nearly null. . . .
>
> The inevitable fault of beginners is not to be too brief. To the contrary, it's to speak too much for fear of being too brief. It's also a fault to speak all at the same time, and not know at what point to be silent for another actor who is developing a more important situation. It's up to the impresario to be very severe during the first days in order to establish calm and orderliness. Individual genius is always too abundant. Collective genius is the result of a certain amount of work, but full of interest and originality.
>
> When you've reached a block in a scenario, take up the first play that comes to you and dissect it, summarize it in a scenario and resume by playing that scenario. Here we've played a scenario of Molière's *Don Juan,* modified by Mozart's opera, and plays by Shakespeare arranged in that fashion. You can try anything . . . invent anything with this method (*Corr.* 9:787–90).

This letter shows to what high degree of finesse the Nohant players had arrived in their commedia skills, and how firm and organized the impresario, George Sand, had become. No sloppy lapses in concentration were permitted. What had begun as a plaything had developed into a disciplined art. Sand and her Nohant troupe achieved the practice of breaking down a script, paraphrasing and improvising character roles, similar to the practice of many directors and actors in our modern-day theatre.

The plays by Shakespeare which Sand shaped into commedia scenarios were *Much Ado About Nothing,* or *Beaucoup de bruit pour rien,* which played the Nohant stage 24 November 1849; and *Henry IV,* parts one and two, renamed *La Jeunesse d'Henri V,* performed 6 January 1850, with Sand playing the part of Hotspur![20]

An article by George Sand with illustrations by Maurice, "La Comédie Italienne," culminated the Nohant Theatre's middle period of commedia dell'arte revivals. Published in the journal *L'Illustration* of 5 June 1852, the article gives no hint of the goings-on in Nohant, but rather summarizes the history of commedia character types. Seven years later George and Maurice would extend this study to two volumes, *Masques et bouffons.* The ideas Sand had developed in her letters to Bocage and René Vallet de Villeneuve find similar expression in the published article, principally Sand's regret that France's modern actors have lost the facility to improvise and would not dare to give it a try. Commedia demands superior talents, and Sand finds the majority of French actors unequal to the demand.[21]

Sand's burgeoning professional stage career, and ensuing changes in Nohant Theatre's personnel and space, caused Sand to shift the little theatre's operation from commedia dell'arte improvisations to more fully developed plays. The unexpected success of her play *François le Champi* (performed over a hundred times at the Odéon Theatre in Paris during the winter of 1849–50) inspired Sand to spend more of her time and energy on writing fully scripted plays for the professional stage, rather than commedia scenarios for her amateur theatre.

Then, in November 1849, the Nohant Theatre moved to its permanent quarters, a southeast bedroom on the ground floor of the mansion, with direct access to the entrance foyer. At the same time, Maurice moved his puppet theatre into its final resting place, a corner room formerly known as the "salle des archives," contiguous to the "big" theatre's room. George's adaptation of Perrault's "Cinderella" officially inaugurated the new theatre space and consecrated it to the muses on 12 November 1849.[22]

After spending the Christmas holidays in Paris to witness the success of her *Champi* at the Odéon, George Sand returned to Nohant the first week in January 1850 with elaborate new costumes and three new members for the Nohant troupe. Müller-Stübing, a jolly German political exile, came to Nohant for a brief stay, long enough to play Douglas in Sand's scenario of Prince Hal, to play the piano for her pantomimes, and to be her lover, before passing on into England, the home of many socialist exiles. Leon Villevieille, an artist who later became an accomplished landscape painter, came to Nohant and spent a year; Sand found him a gifted painter, a handsome blond, but lazy. The third most important addition to the Nohant players, Alexandre Manceau, a young painter-engraver, immediately took over as the director of Nohant's little theatre, and soon became Sand's devoted companion, remaining her helpmate and lover until his death fifteen years later. George immediately recognized Manceau as their new leader: "Manceau is our lead actor now. . . . He plays serious and comic, and for costumes . . . [and] for arranging the set, he is the leading force" (*Corr.* 9:427).

When Manceau took a look at the theatre of Nohant everything had to be redone:

> Manceau came, saw, and criticized. In effect the backstage was too narrow, the masking too low, the set changes too long and tiring. Everything's been turned upside down. Lambert has courageously started all over again painting the drops, and Bonnin has redone all the carpentry.

Apparently Manceau had an opinion on everything, including the kinds of plays Sand should write for the Nohant stage. Something more than her usual playful scenario would be required for his new and improved space:

> It's a question of opening this new theatre with a *serious* piece. I've made one, that, parenthetically, I want for Bocage. I've given my actors a carcass adapted to their means and number and memories. It's a mélange of written and improvised scenes.

The "serious piece," the one intended for Bocage to act professionally, is of course *Lelio*, performed on the Nohant stage on 10 February 1850, and later published under the title *Marielle*. Sand herself played the part of Fabio, the young male lover role. For the first time, a small, severely restricted audience could be admitted: "Our public is made up of the mayor, a dressmaker, and actors not performing on stage. We won't suffer any others. For admission you would have to be the prompter or a technician." Now with their new space, new players, and new material, the Nohant Theatre troupe modified their playing schedule:

> The three-act play finishes at midnight. The pantomime, equally in three acts, at three o'clock. We then go to the salon for supper where we laugh about our adventures until five or six. The next day we start all over again . . . two times a week or every ten days (*Corr.* 9:419–22).

After *Lelio*, from 1850 to 1856, George Sand wrote only a handful of commedia scenarios for the Nohant Theatre. Manceau, and the lure of professional Parisian theatre, preempted her less "serious" work and play in commedia dell'arte.

Sand and her partner Manceau remodeled the little theatre of Nohant during the winter of 1850–51. They needed an auditorium for a growing audience of neighbors and friends. So they removed the wall between the room currently being used as the "big" theatre, and the "salle des archives" where the puppet theatre was set up. Rather than remove the entire wall, an arcade was constructed, the thick wall serving as an arch over the opening:

> A beautiful arcade now joins the two rooms. . . . The wings of the stage can now extend far enough to permit loges where the actors can sit and watch the performance without being seen by the audience. The stage curtain no longer opens in two but descends from a cylinder (24 January 1851; *Corr.* 10:47).

Raised benches placed on a stepped platform in the "salle des archives" could accommodate the little theatre's growing audience of fifty to sixty persons.

Sand expressed pride in the new lighting techniques incorporated into the Nohant Theatre. Instead of footlights, lights were directed onto the stage from above, and the spectator sat in relative darkness, "fooled as to the dimensions and depth of objects exhibited in front of him, obtaining the effect of a diorama which permits remarkable distances and reliefs in a paltry space." Sand stressed the importance of having the audience seated in the shadows of a darkened auditorium:

> Italians know well how the auditorium should be darkened in order that the stage appear more luminous, and that the eye loses its faculty to distinguish clearly when light crowds it and penetrates it nearby and from all sides. But the French, especially the French, go to the theatre to be seen and the stage performance is often passed off as part of the bargain.[23]

She suggests in the same essay that candles placed on the back wall of the auditorium should be sufficient for the audience to find its place. All of the bright lights could then concentrate their attention onto the stage.

A visitor to the château of Nohant today will find the theatre exactly as George Sand describes its appearance after the remodeling in 1851. An interesting anomaly of this particular theatre space arose when the hole in the wall between the two rooms was created: viewing the stage from the audience's room favors stage left where the audience can look straight on ahead, whereas stage right is skewed farther to the right than the audience can see. Downstage right is definitely not visible to people sitting at the far left of the auditorium. This occurs because the two rooms do not abut; the outer walls of the auditorium jog further out than do the

10. Nohant Theatre Troupe, by Maurice Sand, January 1850.
Alexandre Manceau, center, acts as director and gives new rules. George Sand sits smoking to his left. On Sand's left (going around the table clockwise) are "Titine," Victor Borie, Müller-Stubing, Emile Aucante, Eugène Lambert (with his head in his hand), Villevieille, and Maurice seated on the fringed cushion. To Manceau's right are neighbors and friends, the Fleury and Duvernet families.
Courtesy of the George Sand Museum, La Châtre.

theatre's walls (drawing on p. 126).[24] Where the red tile floor of the auditorium meets the hardwood floor of the theatre's room a solid, meter-
high barrier, or fence ("a" in drawing), serves to delineate the two spaces
further. The arcade, with its thick arch above the opening ("b"), makes
the audience's window onto the stage look much like a traditional proscenium arch. Interestingly enough, however, a second proscenium arch
exists on the stage proper ("c"). The effect is almost like a double or
mirror image of prosceniums, with a neutral space between them, the
orchestra pit ("d"). On either side of the stage apron, where the stage
meets the walls, proscenium columns have been painted on the walls,
framed above by a false proscenium arch and the curtain drop. The curtain
that Sand proudly announced drops from a cylinder rather than parting
in two still hangs there, a pattern of little squares in orange, green, yellow,
and ochre.

It is very clear what Sand meant about lighting the stage from above.
Over the arcade's opening, mounted on the wall which faces the stage,
hangs a batten or frame for lighting instruments, invisible to the audience's
side ("e"). Lights hung along this batten would shed light at about a forty-
five-degree angle down onto the stage six feet away. The batten hangs
there yet, a long rectangular frame with an outer covering made of netting
and green paper, now badly deteriorated. The green translucent paper
may have been changed to suit the occasion, for Sand talks about different
colored lighting effects, such as blues for moonlight. Along the top of the
batten and paper cover are grommets and cords to fasten the entire piece
to the wall. On ground level the candlelight fixtures would be lit, then the
whole thing would be raised and lashed to the wall of the arcade, like
hoisting a ship's sail. Four existing backstage lights give evidence of side
and back lighting ("f"). Two of the fixtures are mounted on the upstage
flat frame and directed to shine onto the backdrop. The other two are on
either side of the stage, mounted to the outer walls, and directed to shine
through foot-and-a-half-wide openings between the side wall flats and the
upstage wall flats, thus lighting up the stage area which the arcade's lamps
cannot reach. These fixtures, mounted eight to ten feet above the stage
floor proper, are traditionally made candle mounts: a double-faced metal
reflector backing and base for the candle, with an outer semicircular covering made of the same netting and paper as covers the arcade's long
batten.

One can see what Sand meant by loges for the actors, where they
could watch the performance when not onstage themselves, and not be
seen by the audience. Having the actors watch the proceedings was as
important to Sand as having an audience, if not more so, for her theatre
was an actors' workshop for years before it admitted a public. Maintaining

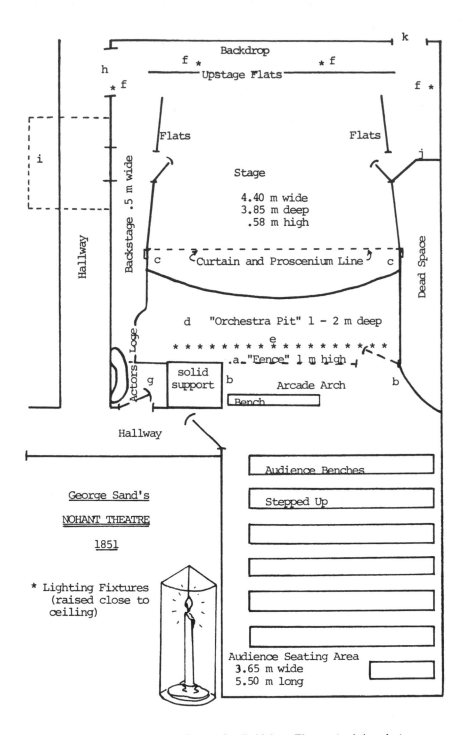

11. Scale Drawing of George Sand's Nohant Theatre (as it is today).

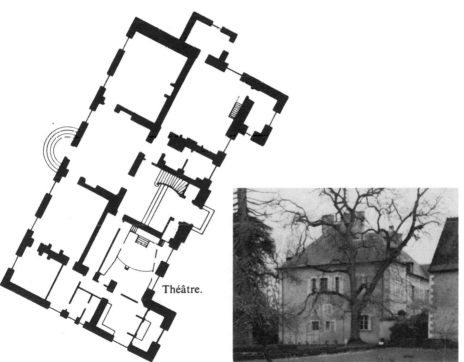

12. Nohant Theatre and Château.
   Top: the stage seen from audience seating with arcade arch
   visible to the left and the meter high "fence" at the base of picture.
   Bottom: ground plan of château's first floor showing theatre at
   bottom right; and photograph of the theatre's corner of the château.

a place where the actors could watch with a good view of the stage (not through a crack of light backstage) took priority in the planning of the new space. Because of that architectural anomaly, the jog of the theatre's room farther into the interior of the château than the audience's room, a corner of the orchestra pit remains entirely hidden from audience view. An actor could exit upstage right, walk along the narrow passageway backstage behind the stage right flats, along the stage floor onto an extended platform masked by a false wall, into the down right corner of the orchestra pit (or that neutral space between the two prosceniums). In this corner is a closet-like cubbyhole ("g"), raised to stage level, with a narrow, long kidney-shaped padded bench extending out of the cubbyhole along the wall toward the stage—the actors' loge where they could sit and watch unobserved. An odd little door in the cubbyhole gives access to the outer hallway where an actor could race off to the nearby dressing room and change his costume.

One other exit from the backstage exists in the far upstage corner of stage right ("h"). It leads into a hallway which connects the entrance foyer of the château to the theatre's entrance, backstage and dressing room, and has a back stairway leading up to the second floor of the château. Back inside the stage's room, on stage right, backstage, a curious little room, elevated five or six feet above the stage floor, accessible only by a small ladder (two ladders still hang nearby), cannot be explained by any of Sand's letters or essays. One can only speculate on its use: based on Nohant playscripts which call for an upstairs in the stage setting, this little room ("i") would have aligned nicely with an onstage staircase, permitting actors to climb the stairs, move offstage, and then descend by ladder from their little room into the backstage area.

Backstage left ends abruptly half way or less down the side ("j"). In the up left corner one steps down two or three steps into an enclosed cellar room the size of a large closet ("k"). This space seems suitable for storing stage properties and small pieces of furniture needed to change the set during a performance. But again its use can only be surmised, since there is no written evidence.

The stage floor is now covered with a rug pieced together, of a brown floral pattern. Underneath, the stage floor proper has been covered with canvas and painted or varnished with a reddish brown color. Big pieces of this canvas are nailed to the stage boards with little nails, the heads of which are no more than an inch apart all along the edges of each patch.

An original setting from the 1850s stands on the stage today. Backing the flats are newspapers, *Le Siècle* and *Le Monde Illustré*, dated 1853 and 1854. The scene represents a garden wall and gate connecting two houses, one on either side of the stage. The flats are traditional canvas nailed to wood battens, but painted with extraordinary artistry. The house on stage right, made of flats painted to represent brick with traditional gray-white corner stones, has a practical door in the center of the flat and a practical window above the door. An actor in that curious little room offstage right and elevated five or six feet above the stage level could lean out through the flat's window opening, giving the impression of a second story. The stage left house has a practical door with a nonpractical oval window above it. Upstage center five steps lead up to the garden gate, a double practical door which leads to a very narrow platform backstage with steps going down on either side. The painted backdrop hangs on the back wall, suspended from above, and represents a distant view of landscape and château, so small and detailed that only the actors at close proximity could have appreciated it. Original stage furniture made of wood, painted green and decorated with a brown diamond pattern, finishes the garden setting.

A yellowing and almost illegible seating chart glued to a wall shows how the benches were arranged for the audience. An aisle bordered the stepped-up benches on the audience's left where sightlines would have been poor and the space conveniently sacrificed. The cases of puppets now distort the impression of size in the auditorium, but even so, it must have been very cramped for fifty or sixty people to sit there.

On 9 February 1851 Sand and her Nohant troupe formally dedicated this new theatre with a prologue by George called *La Malédiction* and a scenario by Manceau and Maurice, *Les Deux Pierrots*.

A series of Sand's fully scripted plays intended for professional theatres in Paris played the boards of Nohant from 1850 to 1853. *Claudie* had been the first, performed on 8 August 1850, and then again on 17 August 1850 for Bocage. Sand played Claudie, Manceau opposite her as Sylvain in the romantic duo; son Maurice was the cad Ronciat, Lambert the père Remy, and Villevieille the bagpiper. Sand wrote to Bocage how useful she finds this trial run of *Claudie* at Nohant:

> The little toy theatre of Nohant is most useful to me. In seeing rehearsals and in rehearsing myself I begin to see the tasks, the difficulties, the impossibilities, the blunders. Each evening we change, we cut, we transpose a word, a phrase (*Corr.* 9:946–47).

Two months later she wrote to her friend Emmanuel Arago that she sees her subjects and their effects more clearly on the Nohant stage than on paper (*Corr.* 9:704–7).

The first performance of Sand's *Mariage de Victorine* played at No-

13. Nohant Actors Performing Roles in *Claudie*.
Top left: Eugène Lambert as Remy in *Claudie* performed at
theatre of Nohant, 8 August 1850, in *Recueil* 1:160.
Top right: Manceau as Sylvain in *Claudie*, *Recueil* 1:162.
Bottom left: Maurice Sand as Ronciat in *Claudie*, *Recueil* 1:164.
Bottom right: Villevieille as le Cornemuseux, *Recueil* 1:166.
Phot. Bibliothèque Nationale, Paris.

hant on 17 July 1851, under the title *Famille de Vanderke*. That same year on 4 October, the Nohant players performed *Nello,* an early version of *Maître Favilla*. *Le Démon du foyer* previewed at Nohant on 15 July 1852, two months before its successful opening in Paris. *Le Pressoir* received two Nohant performances, 29 July and 1 August 1853, before moving to the Gymnase Theatre in Paris. In a letter to Maurice in April 1853, Sand observes that her plays which received a trial run at Nohant first, before moving up to Paris, all succeeded with the Parisian public; whereas those not performed and revised at Nohant did not succeed in the professional theatre:

> Everything played here has succeeded, everything not played hasn't: *Pandolphe, Molière;* whereas *Claudie, Victorine,* and *Démon* went swimmingly. It's so different to be able to see and hear what one has put down on paper! (*Corr.* 11:659).

But watching her amateur troupe of family and friends, Sand realized that her professional writing could be enhanced even more by seeing and hearing it spoken by trained actors. None of her amateurs could play the young romantic hero well.[25] So for her production of *Nello* Sand wrote to Hetzel asking him to find her a young actor from the Paris conservatory. She would pay his expenses.

> Find us a little student from the conservatory, not ugly, without pretensions, a nice, good boy, who will come do us a favor or earn a few sous by his choice . . . not too tall, or big, that would be awful on our little stage . . . with talent, but the most elementary notions of his craft will suffice. You know our manner of playing, an intimate manner that doesn't require actors, but represents a sort of calm reading placed on stage . . . of course his travel expenses will be paid. . . . The actor must not have a beard because we are in costumes of 1795. Without this problem of men's beards, we would have lovers at our choice. I'm surprised to see this love the men have for their fur (*Corr.* 10:421 22).

The actor sent by Hetzel had a beard, but since he could not do the part to Sand's satisfaction, he was happy to keep his beard and go home. Sand wrote to Hetzel again and asked him to find another young professional. Sand received her young actor on 25 September 1851. He would play Herman the lover in *Nello*. Her first impression of him was favorable—he was not too big and he did not have a beard—but he did have difficulties dropping the affected manner of the conservatory:

> He went into rehearsal right away with a lot of intelligence. He speaks the way they all speak at the conservatory, following very well that method, very false, if you ask me. But we can show him that fault and aid him (we, who seek the natural and the real with perhaps too much zeal) to play with more spirit (*Corr.* 10:445).

The young conservatory student was Sully-Levy (Isaïa Levy), who later became a *sociétaire* (full member) of the Comédie Française and performed for several decades. In 1913 Sully-Levy published a memoir of that Nohant experience, how nervous he was to meet such a famous woman as George Sand, and how the stage fright he experienced on the opening night of *Nello* in the Nohant Theatre surpassed any fright in the professional theatres of Paris. He reports that the Nohant *Nello* was an enormous success, played with *ensemble* by all the actors. His only regret was that when the play was cast for the professional production at the Odéon he was not cast in his old part of Herman, or any other part. (Sand's playscripts went from Nohant to professional productions in Paris, but her Nohant actors did not). Sully-Levy's observations on individual members of the Nohant troupe give us an inside look at their talents and personalities:

> The author of *Champi* herself lent her little hand to the velours, silk, and laces of the actors. Maurice swept the stage, surveyed the hand props and the lights. Eugène Lambert was charged with making the posters and flyers. Manceau, a serious and calm manager, gravely numbered the reserve seats . . . he is that type of active, intelligent, obliging, devoted, methodic artisan whose theories sometimes have the logic of a square and compass. [26]

Other professional actors were to follow in Sully-Levy's footsteps on the Nohant stage. George Sand pointed out to these actors that the benefits of playing at Nohant were mutual. Writing to the actor Henri Lafontaine in May 1852, Sand invited him to Nohant, where she could watch him perform and discover new types of characters to write for him; he in turn could discover within him qualities he had not had occasion to bring to light before (*Corr.* 11:93). Sand sent a similar letter to the actor Francis Berton in November 1854; she had seen him perform in *Le Gendre de Monsieur Poirier* and says he has talent of the first rank—would he like to come to Nohant for a few days so that she could study him and write new roles for him (*Corr.* 12:625)? Actresses Amalia Fernand (who was a little too tall for their little theatre), Rose Cheri, Arnould-Plessy, Marie Lambert, Bérengère, all well-known professionals of their day, performed in Sand's plays at Nohant, and in each instance became a lifelong friend of George.

Sand's little handkerchief theatre with its small space, intimacy, modern lighting, and equipment, actors who moved and spoke naturally on the stage, already firmly established in the 1850s, foreshadows the little theatre movement of the 1890s.

Due to a personal tragedy the Nohant Theatre was dark for the two years 1854–55. [27] Sand's drive to produce plays for the professional theatre was diminishing.[28] But Sand's companion Manceau acted as the needed catalyst to rejuvenate George's interest in the theatre. In the summer of 1856 he got to work on the theatre space:

> Manceau is busy morning to night supervising carpenters and painters by day, trying out the new lighting system at night. His love of perfection is devouring him. God knows when one will be able to actually play in the theatre. But it will be there for that day of inspiration (Sand to Ida Dumas, 3 September 1856; *Corr.* 14:36).

A professional scene painter from the Gymnase Theatre, Bolard, came to Nohant in July and stayed two months to help Manceau with the new decorations. Sand gives an inventory list of the Nohant Theatre's sets in an October 1856 letter:

> Rich salon (Renaissance or modern with a fireplace and furniture)
> Garden (where building can be placed to the right or to the left)
> Park or Forest
> Street with houses on either side (not very usable houses)
> Courtyard (of aristocrats)
> Farm courtyard
> Dining room (without fireplace and furniture)
> Library (without fireplace and furniture)
> Rustic Interior (with fireplace and furniture)
> Prison

Sand explains that any of these sets may be used to represent the epoch of Louis XIII or modern times.

The Nohant Theatre reopened on September 8 with Sand's *Ote donc ta barbe*. Sand wrote another twelve new improvisational scenarios for the 1856 season, which closed on November 23 with her *Le Datura fastuosa*, a full-length fantasy based on Hoffmann. Marie Dorval's daughter, Caroline Luguet, and two of Caroline's children all joined the Nohant players that season. In October the professional actress Bérengère returned to Nohant to perform.

Sand wrote another eight pieces for the 1857 season, September 6 to November 19, including commedias, Hoffmannesque fantasies, and historical dramas. The 6 September 1857 performance caused a scandal in the Nohant and La Châtre communities: Prince Jerome Napoleon personally attended a private performance in the Nohant Theatre, with his mistress, Comédie Française actress Arnould-Plessy, playing the principal role. Local officials were outraged that such a distinguished person, the "illustrious prince," should visit Sand's château where, they said, the habitual guests were only actors or socialists: "actresses of the boulevard," and the "men the most compromised members of the socialist party" (*Corr.* 14:477–78n, quoting from police report).

A September 25 performance of her scenario *Pierre Riallo* Sand claimed as the best to date, "for movement, *mise en scène,* action," even though Marie Lambert was "too weepy" (*Corr.* 14:461). Sand became more interested in commedia improvisation than ever before, and it may well have been at this time that she wrote her essay "The Theatre and the Actor."[29]

This essay further develops Sand's idea of reviving commedia dell'arte improvisational acting. But rather than fault the French actors for lack of courage, as she had earlier, Sand blames the French public for being too sheepish and slow to accept change, yet disdainful toward anything from the past. But optimistic Sand believes that commedia improvisational techniques, "a scenario well meditated, well studied, rehearsed with care . . . by actors with superior intelligence and education" will not only revive a once highly respected dramatic art, but also lead toward an epoch of grand development when "the Shakespeares of the future will be the greatest actors of their century."

> I don't pretend to say that actors are generally superior to writers who write for them; but I will say that there are some who are. . . . I especially say that the theatre will not be whole until the two professions will have been made into one; when someone capable of creating a beautiful role will be able to create it truly, inspired by his own emotion and finding in himself the sudden and right expression for the dramatic situation.

The seventeenth-century commedia actor created his own role from his own intelligence, according to his own type, wrote his own speeches, developed the nuances of his character. Such an actor must have had an easy and natural manner, a chastened elocution, and an extensive education. "What wouldn't I have given to see such an action, even if it was a nursery rhyme, performed with that reality which would effect a change to the point of carrying you into the domain of complete illusion." But, Sand says, modern theatre has evolved beyond the point of complete illusion; it has lost that savage originality and those naïve emotions. The progress which remains to be made depends on finding again that primitive truth of the commedia stripped of its roughness and inevitable disorder.

In 1858 the Nohant troupe put aside its usually busy season of commedia performances in order to write and illustrate the history of that ancient art. Maurice Sand designed and drew the commedia types. Manceau engraved them. Maurice translated commedia materials written in the Italian Piedmont dialects. George Sand translated all the others in the Adriatic dialects. Maurice worked on the first draft for three or four months. Then George corrected it and interjected her own material. When the proofs came back from the publisher, it was George who made all the corrections and revisions (*Corr.* 15:155, 158–59, 243). The final result, *Masques et bouffons*, came out in two volumes at the end of 1859.

The Sands, George and Maurice, made an important discovery and contribution to theatre history while researching *Masques et bouffons*. They discovered the plays of Beolco, better known by his stage name, Ruzzante, an early sixteenth-century Italian (Paduan) commedia actor and playwright. Through Ida Dumas, longtime resident of Italy, George got the name of a Paduan scholar to help her with Ruzzante translations (*Corr.* 15:339). The two Ruzzante pieces published in *Masques et bouffons*, *Monologue of Ruzzante Returning from the Wars* and *Bilora*, fulfill Sand's dream for primitive truth created by an actor-writer. The *Monologue*, spoken by a Falstaff-like character, all bravado, creates an incident in which the Ruzzante character plays dead to save his skin and then claims he was attacked by a hundred men, whereas in fact a single one attacked him. (Shakespeare used a similar comic incident in *Henry IV*, Part II three-quarters of a century later.) *Bilora* (the name of the play's lead character, a hungry peasant) reveals an environment of poverty and misery, the precarious and savage life of fifteenth-century Paduan peasants. Bilora's wife has been carried off to live with a rich merchant. The hungry husband calls on her in her new home. She will not leave, but gives him some coins to buy food. Insulted and angry, he awaits the return of the merchant and brutally kills him, stabbing him until his arms and legs cease their "frightening *lazzi* [antics]." The Sands' text describes Bilora as an "enfant de la nature," without any bravery, pride, or a gentleman's honor. He loves his wife, he misses her, he will have her, he beats her, he loves her again. There is no fiction, no ideal. The characters speak as in real life. "One can understand what an intelligent actor could do with such a part, the laughter, the tears, the terror. . . . What strange gaiety, what rugged sensibilities when a public can laugh at such scenes of despair and murder accompanied by frightening antics."[30] Sand solved the problem of translating the Paduan dialect into French by choosing to use her own Berrichon peasant patois rhythms and expressions combined with French, which she had developed for *Champi* and *Claudie*.

The Nohant players performed *Bilora—L'Amour et la faim* on 4 September 1859, announcing its first performance since 1530! George Sand wrote a prologue for the occasion, of which several versions exist. Marie Dorval's grandson, Jacques Luguet, played the "esprit follet" (sprite) who delivered the prologue. Sand describes Ruzzante in her prologue as a likeable young man, well educated and highly esteemed, whose dramatic work places him in the company of Shakespeare and Molière, Plautus and Aristophanes.

> He loved the country, he knew the peasants well; he saw their miseries, their habits, their virtues, their faults. He composed and played himself with his friends, in the château of an amiable lord, and then in Padua's theatre . . . plays he called *dialogues rustiques*. . . . Each character speaks the dialect of his native region.[31]

The description could almost be of George Sand. The Nohant Theatre gave *Bilora* two revivals, one on 14 October 1860, and the other on 10 November 1861. The role of "esprit follet" in Sand's prologue was played by Marie Lambert these last two times.

George Sand wanted her adaptation of *Bilora* to be produced professionally by a good actor. She wrote to Comédie Française actor François Regnier hoping to interest him in the piece. She assured him that the expenses and effort involved would be minimal, and the results grand. The one-act play, "naïve and terrifying," needed only one set, four actors, no costumes, no expense, and twenty minutes to perform. Sand assured Regnier he would be admirable in the lead role (23 December 1859; *Corr.* 15:623–24). As late as 1872 Sand tried to get her *Bilora* professionally produced, when she asked a friend to prevail upon the Odéon management.[32] But public recognition of Ruzzante's rustic dialogues and commedia acting would have to wait until Copeau adapted and produced one of his plays in the 1920s, an adaptation one modern scholar finds remarkably similar in style and technique to Sand's adaptation.[33]

The same year, 1859, that *Bilora* first appeared at Nohant, George Sand indulged her taste for melodrama; "There's nothing but that which amuses me at the theatre."[34] Crime, mystery, and romance characterize her three major scripts performed at Nohant that season: *L'Auberge rouge* on October 11, *Octave d'Apremont* on October 23, and *Tulipe noire* on November 13. Sand considered these melodramas suitable for the children to be included in the audience (*Corr.* 15:524). In Sand's hierarchy of dramatic literature, melodramas have the broadest appeal because they are simply amusing and entertaining. Sand found melodrama less difficult to write than her more instructive and more artistic pieces; therefore when she needed diversion, and she wanted to divert her family and friends, melodrama came most easily.

The kind of frank, brutal violence which occurs at the end of *Bilora* reappears in Sand's *L'Auberge rouge*, an adaptation of Balzac's novel of the same title. In the first of two acts, scenes ten and eleven, a young man guarding a box of money in the inn decides to steal it. Unable to sleep in the adjoining room, the owner of the money box sees what is happening

Prologue
des
Ruzzante

———

Ruzzante au public
devant le rideau.

———

Q u'aucun de vous ne s'étonne,
braves gens, car je vous tiens pour
braves gens, tous tant que vous
êtes ici, si je ne vous parle
point en vers ou en langage
fleuri de métaphores. J'ai
toujours détesté le

14. Ruzzante's Prologue in George Sand's Hand.

and throws himself on the thief. But the criminal pulls his victim to the floor, holds him down with one hand and stabs him with the other, cursing him under his breath: "What are you doing, you imbecile?! *Allons,* you asked for it. . . . Dead? Already?" In a last gasp the dying man speaks in a muffled voice, "Assassin . . ."—struck again, he finally lies immobile. The thief throws his knife down and jumps out the window.[35] Manceau played the murderer and Maurice the murdered man. Marie Caillaud, a Berrichon peasant girl whom George Sand taught to read and write, then nineteen years old, played one of the two female leads, "ravishing, beautiful, touching, simple, delicious in the part" according to Sand's Agenda. A professional actress, Irma, played the other female roles, "sad, gay, funny, serious, pretty, gracious, spirited, and very intelligent." The play's manuscript shows Sand and her helpers' great attention to detail: set, props, blocking, gesture, are all indicated in the text. Rehearsals for the production began early in September 1859 and continued both morning and evening until the play opened on October 11—almost six weeks of preparation. Sand was again shifting away from writing scenarios for commedia improvisations, towards fully scripted plays with staging instructions carefully detailed.

Sand reworked her play *Gabriel* into *Octave d'Apremont* by completely changing the last act. Unfortunately the manuscripts for these two pieces, both given to Paul Meurice, have not been uncovered, so that the details of that changed last act remain a mystery. The professional actress Irma played the role of Gabriel in Nohant's 23 October 1859 production. Sand's play adaptation of Dumas père's novel *Tulipe noire* finished Sand's theatrical efforts for that fall.

The 1860 Nohant theatre season was cut short by George Sand's grave illness, which struck her in the last days of October. Her months of recovery from near death were partly accomplished in the south of France where she gathered new material for her novel *Tamaris* and a play, *Le Drac*. When the Nohant Theatre resumed its busy schedule at the end of summer 1861, Sand produced four new scripted plays, three of which would be published in the volume *Théâtre de Nohant* and best characterize the finesse and innovation of her fully written original plays performed at Nohant.

Before looking at these last Nohant play productions, it is important to note the influence of her little get-away house in the tiny village of Gargilesse, situated on a steep slope of the lovely Creuse River canyon (to Berry what the Ozarks must be to Missouri). Manceau bought the cottage there in 1856, making it a gift to Sand in his will. At the north end of a row house (containing two or three dwellings), the cottage's three rooms, plus closet-size kitchen, have less of a view of the out-of-doors than Nohant has. The tiny dwelling is closed up, cozy, nest-like, with only glimpses of the tree branches and rooftops outside small windows. The scale and ambience of this little retreat resemble Nohant's little theatre. The intimacy of settings in *Le Drac* (a fisherman's cottage), in *Le Pavé* (an amateur mineralogist's workroom), and *La Nuit de Noël* (a clock-maker's living room–work room combination) could all have been played in the Gargilesse cottage; and indeed must have been influenced by the cottage's miniature scale as well as that of the Nohant Theatre.[36]

Le Pavé opened Nohant's 1861 season on September 7. The original manuscript version differs somewhat from the two published versions, both the single volume published from the Gymnase's production copy, and the entry in the anthology *Théâtre de Nohant*. The manuscript has only three characters, no neighbor as in the other two versions. Manceau played Durand, the forty-year-old amateur mineralogist, Marie Caillaud the eighteen-year-old servant girl, and Auguste Jallas, a house painter, played Coqueret, the twenty-two-year-old valet. The entire action takes place in Durand's "cabinet de travail." Much more talk about fossils and stones, and more handling of them, occur in the original manuscript. And there is not the scene with the gun in the original. So the overall effect of Sand's original work is one of intimate psychological realism, without any resort to theatrical tricks. In the end Durand feels foolish for having made a fuss over Louise and her love for Coqueret: "The devil lodges in us like a fossil in its matrix. Fortunately a geologist has a solid head; when a *pavé* falls on him, he picks it up and studies it."[37] What a contrast to the Gymnase's production publication: Louise appears dressed in silk, and the door to Durand's elegant quarters opens onto a formal park, making the play's decor much grander and more artificial than Sand had intended. Much of the word play is out. And the female neighbor character added to the script makes final marriage arrangements for Durand to marry her niece. Worst of all is the scene with the gun when Durand threatens to kill Coqueret,[38] whereas in Sand's original manuscript the two men conduct a duel in words.

The distortions of Sand's plays caused by theatre professionals and public taste appear even more strikingly in *Le Drac* than in *Le Pavé*. *Drac*'s first performance at Nohant, 26 September 1861, was called *Un Homme double*, the second on 25 October became the *Drac*. A text of the play appeared in *Revue des Deux Mondes*, 1 November 1861. The play was again published in *Théâtre de Nohant*, 1865, the same year as a much altered version appeared adapted for the Vaudeville production in 1864 by Paul Meurice.

Paul Meurice had already adapted Sand's novel *Les Beaux Messieurs de Bois-Doré* for the stage in 1862, a highly successful production starring

Bocage. And Meurice would work with Sand on an adaptation of her novel *Cadio* in 1868. Sand's expectation that Meurice would adapt *Gabriel* has already been mentioned. So, evidently, she trusted him to write plays suited to the professional stage and public. However, what he did to the *Drac* appears almost absurdly comical.

Sand's original play, a "fantastic reverie in three acts," was based on a Provençal superstition that the Drac, a spirit, may enter and animate someone's dead body. The play concerns itself less with this spirit's supernatural powers and more with how he adjusts to being human. The Drac experiences human emotions—love, jealousy, and hatred—for the first time. All three acts take place in a fisherman's cottage situated on a cliff overlooking the sea (a backdrop view), and built into the rocks so that a staircase (stage right in the Nohant Theatre) leads up the cliff. The cast of four (plus voices) consists of the Drac, an aging fisherman named André, his daughter Francine, and Francine's fiancé Bernard, who has just returned from two years at sea. The Drac falls in love with Francine when he takes on the body of a drowned pubescent boy. Jealous of Bernard, the Drac plots to get rid of him. To do so he tricks André; appealing to the old fisherman's greed, the Drac makes him think a bag of shells is gold. In his efforts to alienate Francine's affections for Bernard, the Drac conjures up a double of Bernard, whose cynical, disrespectful, and cocky spirit does indeed confuse Francine. Of course the same actor would play both Bernards, the device referred to in the play's first title, *Un Homme double*. Finally Bernard's and Francine's prayers send the Drac back to his spirit world and peace is restored.

A strong feature of Sand's original *Drac* is her creation of mood: old André sitting at a wooden table lit by a single candle in the dark of a late evening, the glint in his eye matching the glint of the seashells by candlelight as he counts out his "gold"—the scene evokes the harsh edges of peasant life seen in Synge's *In the Shadow of the Glenn,* for instance. The Drac appearing at Francine's window also calls to mind Poe's raven or Yeats' words on a window pane. In each instance the environment is small, enclosed, dense with expectancy, sparse of population.

Now contrast this version to Meurice's. In a long letter written on 7 September 1862, Meurice outlines his plans for the play.[39] First he would like to cut some of Sand's "grand thoughts," for example the Drac's puzzlement, "What is there that is so strong in the human heart it can have power over me?" Meurice proposes a new peripety and a new denouement: Francine's prayer, which saves the Drac, strikes Meurice as too religious, especially for the anticlerical Sand. His Act III is to be set down by the sea, at the Grotte des Elfes, where Bernard has decided to commit suicide. A heroic act on the part of the Drac—he throws himself against the rocks—saves Bernard's life; at the same time it liberates the spirit Drac from a mortal body. When the Drac then returns to his natural element:

> The rock upstage center opens; all the fishermen get down on their knees. The Queen of the Elves rises and places on the Drac's head a crown of seaweed and coral, and the curtain comes down as the fishermen sing in a triumphant mixed choir with the elves.

Meurice will also change the location of Act I to the beach in order to give some exposition on the Drac. A comic servant character is added, who falls in love with Francine too. When, at the end of Act I the mortals leave the stage, the world of elves and spirits of the "unleashed sea" arrives and sings in a "bacchanale joyeuse." The Queen of the Elves tries to persuade the Drac to stay with her, as she is in love with him; but he must go to the human world to help and protect Francine. Meurice expressly says to Sand that he wishes to "simplify" Act II; he must make some sacrifices to clarify the line of interest. So he will eliminate all the business with Bernard's double, which only complicates and confuses the action, says Meurice. But the comic servant will be added to this act for comic relief, and some music and singing too. No wonder in a later letter, 11 July 1864, Meurice bemoans to Sand that the Vaudeville's theatre director prefers Sand's original! Undaunted, Meurice persuades the director, and perhaps Sand, that his version will be the more successful with the public, whereas he "fears a negative result" for Sand's (Lovenjoul E935, p. 32). The published production version shows that Paul Meurice prevailed in all of his changes with the exception of the crown of seaweed.[40]

When a theatre director asked to produce Sand's Nohant play, *La Nuit de Noël,* she refused, telling Flaubert in a letter (2 September 1866) that the piece was "too little a thing."[41] One wonders if perhaps Sand feared this lovely intimate piece would be spoiled and made too grandiose, as her *Drac* had been. In any case, *La Nuit de Noël* never went beyond the Nohant theatre. Sand had intended to open her Christmas play on 25 December 1861, as she writes to her friend Charles Marchal: "I'll tell you if you'll keep it a secret, that we are mounting the most fantastic play, with gadgets and ghosts, entitled *La Nuit de Noël*—just for Christmas" (*Corr.* 16:653). However, the play was delayed, and officially opened at Nohant on 31 August 1862, with a revival on 8 February 1863. Manceau played Peregrinus, Maurice was Max, and Marie Caillaud took the role of Nanni. The house painter Auguste played the part of the ghost or Spectre of old Rossmayer. Loosely based on Hoffmann's *Maître Floh,* Sand's fantasy makes use of puppets, a bird at the window, dolls and wind-up toys which jump out of a box, and a ghost who emerges from the stove or the top of the staircase, to create the fantasy. Of course the Nutcracker ballet is based on the same source. But unlike the ballet, Sand's treatment remains human size, with a focus on human problems. Peregrinus, a prospering clockmaker, resembles Durand in the *Pavé;* the two of them have allowed themselves to be too content with their occupations at the expense of human relationships. Max, an acerbic, brittle scholar, accuses Peregrinus of being an overgrown baby. Peregrinus gives off warm imagination and emotion, Max cold logic. Nanni, the loyal servant of Peregrinus, tries to bring harmony and finally succeeds. The ghost, once the master teacher to both Peregrinus and Max when the two were boys, tries to help Peregrinus by giving him the secret of the perpetual clock. Max wants to get to the secret first, and in the attempt almost takes a scalpel to the head of Peregrinus in a kind of mad doctor scene. But Max comes to his senses, Peregrinus and Nanni recognize their love for one another, and they all have a merry Christmas.

The setting for *Nuit de Noël* may be easily imagined on the Nohant stage: downstage right the big stove made of ceramic tiles, out of which the Spectre emerges; center stage right the spiral staircase leading up to the Spectre's old bedroom, and farther up to Nanni's poor artisan attic apartment (actually bridging to the little upstairs room in the Nohant Theatre's backstage); upstage center a double door, through which one goes downstairs to the street level entrance or to the left into an imaginary dining room. A window shows a view of rooftops and Frankfurt's gray sky; downstage left is placed Peregrinus' workbench covered with tools and parts of clocks. There are many clever stage devices, such as the cock mounted over an empty clock face on the wall over the double door, a cock that crows and bats his wings on cue. An owl beats his wings against the windowpane and hoots, "Don't touch, don't touch." Sound effects indicate the downstairs entrance to this city building apartment with Max breaking in the door and stomping up the stairs. Upstairs sound effects are made too, with Max supposedly stomping around in the Spectre's bedroom. Other sound effects include wind, rain, thunder, and the creaking and grinding of weathervanes. (Sand's granddaughter Aurore was impressed with the thunder machine, or sheet of metal rattled backstage, no longer there.)

Like a shriveled up Prospero, Rossmayer's Spectre commands and domesticates all the natural and supernatural elements of the play. He plays the violin while the toys dance, the windmills turn, the toy puppies bark, the wagons roll, the soldiers march. The stove hums and roars prodigiously; the owl and the crickets, even the town's clock, in the tower, all create a "strange hubbub." Rossmayer is able to transform the yule log smoldering in the stove into a fresh green Christmas tree.

At the same time that Sand fills the stage with so many interesting visual and sound effects, she deftly draws her characters Max and Peregrinus. Max attacks his friend:

> Don't you see how deplorably atrophied you've become in the dull comfort and nauseating regularity of your life? . . . passing summers in a cozy spot in the country, espaliering fruit trees and grafting roses; then in the winter coddled in a corner by a good fire amidst a collection of engravings, wooden canes, and snuff boxes. Going along like that, my good friend, with your splendid health and that carefreeness, you're headed straight for idiocy.

Peregrinus responds that he is happy. But Max will not let it stop there. Finally Peregrinus answers back:

> I can't see that your frenzied activity protects you any better than my calm nonchalance preserves me. I see that you fall short by the opposite excess, you neglect your physical life too much. You spend weeks at a time hardly sleeping or eating, deprived of fresh air, drying up in your books. I doubt that that could be a good regime for your body and spirit. . . . You want to be able to touch everything, to submit everything to reason.

Max wants to reform Peregrinus, to destroy his dreams and imagination, so he brutalizes the tangible evidence: toys, Christmas decorations, and the Christmas tree.

The fantastic elements of the play do not exist in order to persuade the audience that such things do exist, but that dreams such as Peregrinus harbors have value too. As he says, "For me everything is summed up in hope, and I'd rather believe in those things that are laughable and a little fanciful, than be absolutely sure they don't exist at all."

In her Preface to *La Nuit de Noël* Sand sums up the experience and accomplishment of her Nohant Theatre experiment, just as the play itself, the last major work Sand wrote for her theatre troupe, achieves a synthesis of Sand's playwriting talents. In the Preface, Sand observes that her play, "this humble fantasy with four characters that we have adapted to the means of our family theatre at Nohant," sets out specifically to "develop the characters." Characterization rather than action had always been Sand's interest and strength in her dramatic writing. Creating a mood and specific environment for her characters to occupy, where they could behave naturally, had always been Sand's objective. The Nohant theatre provided her with the means to discover the values of intimate theatre:

> All that was ingeniously produced at the performance, the scene of the children's toys, the apparition of the little animals, the sounds of their mysterious little voices . . . the effect of these unusual means was due to the smallness of our theatre, to the proximity of the spectator.

Sand had learned that big productions in large professional theatres do not necessarily result in art. She encourages the reader to attempt theatrical experiments similar to her own, and see if these efforts could not develop public taste for a new genre of intimate theatre. One would discover that material done in the small theatre space:

> very carefully done, very studied, where certain developments of ideas, confided to sensitive artists in the presence of a chosen audience, would seize the attention and charm the spirit, the heart or the imagination without having recourse to big and powerful means and effects.

She sounds the call: "we would like to see the conservation and even the creation of a number of little theatres which would rival the big ones in invention and in all the genres, and would preserve the traditions of intimate art."

Sand finishes her Preface with a discussion of what happens to an actor forced to perform in a large house, in contrast to the more natural behavior of an actor permitted to perform in an intimate space. "The larger we make our stages the farther away we push our spectators, and the more we lose the effects that the truth can produce." The big houses lead to banal generalities in the scripts and stretched, exaggerated behavior by the actors:

> One will know more and more how the word, the situation, the effect, the physiognomy, the gesture, the voice must carry to the extremities of a vast enclosure, but facing that necessity which could carry us as far as to the masque, to the megaphone and the stilts of ancient theatre, the delicate sentiment of things, the individual genius of the actor, his natural grace and charm would of necessity become useless qualities.

Sand sees the negative effects of these larger theatres already:

> Already voices no longer resist the conditions of grand opera; already in the big theatres, the playing of the actors has become an inevitable convention which does not produce the same satisfaction up close as far away. Rachel, Rachel herself, breaking the last cords of her admirable instrument in order to move all the waves of her public, appeared up close to be a victim of epilepsy. Mlle Dejazet, that marvel of finesse, endures and will yet endure, because she has always gained by being seen and heard up close.

Sand concludes that "true individualities need a little Greek temple and perish in a vast Byzantine circus."

Sand's little Greek temple of Nohant saved her individualistic talent from perishing in the vast Byzantine circus of Paris, giving revivals of Ruzzante and commedia dell'arte, romantic melodrama, and the precursors of Chekhovian drama in her *Pavé* and *Nuit de Noël,* rather than choruses of singing fishermen and elves, and a crown of seaweed.

15. Selected Scenes from Nohant Play Productions.
     Top: Set for *Tulipe noire*, performed 13 November 1859, *Recueil* 1:72.
     Left: Scene from *La Morte Vivante*, 20 November 1859, *Recueil* 2:74.
     Right: Maurice Sand as Coqueret in *Le Pavé*, performed at
     theatre of Nohant 2 November 1861, *Recueil* 2:90.
     Phot. Bibliothèque Nationale, Paris.

Sand's Theatre in Retrospect

In George Sand's long theatre career (1830–72), the year 1863 may have been the most critical, for it brought an end to Sand's little theatre of Nohant, and therefore an end to Sand's most creative and innovative period of theatre work. A family dispute caused the theatre's closure, when tensions between Maurice, Sand's son, and Manceau, her companion, reached a breaking point. The forty-year-old Maurice had finally married, granting Sand's wish for long-awaited grandchildren. Because Sand had intended all along to give the Nohant estate to Maurice and his descendants, she solved the Maurice-Manceau problem by immediately stepping down from her position as chatelaine of Nohant, and quietly departing for Paris with Manceau. Maurice was furious; he accused Manceau of being a Tartuffe, but he was helpless to change his mother's plans. So in January 1864 Sand left Nohant with Manceau. They eventually purchased a house in a Paris suburb and commuted by train to see friends and theatrical events in the city. But the arrangement was shortlived. Manceau's health degenerated and he died of tuberculosis late in the summer of 1865. Soon afterwards, Sand, in her sixty-second year, returned to Nohant. But without Manceau's serious and disciplined direction to spur George to action, the little theatre of Nohant remained dark. Instead, the family devoted their energies to Maurice's puppets.

The Nohant Theatre served Sand as a halfway house between the pragmatic world of Parisian theatres and the imaginary world of an ideal theatre. It combined Sand's practical experience, gained in the rehearsal halls and audiences of professional theatres, with her dream of a private theatre where artists could grow in their craft and freely express and develop themselves, unrestricted by the demands of bourgeois public taste.

At Nohant Sand achieved an *ensemble* of actors and audience in which class distinctions became immaterial, where only intelligence and talent could be the basis for a hierarchy. The Nohant Theatre was the closest thing in reality to Sand's dream of establishing a "people's theatre." Her Nohant audiences combined the rich and the poor, artists, peasants, politicians, and children. Gautier might be seated next to the provincial town mayor, a house painter next to Prince Napoleon, Dumas fils with the vicar. The acting troupe combined amateurs and professionals, artists and servants.

Sand's work with her Nohant actors anticipated the role of a modern director. She deplored any star system, and instead made every actor's role essential to the whole. Her appreciation of ensemble acting was far ahead of its time. Sand and her troupe not only revived commedia dell'arte techniques, and made the important discovery of Ruzzante in the process, but devised and evolved their own commedia procedure, achieving a disciplined practice similar to modern rehearsal techniques. They broke down a full-length script into a plot outline, then improvised and paraphrased their character roles, got into character before the opening scene and stayed in character between scenes, and then openly discussed the results with their director. To her great satisfaction, Sand discovered that these techniques benefited her children's education and expanded the range of character types for professional actors.

As a professional playwright, George Sand learned in her Nohant laboratory theatre how to cut and revise her scripts more effectively than in the isolation of her writing studio or the confusion of professional rehearsal halls. A woman of highly developed senses, she needed to hear and see her words in action. In some instances, such as *Claudie* and *Marielle,* Sand discovered that by playing one of the roles she could better revise it from the inside out.

Sand's major dramatic achievements, with possibly one exception, owe their origins to the little theatre of Nohant. The exception, *François le Champi,* gave birth to realistic folk drama in France. For the first time audiences listened to dialogue written to resemble a provincial patois, its rhythms and expressions, spoken by characters in authentic folk costumes and set in a realistic Berrichon farmhouse. The success of that experiment led Sand to write a second folk drama, *Claudie,* in which she added more detailed Berrichon folk customs, songs and dances, and developed realism even further than in *Champi* by creating individual tasks and large group activities such as the harvest festival to enhance character development. The play was equally audacious in theme, the forgiveness and rehabilitation of an unwed mother. Sand and her fellow amateurs rehearsed and performed *Claudie* on the Nohant stage before Bocage moved it to Paris for a professional production.

With Sand's efforts to develop a serious, realistic one-act play, she made another significant contribution to the evolution of nineteenth-century theatre. As early as 1844 Sand wrote a one-act play which demonstrates her clear understanding of a play's "through-line." In *Père Va-*

tout-seul a natural progression of conflicts concentrates on a principal character and leads toward one dominant objective or problem. In the realistic one-act play *Le Pavé,* developed on the Nohant stage in 1861, Sand proved that psychological conflict can make a strong dramatic action, even in a short time and in a small space. In so doing, she prefigured the little-art-theatre movement begun by Antoine in 1887, and the naturalistic one-act plays by Strindberg.

The revival of commedia dell'arte on Sand's Nohant stage constitutes another of her major achievements. Her rehabilitation of the commedia actor in *Marielle,* a play that demonstrates the art's complexity and discipline, failed to attract a professional producer. Similarly, Sand's significant work in translating and adapting Ruzzante's *Bilora,* performed three times on the Nohant stage, never received a Parisian production. Therefore, Sand's influence in disseminating an appreciation for commedia dell'arte was limited to the written word, rather than theatrical performance, in sharp contrast to her folk dramas, which became famous upon first production and remained so for half a century.

George Sand posed important problems in many of her plays, from the subject of women's equality in her early dramas, to the conflict of egotism with self-abnegation in her later works. Her imagination and intuition were in advance of her craft. Observing the craft of actor Marie Dorval in 1832, Sand intuited an actor's subtext, the character's inner motives and emotions as opposed to what she might be saying in the text. But Sand wrote romantic plays in which faulty and awkward plots interfere with a character's inner psychological development. For example, *Cosima* (1840) is perhaps the first play to treat a woman's sense of domestic imprisonment with sympathetic psychological realism (thirty years ahead of Ibsen's *Doll House*), but the point is almost lost under the weight of a cumbersome, melodramatic plot. Likewise, *Gabriel* (1839) poses the imaginative and prescient figure of a woman given a boy's education and the occupation of serving as a Renaissance prince. But the plot appears to take a wrong turn and finally finishes with the heroine's gratuitous death. The Nohant Theatre experience refined Sand's playwriting craft. She discovered that contrary to an earlier self-perception, small-scale intimate drama suited her talents better than grand-scale romanticism. As one of her contemporaries observed, Sand's plays are "essentially psychological . . . sometimes badly conducted from the point of view of dramaturgy, always logically deduced from the point of view of psychology." "They persuade by emotion."[1] Sand said of herself at the end of her theatre career, "I've searched too much for the causes to be able to observe well the effects."[2]

In the vanguard, Sand was among those who first denounced roman-

ticism's excesses and promulgated dramatic realism, and then later identified that new movement's limitations. She began writing dramatic fantasies
and symbolic fables when the rest of the world became infatuated with
realism and naturalism. As an individualistic artist Sand went her own
way, retaining qualities from the various schools or movements. Her theatre career demonstrates that she did not deny her romantic origins, she
domesticated them.

The year of Sand's last Paris premiere, 1872, the illustrious critic
Hippolyte Taine wrote to George Sand urging her to write more plays.
He tells her that all the combatants of their century's *"printemps sacré"*
are either dead or mad. Sand and Sainte-Beuve alone have endured, re-
newing and developing themselves. Sand's plays have persuaded Taine
that a heroic world is possible. Her characters perform pure and generous
acts. They give the audience hope by the way they deliver themselves from
the labyrinth of temptation, resolving a "dialectic of the heart."[3] Throughout Sand's theatre career, whether she was creating romantic rebels or
realistic country folk, her characters struggle between self-indulgence and
self-abnegation, between egotism and generosity, between warmth and
coldness, in a dialectic of the heart. In Sand's romantic plays her isolated
heroes and heroines die in despair. In her more realistic plays the individual protagonist is reintegrated into a supportive social fabric. And in the
theatre of Nohant Sand discovered and refined the means to give shape
and substance to this dialectic of the heart.

George Sand's plays have disappeared from the modern stage in part
because they are not great plays, not masterpieces. Those that set new
standards or broke new ground for their day in mid-nineteenth-century
France, such as her realistic folk plays, would strike a late twentieth-
century audience as quaint and old-fashioned. Other pieces which became
sensational *causes célèbres* when first produced in Paris, such as *Le Marquis de Villemer* (1864), would no doubt bore a modern audience, which
has no taste or tolerance for overly idealized and virtuous heroines. The
plays Sand wrote for the public stage are generally sentimental and mor-
alizing, as we might expect for the theatre of Victorian times. At least one
can say that Sand finally knew her audience. On the other hand, Sand
experimented more freely in works for her private stage. Her Ruzzante
adaptations are remarkably unsentimental, simple and even brutal, without any moral lesson to be learned. These characteristics may be equally
applied to her very first drama, the Lorenzaccio piece titled *Une Conspiration en 1537*. Perhaps the feature of Sand's plays we find most contrary to our modern taste is her penchant for overexplaining, for making
her characters and plots too obvious, so that the modern reader feels
cheated by a lack of mystery or discovery.

But the flaws in Sand's plays do not account for the total eclipse of her reputation as a playwright, the complete blackout of information on her rich, varied, and long theatre career. Explanations for this phenomenon go beyond identifying weaknesses in her plays. And they go beyond the scope of this history of Sand's theatre career. But as more scholars and artists examine and produce Sand's plays and take a closer look at her theories and practices, a fuller understanding of this dilemma will emerge. My foray into this undiscovered country is an invitation to proceed further.

16. George Sand Performing Various Roles at Nohant.
Left: George Sand as La Royale in *Boishardy,*
9 March 1851, *Recueil* 1:208.
Top: George Sand as Grand Chef des Eunuques in
L'Incroyable à Constantinople, Recueil 1:24.
Bottom: George Sand as Notaire in Ménéghino,
16 June 1850, *Recueil* 1:141.
Phot. Bibliothèque Nationale, Paris.

Top: George Sand as Inesilla in *L'Aventurière*, 2 October 1849.
Bottom: George Sand as La Comtesse de Villaret in *Ariane*,
20 October 1850, *Recueil* 1:68 and 1:193.
Phot. Bibliothèque Nationale, Paris.

Appendix A

Paris Premieres of George Sand Plays

Date		Play Title[1]	Theatre
1840	April 29	*Cosima*	Comédie Française
1848	April 6	*Le Roi attend*	Comédie Française
1849	November 23	*François le Champi*	Odéon
1851	January 11	*Claudie*	Porte-Saint-Martin
	May 10	*Molière*	Gaîté
	November 26	*Le Mariage de Victorine*	Gymnase
1852	March 3	*Les Vacances de Pandolphe*	Gymnase
	September 1	*Le Démon du foyer*	Gymnase
1853	September 13	*Le Pressoir*	Gymnase
	November 28	*Mauprat*	Odéon
1854	October 31	*Flaminio*	Gymnase
1855	September 15	*Maître Favilla*	Odéon
1856	February 15	*Lucie*	Gymnase
	April 3	*Françoise*	Gymnase
	April 12	*Comme il vous plaira*	Comédie Française
1859	April 23	*Marguerite de Sainte-Gemme*	Gymnase
1862	March 18	*Le Pavé*	Gymnase
1864	February 29	*Le Marquis de Villemer*	Odéon
1866	August 14	*Le Lis du Japon*	Vaudeville
1870	February 25	*L'Autre*	Odéon
1872	November 7	*Un Bienfait n'est jamais perdu*	Théâtre de Cluny

Plays based on George Sand's works (either novels or plays), for which she served as either coauthor or assistant at rehearsals, or both:

| 1862 | April 26 | *Les Beaux Messieurs de Bois-Doré*, by Paul Meurice | Ambigue-Comique |

1864	September 28	*Le Drac*, by Paul Meurice	Vaudeville
1866	August 12	*Les Don Juan de village,* by Maurice Sand	Vaudeville
1868	October 3	*Cadio*, by Paul Meurice	Porte-Saint-Martin
1869	September 15	*La Petite Fadette*, opéra-comique, verse by Michel Carré, music by T. Semet	Opéra-Comique

Appendix B

Nohant Plays and Scenarios by George Sand

Premiere Performance		Title	Provenance If Known
1846	December 8	Le Druide peu délicat	O 33 A & B[1]
	December 9	Pierrot précepteur	
		Cassandre persuadé	O 24
	December 10	Scaramouche brigand	O 52
	December 11	Thomiris reine des Amazons	O 54
	December 12	Les Deux Vivandières	O 32
	December 13	La Belle au bois dormant	Boîte 55[2]
	December 14	Scaramouche précepteur	
	December 17	Pierrot maître de chapelle	O 46
	December 31	Don Juan	
1847	January 1	Pierrot comédien	O 45
	January 3	La Famille Pierrot	
	January 10	L'Incroyable à Constantinople	
	January 11	Le Philtre	
	January 13	La Caverne du crime	O 25
	January 20	La Nuit aux soufflets	
	January 21	Le Mariage au tambour	
	January 24	La Royale, or Boishardy	H 351[3]
	January 27	Le Sourd ou l'auberge pleine	
	January 29	Le Déserteur	
	January 30	Riquet à la houpe	O 50
	July 6	Cassandre assassin	O 23
	December 25	Barbe bleue	O 21
	December 31	L'Auberge du crime	O 19

1849	October 2	L'Aventurière	
	October 18	Arlequin Médecin	O 18
		Maison de bois	O 39
	November 12	Prologue—Cendrillon	O 26
	November 13	Une Nuit à Ferrare	
	November 15	Le Podesta de Ferrare, or Les Enfants du soir	O 47
	November 24	Beaucoup de bruit pour rien	O 22
	November 27	Les Grands Infortunes de Pierrot	
	November ?	Cassandre homme vertueux	
	December 25	L'Inconnu	O 38
		Pierrot enlevé	
	December 26	Pierrot berger	

1850	January 6	La Jeunesse d'Henri IV	
	February 10	Lelio	published as *Marielle*
	July 5	L'Anglais en voyage; Un Lion; Monsieur le maire	
	August 8	Claudie	*Claudie*
	October 5	Le Spectre	O 51
	October 17	Pierrot bergère	H 359

1851	February 9	La Malédiction	H 349
	June 10	Début de Columbine	O 30
	July 17	Famille de Vanderke	published as *Le Mariage de Victorine*
	October 4	Nello	published as *Maître Favilla*
	October 9	Testament du veinturier	

| 1852 | July 15 | Démon du foyer | *Démon du foyer* |

| 1853 | July 29 | Le Pressoir | *Le Pressoir* |

1856	September 8	Ote donc ta barbe	
	September 11	Charlotte et la poupée	
	September 17	Les Cretards	H 366
	September 30	Les Premières Armes de Mario	
	October 13	C'est pour la frime	
	October 18	Le Coeur sensible	
	October 21	Le Vacher de la couronne	

1856	October 24	La Prédiction	
	October 26	Le Bail à Jeannette	O 20
	October 27	Mario	
	November 2	Le Boeuf chauvet	H 358
	November 11	La Femme battue	O 36
	November 23	Le Datura fastuosa	O 29
1857	September 13	Vive le roi! Vive la ligue!	
	September 22	Jacques	
	September 30	Pierre Riallo	
	October 2	Un Héritage	
	October 11	L'Emigré, or Le Chavalier de Tintignac	O 34
	October 21	Les Chevaliers du soleil	
	October 30	Daniel	
	November 19	Le Dalès	
1858	September 23	Eustache ou le petit ramoneur	Arsenal Acq 1963, O 384
1859	September 4	Bilora, L'Amour et la faim	H 316
	September 25	Le Poulailler	O 48
	October 11	L'Auberge rouge	private collection Daniel Sickles
	October 23	Octave d'Aprémont	
	November 13	Tulipe noire	O 55
	November 20	Pantalonnade	
1860	September 16	L'Homme de campagne	
	September 30	Jean le Rebateux	H 380
	October 19	La Légende de Rosily	
1861	September 7	Le Pavé	O 43
	September 8	Le Déjeuner de Léonie	O 31
	September 26	Un Homme double	
	October 25	Le Drac	
1862	August 25	Fiornis	
	August 31	La Nuit de Noël	published as *La Nuit de Noël*
	September 28	Soriani	
	October 26	Le Pied sanglant	Maurice's copy La Châtre
	November 23	Les Paysans	
	December 31	Le Père Raymond	
1863	August 31	Daphnis et Chloë	

Appendix C

George Sand's Acting Roles

Sand pokes fun at herself and her own acting in the following passage, overstating her self-deprecation in a way typical of her humor:

> I, who have never played anything but fill-in roles, the notary in the denouements . . . the domestic who carries a letter, and other utilities, where only my costumes have any success; I don't believe I'm capable of reciting a woman's role. I have no memory, I don't know how to make gestures, I play just like I read aloud, that should tell you everything. . . . It's strange how I have no facility for rendering my emotions by that means, and yet I can cry like a baby at the theatre over the least little thing. I can tell when the acting in others is bad, but I don't know how to draw out myself except with pen and paper (*Corr.* 9:632–33).

Sand obviously enjoyed acting and played several roles on the Nohant stage. Fourteen of these parts were illustrated by her son Maurice in his collection of drawings, *Recueil des principaux types crées avec leurs costumes sur le Théâtre de Nohant,* bound in two volumes and now housed in the Bibliothèque Nationale, Paris, (Estampes Réserves, Tb471). Of these fourteen pictures seven roles are female and seven male. Of course Sand played other roles in Nohant productions, not represented in this list from Maurice's illustrations, such as Hotspur in her scenario of *Henry IV.*

George Sand's Acting Roles on the Nohant Stage
as Illustrated by Maurice Sand

Date		Part[1]	Play or Scenario
1846	December 9	Leandre	*Cassandre persuadé*
	December 14	Duchess	*Scaramouche précepteur*

1847 January 10   Chief of the Eunuchs *L'Incroyable à Constantinople*

1849 October 2   Inesilla   *L'Aventurière*
      October 14   Herminie   *La Soeur de Jocrisse*
      October 16   Edul   *La Famille maudite*
      November 13 Pietro Colonna   *Une Nuit à Ferrare*
      November 15 Pistola   *Le Podesta de Ferrare*

1850 February 10 Fabio   *Marielle*
      June 16   Notary   *Meneghino*
      August 8   Claudie   *Claudie*
      October 13   Madame Baletti   *Le Quatrain*
      October 20   Countess of Villaret *Ariane*

1851 March 9   La Royale   *Boishardy*

Notes

Preface

1. Dorrya Fahmy, *George Sand: Auteur dramatique* (Paris: Droz, 1935).

2. Debra Linowitz Wentz, *Les Profils du théâtre de Nohant de George Sand* (Paris: Nizet, 1978).

Chapter 1

1. *Correspondance,* ed. Georges Lubin, 18 vols. (Paris: Garnier, 1964–84), 6:487 (hereafter cited in the text as *Corr.*) English translations of all quotations are mine.

2. *Histoire de ma vie,* in *Oeuvres autobiographiques,* ed. Georges Lubin, 2 vols. (Paris: Gallimard, 1970), 1:998–1001, 1019–20, 1092–93, 845–47.

3. Patrice Boussel, "George Sand et la technique dramatique," *L'Europe,* June–July 1954, pp. 73–74.

4. *Revue de Paris,* 15 December 1921; Paul Dimoff, *La Genèse de Lorenzaccio* (Paris: Droz, 1936), pp. 83–146.

5. Alfred de Musset's *Lorenzaccio,* written in 1833, was first staged in 1896 with Sarah Bernhardt in the title role. In a 1977 production the director, Pierre Vielhescaze, inserted the assassination scene from Sand's *Conspiration*: Duke Alexander bites his assassin's thumb, and will not let loose, chewing it as Lorenzo stabs him. Perhaps it is this scene that Sand imagined might make the delicate ladies abort. See Bibliothèque Nationale, *Lorenzaccio: Mises en scène d'hier et d'aujourd'hui* (Paris: B.N. Catalogue, 1979), p. 55.

6. In 1836 Sand expressed sympathy for the would-be assassin who made an attempt on Louis Philippe's life and was subsequently executed. She compared him to a character in the 1830 play *Napoléon ou Schoenbrunn et Sainte-Hélène* in which her friend Bocage had played the dissident Schoenbrunn who tries to assassinate Napoleon. Sand saw the play in 1830 and may have had Bocage's character in mind as she wrote her *Conspiration* (*Corr.* 3:456–57).

7. George Sand, *Une Conspiration en 1537,* in Dimoff, *La Genèse de Lorenzaccio,* pp. 113, 144–45.

8. Rose, an actress-singer, abandons the theatre and becomes a nun; Blanche, a nun, abandons her religious life, marries, and goes insane.

9. *L'Ecole romantique en France,* trans. (from German) A. Topin (Paris: A. Michalon, 1902), pp. 140–41.

10. "La Marquise," *Nouvelles* (Paris: Michel Levy, 1869), p. 15. Further references to this edition are cited parenthetically in the text.

11. "I've always looked for serene friends, having need of their patience and wisdom. With Marie Dorval I had the opposite role, that of calming and persuading her, a very difficult role for me, particularly at that time when troubled and frightened myself to the point of despair, I could find nothing consoling to say to her." George Sand, *Histoire de ma vie,* 10 vols. (Paris: Michel Levy, 1856), 9:122 (hereafter cited as *Histoire de ma vie*).

12. Casimir Carrère, *George Sand amoureuse* (Paris: La Palatine, 1967), p. 284.

13. Enid M. Standring. "The Lelio's of Berlioz and George Sand," in *The George Sand Papers,* ed. Natalie Datlof (New York: Hofstra University, 1976), pp. 181–82.

14. *Histoire de ma vie,* 9:130.

15. Maurice Descotes, *Drame romantique et ses créateurs* (Paris: Presses Universitaires de France, n.d.), p. 189 (hereafter cited as Descotes, *Drame romantique*).

16. Descotes, *Drame romantique,* pp. 267–69.

17. George Sand, *"Les Beaux Messieurs de Bois-Doré* au Théâtre de l'Odéon," *Questions d'art et de littérature* (Paris: Calmann Levy, 1878), p. 408. *Les Beaux Messieurs,* a play adaptation of Sand's novel, premiered in Paris in 1861 with Bocage in the lead role. It was his last performance, for he died a few months later. Sand reviewed the revival of the play in 1867.

18. An extraordinary coincidence, and one that has yet to be entirely unraveled, is the fact that Bocage played Berlioz's autobiographical character, the composer named Lelio, in the premiere of *Episode in the Life of an Artist,* performed 9 December 1832, one week after the publication of Sand's "La Marquise." Some of the songs had been composed and performed earlier than 1832, and they related to Berlioz's passionate love for the British actress, Harriet Smithson, whom Berlioz had seen play Ophelia in Paris during that famous touring season of 1826. Following the performance of Berlioz's "Lelio" in 1832, in which the composer dramatized his heretofore unrequited passion, Miss Smithson softened and admitted to loving Berlioz. Within a month of the appearances of both Sand's "Lelio" and Berlioz's, an article in the *Revue de Paris* drew attention to the coincidence. But who influenced whom, who knew whom, if indeed any such connections exist, has not been determined. In 1837 Berlioz asked Sand to write a play for his unemployed actress wife, Miss Smithson; and Sand proposed to do *Love's Labours Lost* with Bocage playing opposite the Shakespearean actress. But the project failed to materialize. See *Corr.* 3:771; 4:131–32, 197. For discussion of the two "Lelios"—Sand's and Berlioz's—see Enid M. Standring's article, "The Lelio's of Berlioz and George Sand."

19. A third famous actress of the nineteenth century, Pauline-Virginie Dejazet (1798–1875), played Cherubin, the part of the pubescent boy whose first feelings of romantic love are for the Countess Almaviva.

20. George Sand, "Mars et Dorval," *Questions d'art,* pp. 14, 22.

21. Sand would create a parallel dilemma in her play *Cosima,* in which Dorval played the

lead when it premiered at the Comédie Française in April of 1840. The dilemma of Cosima is similar to Countess Almaviva's: an older married woman attracted to a younger suitor.

22. "Mars et Dorval," *Questions d'art*, pp. 19–23.

23. George Sand, "Le Drame fantastique," *Revue des Deux Mondes*, 1 December 1839, pp. 596–600 (hereafter cited as "Drame fantastique").

24. Sand said that in the finished version Aldo would either succeed in committing suicide or eventually reconcile himself to life. See Valentine Petoukhoff, "George Sand et le drame philosophique," (Ph.D. dissertation, University of Pennsylvania, 1975), p. 107.

25. A partially staged production of the original French version of *Aldo le rimeur* was presented at a George Sand conference at San Diego State University, California, February 1981.

26. In her essay on "Drame fantastique" Sand discusses staging possibilities for all three of her play examples. Goethe's *Faust* would be easier to stage than Byron's *Manfred* because Faust's boredom is made manifest materially, while Manfred's internal struggle with despair cannot be seen, only imagined. *Konrad* has devils as real and factual as Callot's drawings, says Sand, more medieval and legendary and less poetic and allegoric than Manfred's. Konrad's demon seen as a monstrous despot Sand claims to be the most modern figure of the three, and the most effectively disturbing stage figure ("Drame fantastique," pp. 626–27).

27. Charles Sechan, *Souvenirs d'un homme de théâtre: 1831–1855* (Paris: Calmann Levy, 1883), pp. 273–74.

28. Emile Zola, *Le Naturalisme au théâtre* (Paris: Charpentier, 1893), pp. 377–78.

29. "De Madame Dorval" first appeared in *Journal de Toulouse*, 27 January 1837; rpt. in *Questions d'art*, pp. 62–63.

30. "De Madame Dorval," *Questions d'art*, pp. 62, 64.

31. George Sand, *Les Sept Cordes de la lyre* (Paris: Flammarion, 1973), pp. 182, 189, 110.

32. René Wellek, *A History of Modern Criticism: 1750–1950*, 4 vols. (New Haven: Yale, 1955–65), 3:27–29; Jacques Viard, "George Sand et Michelet disciples de Pierre Leroux," *Revue d'Histoire Littéraire de la France*, no. 5, September–October 1975, pp. 749–73; Jean-Pierre Lacassagne, *Histoire d'une amitié* (Paris: Klincksieck, 1973).

33. Only one voice of enthusiastic praise was raised when *Sept Cordes* appeared: Leconte de l'Isle wrote a letter to the *Revue des Deux Mondes* on 4 October 1839, in which he included the following lines:

> Sister of the spirits, Helene! O Lyre that the wind
> Makes vibrate in the skies like a living perfume
> Helene, answer me, sweet and profound mystery,
> Harmonious voice, are you truly of this earth?

Quoted by René Bourgeois in his Introduction to *Les Sept Cordes de la lyre*, p. 10.

34. Balzac, *Correspondance* (Paris: Garnier, 1966) 4:476.

35. George Sand, *Gabriel* (Paris: Michel Levy, 1867).

36. George Sand, *Cosima, Théâtre complet,* 4 vols. (Paris: Calmann Levy, 1867), 1:33 (hereafter referred to in the text as *Cosima*).

37. Preface to *Cosima,* pp. 11–14.

38. Heinrich Heine, "Letters on the French Stage," trans. Charles G. Leland, *The Works of Heinrich Heine* (New York: Croscup & Sterling, n.d.), 8:295.

39. Théophile Gautier, *Histoire de l'art dramatique en France depuis vingt-cinq ans,* 6 vols. (Paris, 1858; rpt. Geneva: Slatkine, 1968), 2:52–60.

40. *Journal des Débats,* 1 May 1840.

41. During that same year of 1838–39, Sand nursed Chopin and moved him and her two children to Majorca, then to Marseilles and back to Nohant and Paris.

42. *Les Mississipiens* (Paris: Michel Levy, 1869), p. 171.

43. After their meeting in Russia, Turgenev and Pauline became devoted lifelong companions, and perhaps lovers. For one brief romantic interlude Pauline and Maurice Sand, George's son, were in love (*Corr.* 6:618n, 632–33), a tangled relationship which Turgenev appears to have immortalized in his play *A Month in the Country.* A daughter born to Pauline in 1852, purportedly Turgenev's, was named Claudie, after the title of George Sand's successful play about an unwed mother (1851). For Turgenev's literary indebtedness to Sand, see Lesley Herrmann, "George Sand and Ivan Turgenev," in *The George Sand Papers,* pp. 162–73.

44. She gives this description of her cure from that "malady which renders one egotistical and vain," that "skepticism which dries up my French contemporaries," in a letter to her friend George Henry Lewes, British drama critic, in 1843. Byron, her prophet in the 1830s, had sent her into a "rude purgatory," but now she has arrived at "heaven's gate" ("Quarante-quatre lettres inédites," ed. Georges Lubin, *Présence de George Sand,* October 1982, pp. 32–33).

45. "A propos de la traduction de *Werther* par Pierre Leroux," in *Jean Zyska* (Paris: Michel Levy, 1867), pp. 341–50.

46. George Sand, *Le Père Va-tout-seul, Questions politiques et sociales* (Paris: Calmann Levy, 1879), pp. 118–19 (hereafter cited as *Questions politiques*).

47. Sand's socialism did not favor big government or centralization of political power. See *Questions politiques,* p. 27.

48. E. J. Hobsbawm, *The Age of Revolution: 1789–1848* (New York: Mentor, 1962), pp. 286–87.

49. *Questions politiques,* p. 80.

50. *Corr.* 6:643n. Sand's vision of a proletarian poet had appeared in her novel *Le Compagnon du Tour de France* (1840), based on her friend Perdiguier, a man of the people, craftsman and poet. A review of an English translation of this novel, entitled *Journeyman Joiner,* appeared in the *Brooklyn Eagle* on 27 September 1847, written by Walt Whitman. The reviewer later (1850s) adopted the persona of a proletarian poet and celebrated the open road in the manner of Père Va-tout-seul, in such passages from *Leaves of Grass* as: "I tramp a perpetual journey . . . /I have no chair, no church, no philosophy" ("Song of Myself"), or "Afoot and light-hearted I take to the open road,/ Healthy, free, the world before me,/ The long brown path before me leading wherever

I choose" ("Song of the Open Road"). Some of Whitman's lines are said to be word-for-word translations of Sand's Epilogue to her novel *Consuelo,* a favorite of Whitman's mother in the 1840s (and of Ibsen's wife, too). See Esther Shephard, *Walt Whitman's Pose* (New York: Harcourt Brace, 1936).

51. B. Juden and J. Richer, "L'Entente cordiale au théâtre: Macready et Hamlet à Paris en 1844," *La Revue des Lettres Modernes,* nos. 74–75, 1962–63, pp. 15, 19, 21, 30.

52. Macready's classical liberal arts education and years of acting experience made him an ideal spokesman for reform in the art of acting. His careful attention to the art is aptly described by another of Sand's British friends, George Henry Lewes, in 1851, the year Macready retired:

> Macready . . . seemed to have stepped from the canvas of one of the old masters. . . . By his intelligence he was fitted to conceive and by his organization fitted to express *characters,* and was not like a melodramatic actor—limited to *situations.* . . . Whenever he had an emotion to depict he depicted it sympathetically and not artificaly; by which I mean that he felt himself with the character. . . . In the great scene of the third act of *The Merchant of Venice,* Shylock has to come on in a state of intense rage. . . . Macready it is said, used to spend some minutes behind the scenes, lashing himself into an imaginative rage by cursing *sotto voce,* and shaking violently a ladder fixed against the wall. . . . He had a powerful voice . . . He spoke in broken and spasmodic rhythms. . . . In tenderness he had few rivals . . . the noble tenderness of a father . . . the chivalrous tenderness of a lover.

On Actors and the Art of Acting (New York: Grove, n.d.), pp. 40–44. This is one from a collection of essays Lewes wrote in the 1850s which constitutes a first comprehensive analysis of acting theory. Lewes' lover and companion, George Eliot, assumed for her own Sand's pen name, George, out of friendship and admiration.

53. George Sand, "Hamlet," *L'Almanach du Mois,* February 1845, pp. 65–72.

54. George Sand, "Debureau," *Le Constitutionnel,* 8 February 1846; rpt. in *Questions d'art,* pp. 215–22 (hereafter cited in the text as "Debureau").

55. Robert F. Storey, *Pierrot: A Critical History of a Mask* (Princeton, New Jersey: Princeton Univ. Press, 1978), p. 103.

Chapter 2

1. See excerpts of Rolland's essay in *The Theory of the Modern Stage,* trans. Barrett H. Clark, ed. Eric Bentley (New York: Penguin, 1979), pp. 455–70.

2. A correspondence between Sand and Michelet began in 1845 after Michelet sent several of his works to Sand for comment. She responded by telling him he spent too much energy and genius on too little, on the less significant. For example, he talked about reforming the Church; she would rather take action, take up the hammer and destroy it, and then talk about it afterwards! (*Corr.* 6:836, 855). Michelet called Sand "the first socialist writer," quoted in Jacques Viard, "George Sand et Michelet, disciples de Pierre Leroux," *Revue d'Histoire Littéraire de la France,* no. 5 (September–October 1975), p. 773.

3. *Questions politiques,* pp. 80–81.

4. Théodore Muret, *L'Histoire par le théâtre: 1789–1851* (Paris: Amyot, 1865), vol. 3 pp. 306–7.

5. "Théâtre de la République," *La Cause du Peuple*, 8 April 1848; rpt. in *Questions d'art*, p. 225 (hereafter cited as "Théâtre de la République").

6. "Théâtre de l'Opéra," *La Cause du Peuple*, 15 April 1848; rpt. in *Questions d'art*, p. 232.

7. "Théâtre de la République," p. 230.

8. "Théâtre de la République," p. 228.

9. *Le Roi attend, Théâtre complet*, 1:141.

10. Gautier, *Histoire de l'art dramatique*, 5:253–54.

11. 1848 Preface to *La Petite Fadette*; rpt. in *Questions d'art*, p. 284.

12. Had Sand not made the hasty decision to let others dramatize it first, *Fadette* might have been one of Sand's popular plays as well. The first stage adaptation by Anicet-Bourgeois and Charles Lafont played at the Variétés in Paris on 20 April 1850. A German translation by August Waldauer was translated into English anonymously and performed in America by Maggie Mitchell. Henry James saw one of Mitchell's performances in Boston in 1863 while still a student; his review of that *Fadette* started him on his literary career. Later Mary Pickford played *Fadette* on film.

13. Writing to Regnier, a highly respected actor of the time, Sand praised his performance of Figaro in Beaumarchais' *Marriage of Figaro* at the Comédie Française, March 1856: "The long monologue of the fifth act grabbed me in the reading, but I didn't think it scenic. To the contrary it is very much so. It is natural to that moment" (*Corr.* 13:564).

14. See Charles Constant, *Code des théâtres* (Paris: Durand et Pedone-Lauriel, 1876).

15. Preface, *François le Champi, Théâtre complet*, 1:145.

16. George Sand to Maurice Sand, 26 April 1869, Lovenjoul Collection E925, Chantilly, France (hereafter cited as Lovenjoul).

17. Sarah Bernhardt to George Sand, 10 August n.d., Fonds Sand, G3523 and G3524 Fol. 184, Bibliothèque Historique de la Ville de Paris (hereafter cited as B.H.V.P.): "I will do my best and it would make me very happy if I could play for you one day."

18. Quoted in George Sand's *Histoire de ma vie*, 9:162–63.

19. *Corr.* 15:153n. Proudhon's attack on Sand in 1858 included the statement that giving emancipation to women would give reign to their lascivious natures and obscene thoughts.

20. Emile Zola, *Nos auteurs dramatiques* (Paris: Charpentier, 1889), pp. 370–71 (hereafter cited as Zola, *Nos auteurs*).

21. Antoine Benoist, *Essais de critique dramatique* (Paris: Hachette, 1898), p. 10 (hereafter cited as Benoist, *Essais de critique*).

22. "L'Amitié de George Sand et d'Eugène Delacroix," *Revue des Deux Mondes*, 15 June 1934, p. 858.

23. *La Presse*, 4 December 1849; Zola, *Histoire de l'art dramatique*, 6:135.

24. Fonds Sand G6123, B.H.V.P.

25. Zola, *Nos auteurs,* pp. 367–69.

26. *Corr.* 9:446–47, 532. Sand's inspiration may have been derived in part from Goethe's Wilhelm Meister, who made a similar observation about the possibility for a people's theatre which gives an honest portrayal of all classes:

    > . . . how useful the theatre might be to all ranks; what advantage even the state might procure from it, if the occupations, trades, and undertakings of men were brought upon the stage, and presented on their praiseworthy side. As matters stand, we exhibit only the ridiculous side of men; the comic poet is, as it were, but a spiteful tax-gatherer, who keeps a watchful eye over the errors of his fellow-subjects, and seems gratified when he can fix any charge upon them. Might it not be a worthy and pleasing task for a statesman to survey the natural and reciprocal influence of all classes on each other.

    Wilhelm Meister's Apprenticeship, trans. Thomas Carlyle (London: Moore, 1901), p. 91.

27. "Quarante-quatre lettres inédites," *Présence de George Sand,* pp. 42–43.

28. A useful estimate: an 1850 French franc equals approximately five 1985 dollars.

29. *Marielle, Théâtre de Nohant* (Paris: Michel Levy, 1865), p. 286 (hereafter cited in the text as *Marielle*).

30. Debra Linowitz Wentz, *Les Profils du théâtre de Nohant de George Sand* (Paris: Nizet, 1978), p. 57 (hereafter cited as Wentz, *Les Profils*).

31. Wentz, *Les Profils,* p. 70.

32. Descotes credits Dumas fils with having been the first to introduce the subject of a sympathetic unwed mother on the French stage. Actually, Sand, a close friend and collaborator of Dumas fils', set the precedent for Dumas' later three plays on the same subject. See Maurice Descotes, *Le Public de théâtre* (Paris: Presses Universitaires, 1964), pp. 330–35.

33. Two English adaptations of *Claudie* were made by Charles Reade: *The Village Tale* in 1852, and *Rachel the Reaper,* which opened at London's Queen's Theatre on 9 March 1874, with Ellen Terry in the principal role. Miss Terry complained that the stage set was far too real, as it included live pigs. Neither adaptation enjoyed a success.

34. It was Charles Fechter's version of *The Count of Monte Cristo* that James O'Neill first played in 1883.

35. In Sand's original manuscript of the play, Madame Fauveau arrives carrying wine bottles and glasses to set up for the evening's harvest festival (Lovenjoul E777, p. 10).

36. Sand could be just as equivocal in her management of the Nohant estate. Looking for a new cook during the time *Claudie* was still on the boards in its first run, Sand said she would pay 200 francs a year for a male chef, 150 for a female! (*Corr.* 10:118).

37. Sand insisted on seeing final proofs for her plays' publications, so that she could correct them to correspond exactly to her staging instructions (*Corr.* 12:116). A look at those plays which have been published but never produced gives further evidence of Sand's precise and detailed stage pictures and activities accompanying the dialogue.

38. In 1856 Sand wrote to another stage director who was reviving *Claudie,* "Don't put

oxen in front of the harvest wagon. It's awful, those oxen made of cardboard . . . have the wagon pulled by workers" (*Corr.* 14:52–53).

39. "Moeurs et coutumes du Berry," *L'Illustration,* 11 September 1852.

40. "Moeurs et coutumes du Berry," *L'Illustration,* 30 August 1851.

41. The melancholy plains of Berry that Sand knew and described so well could have an unhappy effect upon her:

> I have a passion for grand mountains, and since I was born I have had to submit to the chalky plains and puny vegetation of my home with a real fondness, but a very melancholy one. My liver moans in this muggy air we breathe here, and I become like one of these apathetic oxen that works without knowing for whom or why. When I'm able to get out of here, which is now very seldom, when I can see the snowy heights and the precipices, my nature changes, my liver complaint disappears, my work becomes clear to me and I understand why I am in this world. I don't pretend to be able to explain this phenomenon but I feel it so enduringly and so completely that I cannot deny it (*Corr.* 14:759).

42. When *Claudie* played in the town of Nantes in March 1851, it was so popular with the people, the workers, that the town officials closed it down, fearing "popular enthusiasm" or uprisings might be caused by the play's "socialist ideas" (d'Arpentigny to Sand, 12 March 1851; *Corr.* 10:185n).

43. 13 January 1851; rpt. in *Histoire de l'art dramatique,* 6:210–16. Gautier goes on to commend Sand's realism. He notes that Sand writes from experience "intimate, familiar" portraits of Berrichon peasants. They speak their native patois, wear coarse linen and threadbare vests, rather than satin breeches familiar to shepherds in opéra-comique. He likes especially the image of Claudie ironing.

44. "Lettres de George Sand et H. Taine," *Revue des Deux Mondes,* 15 January 1933, p. 347.

45. Gustave Planche, review in *Revue des Deux Mondes,* 1 February 1851, pp. 497–511.

46. Lovenjoul, E777, pp. 108–9.

47. Francisque Sarcey, *Quarante ans de théâtre* (Paris: Bibliothèque des Annales, 1901), 4:199–230 (hereafter cited as *Quarante ans*).

48. Benoist, *Essais de critique,* pp. 28–39.

49. Millet's circle of artist friends overlapped Sand's as early as 1840. Theodore Rousseau, a comrade of Millet's in the Barbizon school, spent some time with the Sands in Nohant when he was engaged to marry George's adoptive daughter "Titine" in 1847. Reviewing the Salon of 1851 Gautier observes that Millet's "Sower" recalls Sand's rustic novels. See his "Salon de 1850–51," *La Presse,* 15 March 1851; and T. J. Clark, *The Absolute Bourgeois: Artists and Politics in France 1848–1851* (Greenwich, Conn: New York Graphic Society, 1973); and *Corr.* 12:295.

50. Vladimir Karénine, *George Sand: Sa vie et ses oeuvres,* 4 vols. (Paris: Plon, 1926), 4:637–45, 648.

51. In *Remembrance of Things Past* Proust recalls his excitement and sleepless night after his grandmother read *François le Champi* to him.

Chapter 3

1. Odéon director Altaroche offered to take three of Sand's plays into his repertory as compensation; but Sand thought that would be overcompensation. She offered to give him *Claudie* and *Molière*, but not her new piece too (*Corr.* 10:277–80).

2. A year later Sand wrote to the ministry of arts on behalf of Barthelemy's innovations: "We do not have true scenic art . . . our old notions are exhausted . . . Monsieur Barthelemy is making immense progress" (*Corr.* 10:793–94).

3. *Molière, Théâtre complet*, 1:319 (hereafter cited in the text as *Molière*).

4. Hostein, the Gaîté manager, places the blame for *Molière*'s failure squarely on Bocage:

   > He pretended that his disfavor with the Empire provoked a cabal in the audience against him. . . . The truth is that Bocage gave a mortally boring *physionomie* to the role of Molière. . . . The piece contains grand merits which remain little known.

   H. Hostein, *Souvenirs d'un homme de théâtre* (Paris: Dentu, 1878), p. 75.

5. *La Presse,* 12 May 1851; rpt. in *Histoire de l'art dramatique,* 6:238–40.

6. *Molière* (Paris: Hetzel, 1851), pp. 7–8.

7. *Molière, Théâtre complet*, 1:313–18.

8. Paul Meurice to George Sand, 14 June and 1 August 1863, copies in George Sand papers, Bibliothèque Municipale, La Châtre. In these letters Meurice discusses his plans for adapting *Gabriel:* he will make the grandfather more important, a "Machiavellian Talleyrand," and give Astolphe a brother who will take on the truly bad characteristics Sand has given to Astolphe, "to leave Gabriel's beloved noble and proud in his debauchery." He wants the play to be amusing and dynamic, in the "admirable sense of Shakespeare's *Cymbeline.*"

9. *Mercadet,* originally by Balzac, rewritten after his death by Dennery, and successfully staged at the Gymnase (August–October 1851) took Sand's time slot for *Victorine,* so that her piece opened later than originally planned.

10. *Le Diable aux champs* (Paris: Michel Levy, 1865), p. 215. In an article published in 1965, Frank Paul Bowman claims that *Diable* is more dramatic than Sand's "supposed plays." He finds it one of her "most readable and interesting compositions . . . its scenes about love, theology, or politics, are quite realistic even if managed in a pleasantly witty manner." See "Notes Towards the Definition of the Romantic Theater," *L'Esprit Créateur* 5 (Fall 1965): 128.

11. Germain Bapst, *Essai sur l'histoire du théâtre* (Paris: Hachette, 1893), p. 584.

12. Marvin Carlson, *The French Stage in the Nineteenth Century* (Metuchen, New Jersey: Scarecrow, 1972), p. 124.

13. *Le Théâtre contemporain (1866–1868)* (Paris: Stock, 1908), p. 30. See also Descotes, *Le Public de théâtre,* pp. 317–18.

14. This and succeeding quotations in this paragraph are drawn from *Corr.* 12:48–49. See also Georges Lubin's article "Quelques lettres inédites de George Sand à Gustave Vaez," *Harvard Library Bulletin* 14 (Autumn 1960): 416–25.

15. But even after she found another space, the Gymnase, with its poorly paid acting troupe, remained the theatre where Sand had the least trouble. Only in the next decade, the 1860s, after Lemoine-Montigny lost his wife and leading lady, Rose Cheri, did relations between the director and Sand cool. Their correspondence ceased and Sand complained to others that he made no effort to revive any of her plays which remained in his repertory. She finally arranged that they be moved to other theatres for production.

16. Sarcey, *Quarante ans,* pp. 211–18; Zola, *Nos auteurs,* pp. 371–73.

17. *Souvenirs dramatiques,* 2 vols (Paris: Calmann Levy, n.d.), 2: 295–313. Dumas adds that Sand does not like to attend rehearsals because she cannot smoke in the rehearsal hall, "her repose is a cigarette."

18. Preface, *Maître Favilla, Théâtre complet,* 3:229.

19. *Petite Revue,* 18 October 1865; quoted in *Corr.* 13:366n.

20. Sand to Janin, *Corr.* 13:371–79; same source for succeeding quotations.

21. George Sand, Preface, *Françoise, Théâtre complet,* 4:3.

22. Preface, *Comme il vous plaira, Théâtre complet,* 4:112–22.

23. Georges d'Heylli, *Journal intime de la Comédie Française (1852–1871)* (Paris: Dentu, 1879), p. 141.

24. Albert Lacroix, *De l'influence de Shakespeare sur le théâtre français* (Brussels: Univ. of Brussels, 1856), p. 779.

25. Paul G. Blount, "George Sand's Misquotation of Shakespeare," *American Notes & Queries* 12 (1973): 34–35. Dickens complained: "Nobody had anything to do but to sit down as often as possible. When I had seen Jacques seat himself on seventeen roots of trees and twenty-five grey stones, which was at the end of the second act, I came away." Quoted in John Forster's *Life of Charles Dickens* (London, 1874), p. 109.

26. *Le Réalisme,* eds. Geneviève and Jean Lacambre (Paris: Hermann, 1973), pp. 171–76.

27. Sand to Flaubert, 25 March 1876, *Correspondance Flaubert-Sand* ed. Alphonse Jacobs (Paris: Flammarion, 1981), p. 528.

28. See his thank-you letter in B.H.V.P., G3528, Fonds Sand.

29. Contrary to what Wentz claims in her study, *Les Profils,* pp. 44–45.

30. Preface, *Le Pavé, Théâtre de Nohant,* pp. 159–60.

31. *Letters of George Sand,* trans. Raphael Ledos de Beaufort, 3 vols. (London: Ward and Downey, 1886), 2:362–63.

32. Sand wrote other play adaptations of her novels, such as *Mademoiselle la Quintinie, La Dernière Aldini, Mont-Revêche, Nanon,* and *Flamarande,* all unpublished and, with the exception of *Quintinie,* unproduced. *Quintinie* was scheduled for an Odéon production, but the censors sat on it so long it never reached a Paris stage. A copy of the manuscript reached Brussels for a production at the Théâtre Molière in 1879. The Odéon manuscript is in Lovenjoul, E 814.

33. When Chilly suddenly died in 1872 the Odéon company prevailed upon Sand to intercede with the ministry and assure a good replacement—not Duquesnel, whom Sand

describes as vacillating and indecisive as a windmill. This opposition may account for Duquesnel's later comments which belittle Sand as a playwright, published at the turn of the century. Lovenjoul E 925, pp. 324, 392.

34. Unpublished correspondence, Lovenjoul E 925, p. 135.

35. Lovenjoul E 925, pp. 141, 143, 162. In turn, Sarah Bernhardt remembers Sand in her memoirs as her "petite madone." During the rehearsals Sand always had a cigarette in her "heavy and vulgar mouth," but Bernhardt loved Sand's big, dreaming eyes, and sweet voice. The actress purportedly took Sand's direction and performed her part more naturally, "like an honest young girl." Quoted in Dorrya Fahmy, *George Sand: Auteur dramatique* (Paris: Droz, 1935), p. 57.

Chapter 4

1. "Dossier Commedia" in Copeau's unpublished archives, quoted in Renée Lelièvre, *Le Théâtre dramatique italien en France, 1855–1940* (Paris: Colin, 1959), p. 505.

2. For a chronological list of Sand's Nohant plays and their dates of performance, see Appendix B.

3. See Sand's novel *Jeanne* (1844) for a story set among the Druidic monuments of Berry.

4. George Sand, "Le Théâtre et l'acteur," *Oeuvres autobiographiques,* 2 vols, ed. Georges Lubin (Paris: Gallimard, 1971), 2:1241, 1559n.

5. Leo Clarétie, *Histoire des théâtres de société* (Paris: Molière, n.d., ca. 1900), pp. 265–66.

6. "Le Théâtre des marionnettes de Nohant," *Oeuvres autobiographiques,* 2:1249.

7. Maurice Sand, *Masques et bouffons: Comédie italienne,* 2 vols. (Paris: A. Levy, fils, 1860, 1862), 1:2–3.

8. B.H.V.P., Fonds Sand, 033 A and 033 B.

9. Provenance of original manuscript is not known. A typed copy of twenty-two pages now resides in the George Sand Room of the Bibliothèque Municipale of La Châtre, Boîte #55.

10. *Le Château des Désertes* (Paris: Michel Levy, 1869), pp. 20–23.

11. Description of *Don Juan* performance in *Château des Désertes,* pp. 96–110.

12. Sand's source for this dramatic moment is of course Goethe's *Wilhelm Meister's Apprenticeship* (1795). In Book 5, Chapter 11, Wilhelm and his troupe are putting on a performance of *Hamlet.* They have no one to play old Hamlet's ghost. But suddenly at the appropriate place in the script a mysterious figure appears on stage as the ghost, and so frightens all the other actors that they give new energy and credibility to their performances.

13. Jean Rousset, *L'Intérieur et l'extérieur* (Paris: Corti, 1968), p. 160. Apparently Rousset imagines that an actor can be a tabula rasa at the commencement of taking on a character role; whereas Sand, like Stanislavski after her, thinks that the more thought, imagination, intuition, experience an actor can bring to bear upon his character, the richer the interpretation will be.

14. Sand expands upon this point in a later novel, *Pierre qui roule* (Paris: Michel Levy, 1870) in which the young would-be actor, Pierre, is counseled to study for a minimum of three years, to take dance lessons, to research, invent, create, and ultimately learn to divest himself of himself (pp. 95–97). He must create characters opposite to his own nature, ones he considers insignificant or even dislikeable, in order to efface his own personality and render himself more supple and open (p. 102). Pierre discovers he is his own worst enemy; he's too self-conscious and critical of himself on stage (p. 288). He needs to look outside of himself, everywhere, for character details; good actors are good observers (pp. 188–89).

15. "Théâtre des Marionnettes," *Oeuvres autobiographiques*, 2:1266.

16. Joseph-Marc Bailbé, "Le Théâtre et la vie dans *Le Château des Désertes,*" *Revue d'Histoire Littéraire de la France* 79 (1979): 609.

17. Ross Chambers, *La Comédie au château* (Paris: Corti, 1971), pp. 118–19.

18. Daughter Solange and her husband Clesinger violently ruptured relations with George Sand in the summer of 1847. Titine's marriage to the artist Rousseau was called off at the same time because of Solange's interference; but she married someone else that Sand found for her and remained in the Nohant troupe for another two or three seasons. But in 1848 only son Maurice and his friend Eugène Lambert were left at Nohant of the original troupe. George Sand and Victor Borie (socialist writer and close friend who became George's lover in 1847–48) constituted the only audience for the puppet shows. Soon afterwards Borie was forced to leave France for a time because of his politics.

19. Maurice Sand, *Plays for Marionettes,* trans. Babette and Glenn Hughes (New York: Samuel French, 1931).

20. Sand confides in her Agenda that her performance was not "full-bodied" enough (*Corr.* 9:421); (see Appendix C for Sand's other roles).

21. *L'Illustration,* 5 June 1852, pp. 380–82.

22. George Sand, "Théâtre des marionnettes," *Oeuvres autobiographiques*, 2:1254–55.

23. "Théâtre des marionnettes," *Oeuvres autobiographiques*, 2:1254–55.

24. When the Nohant troupe conceded to having an audience, they provided space enough to sit and watch, but kept their original theatre space intact.

25. With the exception of Eugène Lambert, who briefly trained with the actor Got at the Comédie Française conservatory in 1856 (before returning to his vocation of painter and becoming famous for his pictures of cats), none of the amateurs had professional aspirations.

26. Isaïa Sully-Levy, "Souvenirs du doyen des comédiens français: Une représentation à Nohant," *Revue de Français,* 30 October 1913, pp. 490, 494.

27. For a few years Sand and Manceau had been raising Sand's little granddaughter, Jeanne, daughter to Solange and Clesinger. The child's father kidnapped her, and for months George tried to regain custody. When finally the courts decided in George Sand's favor it was too late; the child had just died in a boarding school. To assuage Sand's intense grief, the family took her on an extended voyage to Italy.

28. "I've arrived at the point where I really cannot participate in the public theatre anymore. . . . I don't gain enough money for the directors" (*Corr.* 14:141–42).

29. George Sand, "Le Théâtre et l'acteur," *Oeuvres autobiographiques,* 2:1239–44. First published in 1904, the title was given to the essay by George's granddaughter Aurore.

30. *Masques et bouffons,* 2:97–98.

31. Renée Lelièvre, "Un Prologue inédit de George Sand imité de Ruzzante," *Revue de Littérature Comparée* 42 (1968): 572–83.

32. Sand to Charles Edmond, 6 November 1872, Lovenjoul E925, p. 366.

33. Renée Lelièvre, *Le Théâtre dramatique italien,* p. 509.

34. Sand to Charles Edmond, 25 April 1872, Lovenjoul E925, p. 287.

35. Text of *L'Auberge rouge* first published in *Présence de George Sand* (June 1982), with an introduction by Thierry Bodin and illustrations of original costumes and actors. Original manuscript in private collection of Colonel Daniel Sickles.

36. One needs to remember that George Sand and Alexandre Manceau were themselves very diminutive in size.

37. B.H.V.P., Fonds Sand, 043 for Sand's original manuscript, which, however, is not written in her own handwriting. It is interesting to note that Sand creates a scene in the original with Louise and Coqueret alone on stage hearing Durand ringing for his valet, neither of them wishing to answer. In a later published, unproduced, one-act play, *La Laitière et le pot au lait,* Sand creates the same scene. But this time the master is much more severe than Durand, and he's sure the cook is trying to poison him. Strindberg's *Miss Julie* and *Ghost Sonata* have parallel features: the ringing, the class distinctions, and the paranoia about poisoning.

38. George Sand, *Le Pavé* (Paris: Michel Levy, 1862).

39. Lovenjoul copy, E935, pp. 8–15; original in B.H.V.P. collection.

40. George Sand and Paul Meurice, *Le Drac* (Paris: Michel Levy, 1865).

41. *Correspondance Flaubert-Sand,* p. 73.

Chapter 5

1. Camille de Chancel, "Le Théâtre de George Sand," *Revue des Cours Littéraires,* 6 May 1865, p. 379; 24 June 1865, p. 490.

2. Lovenjoul, E 925, p. 287.

3. Taine to Sand, 30 March 1872, "Lettres de George Sand et H. Taine," *Revue des Deux Mondes,* 15 January 1933, pp. 346, 348.

Appendix A

1. Each of the plays in this list has been published.

Appendix B

1. O Series, Fonds Sand, B.H.V.P.

2. Bibliothèque Municipale, La Châtre. Gift of Ch. Smeets-Sand.

3. A Nohant catalogue of plays (H 320) attributes authorship of certain H series plays to George Sand, rather than to her son Maurice. The B.H.V.P. attributes all H series to Maurice.

Appendix C

1. Volume and page number of Maurice's *Recueil* for each of the listed illustrations, in the same order as listed, are as follows: 2:9, 1:16, 1:24, 1:68, 2:75, 1:82, 1:99, 1:106, 1:126, 1:141, 1:161, 1:185, 1:193, 1:208.

Bibliography

Selected Works by George Sand

Aldo le rimeur. Revue des Deux Mondes, 1 September 1833, pp. 473–512.
"A propos de la traduction de Werther par Pierre Leroux." In *Jean Zyska,* pp. 341–50. Paris: Michel Levy, 1867.
"Avant-Propos." In *Masques et bouffons: Comédie italienne,* by Maurice Sand. 2 vols. Paris: A. Levy fils, 1860.
Le Château des Désertes. Paris: Michel Levy, 1869.
"La Comédie italienne." *L'Illustration,* 5 June 1852, pp. 380–82.
Une Conspiration en 1537. In *La Génèse de Lorenzaccio,* pp. 83–146. Edited by Paul Dimoff. Paris: Droz, 1936.
Consuelo. New York: A. L. Burt Co., n.d.; reprint ed., New York: Dacapo, 1979.
Correspondance. Edited by Georges Lubin. 18 vols. Paris: Garnier 1964–84.
Correspondance Gustave Flaubert–George Sand. Edited by Alphonse Jacobs. Paris: Flammarion, 1981.
Le Diable aux champs. Paris: Michel Levy, 1865.
"Essai sur le drame fantastique." *Revue des Deux Mondes,* 1 December 1839, pp. 593–645.
Fanchon the Cricket. Translated by Jane Minot Sedgwick. New York: Duffield, 1915.
Gabriel. Paris: Michel Levy, 1866.
"Hamlet." *L'Almanach du Moís,* February 1845, pp. 65–72.
Histoire de ma vie. 10 vols. Paris: Michel Levy, 1856.
La Laitière et le pot au lait. In *Journal le Temps,* pp. 65–80. Paris: G. Schiller, 1875.
Letters of George Sand. Translated by Raphael Ledos de Beaufort, 3 vols. London: Ward & Downey, 1886.
Le Lis du Japon. Paris: Michel Levy, 1866.
Lupo Liverani. Revue des Deux Mondes, 1 December 1869, pp. 513–54.
"La Marquise." In *Nouvelles,* pp. 1–44. Paris: Michel Levy, 1869.
Les Mississipiens. Paris: Michel Levy, 1869.
"Moeurs et coutumes du Berry." *L'Illustration,* 30 August 1851, pp. 135–37; 11 September 1852, pp. 103–5.
Molière. Paris: Hetzel, 1851.
Oeuvres autobiographiques. Edited by Georges Lubin. 2 vols. Paris: Gallimard, 1970–71.
Pierre qui roule. Paris: Michel Levy, 1870.
Questions d'art et de littérature. Paris: Calmann Levy, 1878.
Questions politiques et sociales. Paris: Calmann Levy, 1879.
Les Sept Cordes de la lyre. Introduction by René Bourgeois. Paris: Flammarion, 1973.
Souvenirs et idées. Paris: Calmann Levy, n.d.

Théâtre complet. 4 vols. Calmann Levy, 1866.
  Vol. 1: *Cosima, Le Roi attend, François le Champi, Claudie, Molière.*
  Vol. 2: *Le Mariage de Victorine, Les Vacances de Pandolphe, Le Démon du foyer, Le Pressoir.*
  Vol. 3: *Mauprat, Flaminio, Maître Favilla, Lucie.*
  Vol. 4: *Françoise, Comme il vous plaira, Marguerite de Sainte-Gemme.*
Théâtre de Nohant: Le Drac, Plutus, Le Pavé, La Nuit de Noël, Marielle. Paris: Michel Levy, 1865.

Other Sources Consulted: Books and Articles

Attinger, Gustave. *L'Esprit de la commedia dell'arte dans le théâtre français.* Paris: Librairie Théâtrale, 1950.
Bailbé, Joseph-Marc. "Le Théâtre et la vie dans *Le Château des Désertes.*" *Revue d'Histoire Littéraire de la France* 79 (1979): 600–12.
Baldick, Robert. *The Life and Times of Frederick Lemaitre.* London: Hamish Hamilton, 1959.
Bapst, Germain. *Essai sur l'histoire du théâtre: La Mise en scène, le décor, le costume, l'architecture, l'éclairage, l'hygiène.* Paris: Hachette, 1893.
Barbey d'Aurevilly, Jules. *Les Bas-bleus.* 1877; Geneva: Slatkine, 1968.
————. *Le Théâtre contemporain (1866–1868).* Paris: Stock, 1908.
Barry, Joseph. *Infamous Woman: The Life of George Sand.* New York: Doubleday, 1977.
Belmont, Nicole. "L'Académie celtique et George Sand: Les Débuts des recherches folkloriques en France." *Romantisme*, no. 9 (1975), pp. 29–38.
Benoist, Antoine. *Essais de critique dramatique.* Paris: Hachette, 1898.
Bibliothèque Nationale. *George Sand: Visages du romantisme.* 1977 Exposition Catalogue. Paris: Bibliothèque Nationale, 1977.
————. *Lorenzaccio: Mises en scène d'hier and d'aujourd'hui.* Paris: Bibliothèque Nationale, 1979.
Blount, Paul G. *George Sand and the Victorian World.* Athens, University of Georgia, 1979.
————. "George Sand's Misquotation of Shakespeare." *American Notes and Queries* 12 (1973): 34–35.
Bourgeois, René. "Les Deux Cordes de la lyre ou Goethe jugé par George Sand." *Hommage à George Sand.* Paris: Presses Universitaires, 1969, pp. 93–100.
Boussel, Patrice. "George Sand et la technique dramatique." *L'Europe,* June–July 1954, pp. 68–78.
Bowman, Frank Paul. "Notes Towards the Definition of the Romantic Theatre." *L'Esprit Créateur* 5 (Fall 1965): 121–30.
Boxer, Marilyn J. and Quataert, Jean H. *Socialist Women: European Socialist Feminism in the Nineteenth and Early Twentieth Centuries.* New York: Elsenier North-Holland, 1978.
Brandes, Georg. *L'Ecole romantique en France.* Translated into French by A. Topin. Paris: Michalon, 1902.
Brown, Frederick. *Theater and Revolution: The Culture of the French Stage.* New York: Viking, 1980.
Brunetière, F. *Les Epoques du théâtre français: 1636–1850.* Paris: Hachette, 1892.
Brynolfson, Gaylord. "Works on George Sand, 1964–80: A Bibliography." *The George Sand Papers,* Second Conference at Hofstra University. New York: AMS, 1982. pp. 189–233.
Carlson, Marvin. *The French Stage in the Nineteenth Century.* Metuchen, New Jersey: Scarecrow Press, 1972.
Carrère, Casimir. *George Sand amoureuse.* Paris: La Palatine, 1967.

Castex, Pierre-Georges. *Le Conte fantastique en France de Nodier à Maupassant.* Paris: Corti, 1951.

Chambers, Ross. *L'Ange et l'automate: Variations sur le mythe de l'actrice de Nerval à Proust.* Paris: Archives de Lettres Modernes, 1971.

_____. *La Comédie au château.* Paris: Corti, 1971.

Champfleury [pseudonym of Jean Husson]. *Le Réalisme.* Edited by Geneviève and Jean Lacambre. Paris: Hermann, 1973.

Chancel, Camille de. "Le Théâtre de George Sand." *Revue des Cours Littéraires,* 6 May 1865, pp. 378–83; 24 June 1865, pp. 489–95.

Clarétie, Leo. *Histoire des théâtres de société.* Paris: Libraire Molière, n.d.

Clark, T. J. *The Absolute Bourgeois: Artists and Politics in France 1848–51.* Greenwich, Conn.: New York Graphic Society, 1973.

Constant, Charles. *Code des théâtres.* Paris: Durand et Pedone-Lauriel, 1876.

Datlof, Natalie, ed. *The George Sand Papers.* Conference Proceedings at Hofstra University. 2 vols. New York: AMS, 1976, 1982.

David-Sauvageot, A. *Le Réalisme et le naturalisme.* Paris: Calmann Levy, 1889.

Delacroix, Eugène. "L'Amitié de George Sand et d'Eugène Delacroix." *Revue des Deux Mondes,* 15 June 1934.

Dersofi, Nancy. *Arcadia and the Stage: An Introduction to the Dramatic Art of Angelo Beolco called Ruzzante.* Madrid: Turanzas, 1978.

Descotes, Maurice. *Le Drame romantique et ses grands créateurs.* Paris: Presses Universitaires, n.d.

_____. *Le Public de théâtre et son histoire.* Paris: Presses Universitaires, 1964.

D'Heylli, Georges. *Journal intime de la Comédie Française (1852–1871).* Paris: Dentu, 1879.

Dimoff, Paul. *La Génèse de Lorenzaccio.* Paris: Droz, 1936.

Dolleans, Edouard. *Feminisme et mouvement ouvrier: George Sand.* Paris: Les Editions Ouvriers, 1951.

Dumas, Alexandre, père. *Souvenirs dramatiques.* 2 vols. Paris: Calmann Levy, n.d.

Fahmy, Dorrya. *George Sand: Auteur dramatique.* Paris: Droz, 1935.

Fitzlyon, April. *The Price of Genius: A Life of Pauline Viardot.* New York: Appleton-Century, 1964.

Frey, Julia Bloch. "Theatre in an Armchair." *Friends of George Sand Newsletter,* Hofstra University, Spring 1979, pp. 20–22.

Gaiffe, Felix. *Le Rire et la scène française.* 1931: Rpt. Geneva: Slatkine, 1970.

Gautier, Théophile. *Histoire de l'art dramatique en France depuis vingt-cinq ans.* 6 vols. Paris: 1858–59; Rpt. Geneva: Slatkine, 1968.

Gilbert, Sandra M. and Gubar, Susan. *The Madwoman in the Attic: The Woman Writer and the Nineteenth Century Literary Imagination.* New Haven: Yale, 1979.

Goethe, Johann Wolfgang von. *Wilhelm Meister's Apprenticeship.* Translated by Thomas Carlyle. New York: J. H. Moore, 1901.

Green, Tatiana. "De J. Sand à George Sand: *Rose et Blanche* de Sand et Sandeau et leur descendance." *French Studies,* Spring 1976, pp. 169–82.

Guex, Jules. *Le Théâtre et la société française de 1815 à 1848.* 1900; Rpt. Geneva: Slatkine, 1973.

Hammond, William T. "Analysis of the Plot and Character Drawing in the Theatre of George Sand." *Birmingham-Southern College Bulletin* 22 (May 1929): 45–54.

Hauser, Arnold. *The Social History of Art.* Translated by Stanley Godman. 2 vols. New York: Knopf, n.d.; 4 vols. New York: Vintage, n.d.

Hays, Michael. *The Public and Performance: Essays in the History of French and German Theatre 1871–1900.* Ann Arbor: UMI Research Press, 1974, 1981.

Heine, Heinrich. *The Works of Heinrich Heine.* Translated by Charles Godfrey Leland. Vol. 8: *Letters on the French Stage.* New York: Sterling, n.d.

Hobsbawm, E. J. *The Age of Revolution 1789–1848.* New York: World Publishing, 1962; New York: Mentor, 1962.

Hostein, H. *Souvenirs d'un homme de théâtre.* Paris: Dentu, 1878.

Houssaye, Arsene. *Behind the Scenes of the Comédie Française.* Translated by Albert D. Vandam. London: Chapman and Hall, 1889.

Ihrig, Grace Pauline. *Heroines in French Drama of the Romantic Period 1829–1848.* New York: King's Crown, Colombia University, 1950.

James, Henry. *French Poets and Novelists.* London: Macmillan, 1884.

Juden, B. and Richer, J. "L'Entente cordiale au théâtre: Macready et Hamlet à Paris en 1844." *La Revue des Lettres Modernes,* nos. 74–75, 1962–63.

Kahn, Armand. *Le Théâtre social en France de 1870 à nos jours.* Paris: Fischbacher, 1907.

Karénine, Vladimir. *George Sand: Sa vie et ses oeuvres.* 4 vols. Paris: Plon, 1926.

Lacassagne, Jean-Pierre. *Histoire d'une amitié: Pierre Leroux et George Sand.* Paris: Klincksieck, 1973.

Lacroix, Albert. *De l'influence de Shakespeare sur le théâtre français.* Brussels: University of Brussels, 1856.

Larnac, Jean. *George Sand révolutionnaire.* Paris: Hier et Aujourd'hui, 1947.

Latreille, C. *George Sand et Shakespeare.* Macon: Protat, 1901.

Lelièvre, Renée. "Un Prologue inédit de George Sand imité de Ruzzante." *Revue de Littérature Comparée* 42 (1968): 572–83.

_____. *Le Théâtre dramatique italien en France, 1855–1940.* Paris: Colin, 1959.

Lewes, George Henry. *On Actors and the Art of Acting.* New York: Grove, n.d.

L'Hôpital, Madeleine. *La Notion d'artiste chez George Sand.* Paris: Boivin, 1946.

Lough, John. *Writer and Public in France: From the Middle Ages to the Present Day.* Oxford: Clarendon, 1978.

Lubin, Georges. *Nohant.* Paris: Caisse Nationale des Monuments Historiques et des Sites, 1976.

_____, ed. *Correspondance: George Sand.* 18 vols. Paris: Garnier, 1964–84.

_____, ed. *Oeuvres autobiographiques: George Sand.* 2 vols. Paris: Gallimard, 1970.

Lucas, Hippolyte. *Histoire philosophique et littéraire du théâtre français.* Paris: Gosselin, 1843.

Marix, Thérèse. "Les Débuts de George Sand critique dramatique." *Revue du Berry et du Centre,* March–April 1934, pp. 26–33; July–August 1934, pp. 57–65.

Marix-Spire, Thérèse. *Les Romantiques et la musique: le cas George Sand 1804–1838.* Paris: Nouvelles Editions Latines, 1954.

_____. "Vicissitudes d'un opéra-comique: *La Mare au Diable,* de George Sand et Pauline Viardot." *Romanic Review,* April 1944, pp. 125–46.

Maurois, André. *Lelia: The Life of George Sand.* Translated by Gerard Hopkins. London: Jonathan Cape, 1953.

Melcher, Edith. *Stage Realism in France Between Diderot and Antoine.* New York: Russell and Russell, 1976.

Merriman, John M. *The Agony of the Republic: The Repression of the Left in Revolutionary France, 1848–1851.* New Haven: Yale, 1978.

Meurice, Paul, and George Sand. *Cadio.* Paris: Michel Levy, 1868.

_____. *Le Drac.* Paris: Michel Levy, 1865.

Moers, Ellen. *Literary Women.* New York: Garden City, 1976.

Moland, Louis. *Théâtre de Sedaine.* Paris: Garnier, 1878.

Moynet, Georges. *Trucs et décors: La Machinerie théâtrale.* Paris: Librairie Illustrée, 1893.

Muret, Theodore. *L'Histoire par le théâtre: 1789–1851*. Paris: Amyot, 1865.

Pailleron, Marie-Louise. *François Buloz et ses amis: La Revue des Deux Mondes et la Comédie Française*. Paris: Firmin-Didot, 1930.

————. *François Buloz et ses amis: Les Derniers Romantiques*. Paris: Perrin, 1923.

Petoukhoff, Valentine. "George Sand et le drame philosophique: *Aldo le rimeur, Les Sept Cordes de la lyre, Gabriel, Les Mississipiens, Le Diable aux champs.*" Ph.D. dissertation, University of Pennsylvania, 1975.

Picard, Roger. *Le Romantisme social*. New York: Brentano's, 1944.

Poli, Annarosa. *George Sand vue par les italiens*. Paris: Didier, 1965.

————. *L'Italie dans la vie et dans l'oeuvre de George Sand*. Paris: Colin, 1960.

Pommier, Jean. *Les Ecrivains devant la Révolution de 1848*. Paris: Presses Universitaires, 1948.

Remy, Tristan. *Jean-Gaspard Deburau*. Paris: L'Arche, 1954.

Rolland, Romain. *Le Théâtre du peuple*. Paris: Michel, n.d.

Rousset, Jean. "Le Comédien et son spectateur: Don Juan." *Ecriture: Cahier de Littérature et de Poésie* 13 (1977): 132–43.

————. *L'Intérieur et l'extérieur*. Paris: Corti, 1968.

Sainte-Beuve, C. A. *Causeries du lundi*. Vol. 1. Paris: Garnier, 1850.

Sand, Maurice. *Plays for Marionettes*. Translated by Babette and Glenn Hughes. New York: Samuel French, 1931.

Sand, Maurice and George Sand. *Les Don Juan de village*. Paris: Michel Levy, 1866.

————. *Masques et bouffons: Comédie italienne*. 2 vols. Paris: A. Levy, fils, 1860.

Sarcey, Francisque. *Quarante ans de théâtre*. vol. 4. Paris: Bibliothèque des Annales, 1901.

Schaeffer, Gerald. *Espace et temps chez George Sand*. Introduction by Marc Eigeldinger. Neuchâtel: A la Baconnière, 1981.

Schutz, Alexander. *The Peasant Vocabulary in the Works of George Sand*. *University of Missouri Studies* 2 (January 1927).

Séchan, Charles. *Souvenirs d'un homme de théâtre 1831–1855*. Paris: Calmann Levy, 1883.

Seillière, Ernest. *George Sand: Mystique de la passion et de la politique et de l'art*. Paris: Allan, 1920.

Shephard, Esther. *Walt Whitman's Pose*. New York: Harcourt, Brace, 1936.

Standring, Enid M. "The Lelio's of Berlioz and George Sand." *The George Sand Papers*, Conference Proceedings at Hofstra University. New York: AMS, 1976.

Storey, Robert F. *Pierrot: A Critical History of a Mask*. Princeton, New Jersey: Princeton University Press, 1978.

Sully-Levy. "Souvenirs du doyen des comédiens français: Une Représentation à Nohant." *Revue de Française*, 30 October 1913, pp. 486–95.

Szogyi, Alex. "The Dramas of George Sand." *Friends of George Sand Newsletter*, Hofstra University, Fall–Winter 1981. pp. 29–34.

————. "Preface to the Prologue of *Les Mississipiens* of George Sand." *The George Sand Papers*, Conference Proceedings at Hofstra University. New York: AMS, 1982.

Taine, Hippolyte. *Derniers Essais de critique et d'histoire*. Paris: Hachette, 1903.

Taine, Hippolyte and George Sand. "Lettres de George Sand et H. Taine." *Revue des Deux Mondes*, 15 January 1933, pp. 335–51.

Thomas, Edith. *Les Femmes de 1848*. Paris: Presses Universitaires, 1948.

Thomson, Patricia. *George Sand and the Victorians: Her Influence and Reputation in Nineteenth Century England*. New York: Columbia University Press, 1977.

Tricotel, Claude. *Comme deux troubadours: Histoire de l'amitié Flaubert-Sand*. Paris: Société d'Editions d'Enseignement Supérieur, 1978.

Viard, Jacques. "George Sand et Michelet, Disciples de Pierre Leroux." *Revue d'Histoire Littéraire de la France,* September–October 1975, pp. 749–73.

Vincent, Marie-Louise. *La Langue et le style rustiques de George Sand dans les romans champêtres.* Paris: Champion, 1916.

Weiss, Jean-Jacques. *Le Théâtre et les moeurs.* Paris: Calmann Levy, 1889.

Wellek, René. *A History of Modern Criticism: 1750–1950.* 4 vols. New Haven: Yale, 1955–65.

Wentz, Debra Linowitz. *Les Profils du théâtre de Nohant de George Sand.* Paris: Nizet, 1978.

Zola, Emile. *Le Naturalisme au théâtre.* Paris: Charpentier, 1893.

————. *Nos auteurs dramatiques.* Paris: Charpentier, 1889.

Other Sources Consulted: Manuscript Collections

Chantilly, France, Spoelberch de Lovenjoul Collection, Institut de France.

Châteauroux, France, Bibliothèque Municipale.

La Châtre, France, Bibliothèque Municipale.

Paris, Bibliothèque de l'Arsenal.

————. Bibliothèque Historique de la Ville de Paris.

————. Bibliothèque Nationale.

Index